An Alchemy of Living Culture

An Alchemy of Living Culture

Collected Writings on Double Edge Theatre

Stacy Klein

Preface by
Jonathan P. Eburne

BLOOMSBURY ACADEMIC

LONDON · NEW YORK · OXFORD · NEW DELHI · SYDNEY

BLOOMSBURY ACADEMIC
Bloomsbury Publishing Plc, 50 Bedford Square, London, WC1B 3DP, UK
Bloomsbury Publishing Inc, 1359 Broadway, New York, NY 10018, USA
Bloomsbury Publishing Ireland, 29 Earlsfort Terrace, Dublin 2, D02 AY28, Ireland

BLOOMSBURY, BLOOMSBURY ACADEMIC and the Diana logo are
trademarks of Bloomsbury Publishing Plc

First published in Great Britain 2025

A catalogue record for this book is available from the British Library.

A catalog record for this book is available from the Library of Congress.

ISBN: HB: 978-1-3504-4936-7
           PB: 978-1-3504-4937-4
           ePDF: 978-1-3504-4938-1
           eBook: 978-1-3504-4939-8

Series: Theatre Makers

Typeset by Integra Software Services Pvt. Ltd.
Printed and bound in Great Britain

For product safety related questions contact productsafety@bloomsbury.com.

To find out more about our authors and books visit www.bloomsbury.com
and sign up for our newsletters.

*For those who dare
To move, desire, and imagine—
And for the courage to fly through the impossible.*

CONTENTS

3 "Each Person Must Ask Why They Are Here": Training and Performance Creation 75

4 Art, Living Culture, Art Justice 123

FIGURES

ACKNOWLEDGMENTS

My acknowledgments must start with Jonathan Paul Eburne, a friend and scholar, and the first of the many people who encouraged and prodded me to write, who actually put pen to paper, so to speak, dug out my writings from filing cabinets and libraries, and walked me through this process of reflecting on my life's work. Without your partnership, this book would not have been written.

For my teacher and friend Rena Mirecka, of blessed memory, I remain with you. My unending gratitude to all those who have traveled with me along the Double Edge journey for over forty years. Thank you Amrita Ramanan and Daina Robins, friends and colleagues who gave your time to read and question and discuss the contents; Ebony Noelle Golden, for our endless conversations and agreeing, amidst all else, to be interviewed; to my daughters Tadea Klein, for your own unique perspective on this book, and Cariel Klein, for taking on the almost insurmountable task to ensure I had time to write; Milena Dabova, your extraordinary and exacting understanding for detail and depth has made this book and my work much improved; and Adam Bright, for embracing my vision and growing it with me for the last twenty years.

Much gratitude, Jennifer Johnson, my fellow traveler to other dimensions; you scoured all the journals I felt I could share and found selections I dared include; John Peitso, your endless curiosity about the theatre's 42-year-old archive and excitement about my words often outweighs my own; and Travis Coe, our dialogue of the heart over countless hours has hopefully become, with this book, my own "letter to a young artist."

And of course to Carlos Uriona, you are my beshert, my soul, and my everyday inspiration, in my life and in the life of the theatre.

PREFACE

Stacy Klein: A Maker of Worlds

Jonathan P. Eburne

Our job at Double Edge might be: to swim, not to drown. Perhaps even to try to fly. That might be the extent of our job. Sometimes you're just drowning in all the obligations. But then you think: no, I have to be here. And maybe I can take someone's hand as well, so they won't drown while also dying of thirst. And this way I won't drown, either. I can help make sure someone gets the water. That's our job now.

—STACY KLEIN[1]

Stacy Klein claims not to be a writer. This book proves, on the contrary, that she is a writer of tremendous grace and wisdom. It might therefore be more accurate to say that her life's work, as an artist in a living medium, has demanded all the talents at her disposal. Writing is but one of the many facets of Klein's art, yet it is one of the most revealing.

As founder and, for over forty years, Artistic Director of Double Edge Theatre, Stacy Klein has orchestrated ensemble performances

---

[1] Stacy Klein, fragment written during the process of compiling this book, 2023.

of breathtaking vision and beauty, while also directing a permanent, full-time residential theatre company of fellow artists. Klein's writings for and about this company—which include program notes, speeches, essays, interviews, newsletters, journal entries, and working documents—disclose the range, yet also the focus, of her creative imagination. Her writings articulate the practical as well as aesthetic dimensions of her life's work with Double Edge Theatre, offering a window into the creative life of a living, working company of artists. Introducing readers to her visionary approach to collectivizing experimental art, this compilation of Klein's writings testifies to the organizational, interpersonal, political, and even spiritual dimensions of sustaining a creative ensemble.

Double Edge Theatre was founded in Boston in 1982 as a feminist theatre group and laboratory for experimental creative process. Working together as a group of eight women, Klein's ensemble sought nothing less than "to redefine theatre for our society," as she later put it. This meant "reawaken[ing] ourselves and our audience to the forces of imagination and spirit which lay dormant within."[2] Klein has pursued this aim with unrelenting devotion. Today, Double Edge is located on a former dairy farm in the rural village of Ashfield, Massachusetts, on the traditional homelands of the Nipmuc Tribal People. Having celebrated its fortieth anniversary in 2022, Double Edge is a world-renowned theatre ensemble recognized as much for its immersive working culture as for the immersive sensory experience of its strikingly original performances. Throughout the year, in addition to touring, Double Edge Theatre hosts both indoor and outdoor performances at its Farm Center. These performances integrate landscape and spectacle, incorporating live music and large-scale mythic storytelling with masks and pageantry, stilt walking and street theatre, poetry and acrobatics. In the refurbished barn that serves as the ensemble's performance space, actors fly from the rafters, suspending themselves from ribbons, lyra, or bars. At various *plein air* sites around the farm, actors soar through trees, wade through streams, or suspend themselves high above the spectators. Chant and song sweep across the hillside pasture, as dispersed actors recombine in choral harmony. The effects are magical.

---

[2]See Stacy Klein, "We Realized That Something Had Changed," March 23, 2002, intra.

Klein's genius is distributive; it is fueled by collaboration. As in the case of other ensemble-based theatre companies worldwide, Double Edge performances are co-created by the actors in the ensemble over a span of months or even years of intensive physical training. Rigorously exploring the possibilities of physical movement and the relationships between voices, bodies, sounds, objects, and spaces, the company's training process involves a "unique, holistic methodology" that "employs the artist's full potential—emotional, imaginative, physical, vocal—to drive ensemble collaboration, individual exploration, and performance creation."[3]

The ensemble's process of creating a performance proceeds from this training, rather than from a preexisting script or repertoire. In this regard, Double Edge shares in the history of avant-garde performance ensembles that have reshaped the very foundations of theatre over the past century. And indeed, over the decades Klein and Double Edge have collaborated with, hosted, visited, and exchanged ideas with many of the most notable experimental theatre companies around the world. (Klein herself trained with Jerzy Grotowski's Teatr Laboratorium [Poland; founded as the Theatre of 13 Rows in 1958] and wrote her Ph.D. thesis on Eugenio Barba's Odin Teatret [Denmark; founded in 1964]). Double Edge's work is grounded in a practice of co-creation that stems from movement and improvisation exercises that are refined and orchestrated over time. The highly physical, embodied nature of the company's training is bolstered, in turn, by the artists' research, writing, singing, musical training, set and costume construction, and creation of masks and puppets, all of which contribute to the co-creation of the performances Klein directs. In working collaboratively in this fashion, Double Edge seeks to do away with the theatre-world habits (scripts, auditions, industrial repertoires, blockbuster economics) that conspire to form "a barrier, or wall, to the imagination, soul, and autonomy of the actor, and therefore to the creation of a living theatre," as Klein puts it in a 2005 essay.[4]

---

[3] From the Double Edge Theatre website: https://doubleedgetheatre.org/event/summer-intensive/.

[4] Stacy Klein, "Why Devise? Why Now? Creating the Impossible." *Theatre Topics*, vol. 15 no. 1, 2005, p. 69–72. See intra.

The task of *reawakening*, as envisioned in 1982, has evolved into a year-round ecosystem of training and co-creation. This dynamic ecosystem also includes theatre workshops for students and community members, social justice programming, farming and environmental education, large-scale cultural projects, and the company's own self-administration. Herein lies one of the true distinctions of Klein's theatrical vision: Working together daily, the Double Edge ensemble investigates theatre as a living, experimental art form that extends to the very culture of the organization itself. The Double Edge mission statement upholds this "living culture" as one of its three core principles, together with "art" and "art justice."

What this means is that each artist in Double Edge is responsible for creating their own artistic work, while at the same time fulfilling the real-world demands of collaborative co-creation. This includes the design and construction of sets, costumes, and lighting, as well as the research process of gathering, writing, drawing, composing, and playing. But as an independent, artist-run organization located on a farm in rural Western Massachusetts—far from the urban arts centers of Boston, New York, or Chicago—it also means attending to the economic and administrative realities of the company, its physical environment, and its community. "There are many paths Stacy could have chosen to use her brilliant mind and acute way of seeing the world," notes Adam Bright, Double Edge's Producing Executive Director and an ensemble member, "but she chose something that required all of herself. She has needed to master so many things to create the impossible. The same applies to anyone who chooses to follow her." This includes Bright himself: "I have learned almost every job that it takes to make theatre, and every job that it takes to run a non-profit."[5] The artists in Double Edge self-manage the company's physical operations as a farm and a working theatre alike, coordinating the theatre's funding, programming, touring, and payroll. This includes the writing of grants; the articulation of language for publicity, membership development, and internal management; and the project of maintaining active communication with thousands of people. Klein's writing, like her role as Artistic Director, addresses every facet of this work.

---

[5] Adam Bright, email correspondence with the author, May 11, 2024.

***

An Alchemy of Living Culture presents a core selection of Stacy Klein's writings on theatrical and cultural practice, documenting her work with Double Edge Theatre over the course of nearly five decades in its rigorous, impassioned dedication to artistic co-creation, equitable organization-building, and cultural survival. The book also features new writing in which Klein reflects on her earlier texts and comments on their historical and personal significance. In addition to providing an opening "Address to the Reader" that outlines Double Edge's history and approach to theatrical training, Klein introduces each of the book's five chapters, while also presenting brief contextualizing reflections throughout.

The writings collected here, most of which have never been published beyond their distribution in programs and newsletters, document how Klein has shaped and articulated Double Edge's core mission as it has evolved. They outline a lifelong approach to theatrical and cultural work founded on creating physical, bodily, conceptual, and cultural environments in which artistic life can flourish. More broadly, they testify to an artistic practice predicated on relentless searching and questioning—in nonverbal as well as verbal forms—rather than prescribing a fixed set of methods or approaches.

For this reason, *An Alchemy of Living Culture* is not a "how to" guide to creating theatre according to a "Double Edge method." For as Klein insists, her work with Double Edge is based on process, not on "method." As she writes in her introductory Address to the Reader,

> Our method is based on *search*; it's not based on *form*. After a training program, you wouldn't be able to say, "I've got the Double Edge method." Rather, you will be invited, for the rest of your lives, to call upon this training as a means for searching yourself and for asking essential questions. [...] Who do you want to be? How do you want to live your complete self? I think it's important to believe that we *can* remove the things that block us from living as we choose to live.[6]

---

[6]Stacy Klein, "Introduction: An Address to the Reader," intra.

A living art impelled by search, not form: for Klein, the tasks of imaginative and practical worldmaking are fueled by the same fundamental set of questions about what it means to live as an artist. These are questions that can only be answered for oneself; the answers are not provided.

This book documents the working methods developed and practiced by a world-renowned experimental theatre company. Yet just as Double Edge is more than just a theatre group, this book's compilation of Klein's writings is far more than documentary in scope. In attending to the full range of an artist-run organization's local, regional, and international activities, this book explores the intellectual and artistic labor, as well as the organizational forms and strategies, that Double Edge entails. Klein considers herself an artist above all else, yet she is no less a thinker. An uncompromising cultural critic and activist, Klein tends to work in actions rather than in words. Her writings offer a powerful articulation of her artistic and cultural vision because they are so intimately bound to the relentlessly searching practice of the Double Edge ensemble.

Klein's work thus offers powerful insights into the much vaunted "fusion of art and life" championed by scholars and practitioners of avant-garde art since the 1960s—with the added understanding that the definitions of "art" and "life" are to be challenged and continually expanded in the name of inclusivity and social justice. In an age of eviscerated state support for cultural institutions, it is vital to understand how autonomous collective organizations (which tend to operate outside of the attentions of Big Philanthropy) can provide alternative sites for sustaining vibrant, ethical cultures of creativity and imagination. Just as alumni of the Double Edge ensemble and its training programs have gone on to found theatre companies of their own, artists persist in finding ways to survive within current social and civic infrastructures. Klein's writings for and about Double Edge thus have much to teach contemporary artists, scholars, students, and organizers about the urgency, as well as the possibility, of fostering living culture in the contemporary moment. By following the story of Stacy Klein and Double Edge, this collection offers a critical resource for creating new arts organizations and supporting existing ones. For in addition to documenting the profound artistic and political ecology of Double Edge Theatre, this book also offers practical tools and concepts for helping future artists, arts organizations, and autonomous groups to thrive in turn.

✳✳✳

The creation of a living culture, according to Klein, is not a matter of work-for-work's sake. Rather, this culture undergirds the very project of collectivizing artistic creation during a period in US history that has been especially hostile to artists and collectives alike. To live and create imaginatively in such an environment is a perpetual struggle that demands courage as much as inspiration. As Double Edge Co-Artistic Director Jennifer Johnson notes: "Stacy talks about the courage of the imagination, which to me is about being brave enough to meet yourself and everyone with the same spirit of possibility, of uncertainty, that I experienced that first night I saw Double Edge, so that something new can be discovered."[7] This courage has as much to do with meeting the challenges of artistic work as with facing the worldly pressures of living as an artist.

Johnson, an ensemble member since 1993, describes her initial encounter with Double Edge, when she and John Peitso (Co-Musical Director, Lighting Designer, and ensemble member) witnessed a performance of *Song of Absence*. "I was stunned," Johnson writes; "I was almost afraid! I had no idea theatre could behave like that— wild, dangerous, beautiful, heartbreaking, poetic. I'd never seen or even heard about anything like what I had experienced. It was an awakening of possibilities, of creativity." After more than thirty years of collaborating with Klein and Double Edge, Johnson asserts that

> the work is still wild, and dangerous, and beautiful, and it's expanded to embrace all that Double Edge is and does, the whole world of the work, all the artists and partners and students and audiences of the work, and the land of the work. And the futures of the work. It's an adventure we take together every day— with all the triumphs and disappointments and mundanity and poetry.[8]

---

[7] Jennifer Johnson, email correspondence with the author, April 16, 2024.
[8] Johnson, email correspondence with the author, April 16, 2024.

The artists in Double Edge, past and present, all have powerful stories to tell about their decision to work with the company, and, in particular, about Klein's guidance in confronting the gravity of pursuing a life in experimental art. The life of the ensemble, like the lives of the individual artists who comprise it, lies at the heart of Klein's theatrical vision. Co-Artistic Director and ensemble member Milena Dabova, who has collaborated with Klein for over sixteen years, recalls "many occasions in which she [has] brought into focus the deepest questions I needed to face within myself." Dabova continues, "I have never met anyone else whose visions are so ambitious and full, and who is simultaneously as patient and accepting of the often frustrating—and always difficult!—process of meeting them."[9] The task of collectivizing the artistic process, to which Klein has dedicated her life's work, demands creating and maintaining an artistic culture that can accommodate itself, day after day, to the most profound imaginative aspirations of its participants, as much as to their material needs. Such a culture thereby "defines its own reality," as Klein once put it.[10]

---

[9]Milena Dabova, email correspondence with the author, April 23, 2024. I take the liberty here of citing Dabova's account of an early conversation with Stacy Klein that precipitated her decision to join the ensemble on a permanent basis:

> During my second month at Double Edge as a student, I created a brief "étude" as part of our regular assignments within the DE immersion program I was attending. After the étude showings, Stacy asked me to go to her office to talk. I immediately assumed I had done something wrong, as I had barely spoken with her by that point (and was quite intimidated by her strong presence and her authority as a prominent director!). That same week, I had just successfully interviewed for an unrelated-to-theatre job in Boston, as I could not fathom the possibility that I might work in the performing arts. When I went to Stacy's office, it turned out that she had heard about the job interview and, collating that reality with the snippet of artistic work I had just shown, felt that it was important to tell me—in no uncertain terms—that I would be making a grave mistake if I were to accept the job. More specifically, she told me that she could see that I am an artist and therefore, if I were to choose to not follow that path out of fear, I would be imprisoning myself.
>
> I walked out of Stacy's office and cried for two hours. I cried because I recognized the painful truth of my enormous desire and my equally enormous lack of belief in myself. Sixteen years after that conversation, the distance between my desire and my belief is much, much narrower, and I have dedicated my life to being an artist, which for me is one of the most important choices I have ever made.

[10]Stacy Klein, "Introduction: An Address to the Reader," intra.

What does it mean for a group of artists to define its own reality? Klein's statements about the ensemble's working practices speak to a project far more involved than the creation of works of art alone. Rather, Klein's understanding of "living culture" means that the creation of art necessarily extends to the care for and cultivation of real life. Without this, the possibility of creating truly experimental art withers. The magical, surrealist scenes in Double Edge performances may beckon toward the otherworldly, yet they are very much rooted in the demands of *this* world: the artistic, spiritual, as well as bodily and political needs of the here-and-now, as well as the historical and bodily traumas of the past. The artistic work of Double Edge has always grappled with historical trauma and the scars of genocide and cultural erasure; over the past four decades, its performances have championed glorious imagination in the face of usurpation and death. Yet its worldmaking practices likewise extend into the practice of everyday existence; for Double Edge, there is no proscenium arch.

One of Klein's collaborators, Ebony Noelle Golden, describes her first encounter with Double Edge in 2016, when she took the advice of a trusted friend and attended a performance at the farm in Ashfield. Golden is a Harlem, New York-based artist, scholar, and cultural strategist who creates site-specific ritual performances and art installations. Working at the intersection of art, social engagement, and public education, Golden immediately recognized the significance of Double Edge's "spatial politics," as she puts it, describing how the performance inhabited the full dimensions of its farmland setting. "I was very much inspired," she explains,

> by the way in which Double Edge used the space: that is, the farm, the whole space. [...] The initial piece I saw was *Once a Blue Moon—Cada Luna Azul*. I could not stop thinking about the work, about how the work is three-dimensional in scope: its spatial politics. How the work asked us to really lean in, in very significant ways. How the work invites intimacy, but also invites a grand, spectacular approach to thinking about who we are as humans and where we are on this planet.[11]

---

[11]Ebony Noelle Golden, conversation with the author, September 2023.

Klein's art is an art of world-making, understood also as the real-life work of creating environments for imaginative freedom, cultural exchange, and creative survival during trying contemporary times. Writing in 2018, Klein identifies the project of "giv[ing] voice to those unheard or ignored or dismissed" as the very starting point for the ensemble's work.[12] For over forty years, Double Edge Theatre has framed its artistic and social mission as an active resistance to cultural erasure, fostering creative survival in the face of silencing, genocide, and invisibilization. In the 1980s, the fledgling company developed its rigorous practice of feminist collective creation in the teeth of the Culture Wars and AIDs; in the 1990s, Double Edge toured Ukraine and Poland, collaborating with local communities and creating work about the living cultures of Judaism a half century after the Holocaust. After moving from Boston to Ashfield in 1994, the company attended to their local community as well, responding to economic and ecological crises as well as to the legacies of Indigenous life—and its genocidal erasure—on the very land they occupy.

Art, Klein maintains, cannot exist in a vacuum. Yet the exclusion of minoritized communities from the art world dangerously creates such a vacuum. For Klein, as for Double Edge, the de facto exclusion of BIPOC, queer, trans, working-class, disabled, elderly, and youth populations from the arts is both a social problem *and* an artistic problem. So too is it a social and artistic problem merely to pay lip service to diversity and inclusion initiatives, rather than wrestling with the profound and difficult work of structural change. The ensemble culture of Double Edge Theatre is predicated on undertaking the practical and imaginative work such change demands, as a basic prerequisite for artistic survival.[13] By considering the space and land they inhabit, Klein and Double Edge have had to be intentional about who is present in the room with them, so to speak.

Double Edge's commitment to "rooting out appropriation, exclusion, invisibility, marginalization" as the precondition for

---

[12]Stacy Klein, "Living Culture Filled with Art Justice," *Medium*. November 26, 2018. https://medium.com/@DoubleEdgeTheatre/living-culture-filled-with-art-justice-ee23bb3e5b93.
[13]Ibid.

collective creativity is not a utopian abstraction. It describes a concrete social practice consistent with the creative process, though not reducible to it.[14] In the theatrical contact, this amounts to holding space for the emergence of new theatrical voices, including the invocation of people, histories, and stories that have been marginalized throughout the region, if not erased altogether. At the same time, Double Edge's cultural work also extends to the creation of real, concrete forms of funding, land use, and institutional support for queer, Black, and Indigenous artists and communities.

Perhaps closest to home for Klein was the realization of how fully the Indigenous inhabitants of Western Massachusetts have been subject to appropriation, exclusion, and marginalization. While researching the history of their community in Ashfield, Double Edge sought out local Indigenous community leaders, whose people inhabit the region despite their presence having been all but invisibilized. Through this research, Rhonda Anderson (Iñupiaq—Athabascan) and Larry Spotted Crow Mann (Nipmuc) became aware of Double Edge's work. Their ensuing conversations led to the formation of the Okheteau Cultural Center, a Native-led organization that holds a land share agreement with Double Edge for the entirety of its 105-acre farm, and includes full access to the land, the waters, and the surrounding woods.[15] Over the past decade, Klein and Double Edge have also formalized their partnership with Golden and her Jupiter Performance Studio. This partnership has involved a number of projects supporting artists of color whose work explores climate justice, cultural wellness, site-responsive performance, and community-building across rural and urban geographies. The co-curated "Art and Survival" fellowship

---

[14]Double Edge Theatre website: https://doubleedgetheatre.org/about-us/art-living-culture-art-justice/.

[15]On Double Edge's collaboration with Okheteau, see Jonathan P. Eburne, "Worldmaking 101: Imagination and Reparation at Double Edge Theatre and Ohketeau Cultural Center," *Howlround Theatre Commons*. November 14, 2022. https://howlround.com/worldmaking-101-imagination-and-reparation-double-edge-theatre-and-ohketeau-cultural-center. See also Rhonda Anderson and Larry Spotted Crow Mann, with Jonathan P. Eburne, Stacy Klein, and Carlos Uriona, "Where's Decolonization? The Ohketeau Cultural Center, Indigenous Sovereignty, and Arts Institutions." *The Routledge Companion to Decolonizing Art History*. Ed. Tatiana Flores, Florencia San Martín, Charlene Villaseñor Black. London: Routledge, 2024, 185–95.

and festival (2021–3) has since evolved into the development of an Ecowomanist Institute.

Klein's role in such collaborations—as a facilitator of possibilities, as an intermediary, and as a mentor—is continuous with her work as a director. In both contexts, Klein's strong leadership is predicated, above all, on listening. "She was such a good listener," Golden notes of her collaboration with Klein, "and the part of it I was really able to witness and benefit from is what happens when your teacher trusts you to do the thing you say you do." In that regard, she concludes, "Stacy was a partner." Klein's participatory mentorship amounts to "an expansive way of teaching; it's not just 'do what I say.' It's 'let me show you what I do, and you need to pay attention.'"[16] Such a relationship is "challenging," Golden explains, for what it demands of oneself: "you have to determine what's important; your lifestyle has to be woven into the way in which you want to make art, the way you want to build community." Adam Bright shares Golden's appreciation of how Klein leads through listening and participating. "I'm approaching my twentieth year of working with Stacy," he writes.

> Never in that time have I felt like I was working 'for' her. This is important, as she is a leader and a powerful voice and so [...], from the outside, it may sometimes look different. But the truth is that Stacy always listens, almost always has a thought or opinion, and is *always* willing to do the work with me—which could be simply a conversation or even a disagreement, but also it could be months or years of commitment to a person or persons with a faith in something that no one else sees, or can see, until they are ready.[17]

The writings collected in this volume testify to Klein's capacity for attunement, while also emphasizing that the true challenge of artistic commitment necessarily involves each artist's own curiosity, desire, and self-interrogation. As Johnson summarizes,

> she's brilliant and demanding and exciting to work with, but it's up to you to find your work; she's not going to give it to you. No

---

[16]Ebony Noelle Golden, conversation with the author.

[17]Adam Bright, email correspondence with the author, May 11, 2024.

one can give it to you, just as no one can tell you who you really are. But when we all meet each other with imagination—whether in the space or in the pond or the forest or the office—anything is possible.

Klein's closest artistic collaborator, Carlos Uriona, Double Edge's Co-Artistic Director for twenty years and an ensemble member since 1997, is also Klein's life partner. Summing up her leadership and creative genius alike, Uriona refers to Klein as a master artist. "I consider her to be a master," he writes,

not because she has mastered a body of knowledge, but because she has wisdom. Wisdom is the ability to make connections; to connect things beyond their own immediacy, beyond the immediate field of interpretation. The accumulation of knowledge doesn't necessarily give us wisdom, though a lot of people believe it does. It is wisdom, not knowledge, that describes how someone is attuned to associations—the connections between the elements of life.[18]

For Uriona, this capacity for attunement enables Klein to engage critically with the world, as well as to create artistically, with a tremendous clarity of insight. As Uriona puts it:

In our work at Double Edge we mix politics with religion, with art; it's all intertwined. Stacy has an amazing clarity, particularly when dealing with the emotional aspects of this entanglement. We in the West tend to use our emotions as a shield, in a way that impedes us from freeing our imagination, freeing our creativity. I would use my interest in talking with other people as a shield of this kind; by investing my energy in engaging with other people I could avoid committing to my own artistic work. I was afraid to be alone with my own creativity; it was a refusal to sit with myself. Stacy helped me understand that my emotional entanglement was part of the work I needed to do. [...]

---

[18]Carlos Uriona, conversation with the author, April 30, 2024.

When I'm with her I am always at the precipice of my own self. Vertigo is not the fear of falling; it's the fear of wanting to fall. I'm tremendously attracted to her in many ways, not just romantically. Stacy brings me to a place where I can confront my fear of falling into myself. And I did fall, and I didn't die.[19]

***

Born in Maryland, Stacy Klein began her professional theatrical career working with Obie award-winning director Maxine Klein (no relation) as part of the Little Flags Theatre company in Boston, Massachusetts. From 1977 through 1979, Klein, then a recent graduate of the Boston University School for the Arts, worked as an actor, lighting director, stage manager, director, and producer for a variety of Little Flags performances, while also pursuing an MFA degree in Political Theatre Education.

Then as now, Klein's commitment to feminist political theatre remains indefatigable. Yet the signal experience of her young artistic career began a few years earlier when, as a college student, she trained in Poland with Rena Mirecka, a founding actor of Jerzy Grotowski's Teatr Laboratorium. During this same period, Klein also visited Auschwitz for the first time. The former experience led to an intense, lifelong relationship of mentorship and mutual admiration, which ended only with Mirecka's passing in 2022. The latter experience, no less formative, has haunted Klein throughout her artistic career, galvanizing her artistic and social commitments alike. Throughout the decades to follow, Klein's writings have continued to draw upon these experiences. Mirecka's training-based approach to experimental theatre—as well as the physical and emotional rigor her training demanded—left a profound impression on Klein's own approach to ensemble theatre. This approach, documented in Chapters 2 and 3 of this book, draws upon the improvisatory energy afforded by physical training: leaping, running, aerial work, and, in particular, engaging in physical dialogue with other actors through shared and transferred movements, an exercise called *plastiques* in Grotowski's theatre.

---

[19]Ibid.

So too has Klein's commitment to living culture and the artistic imagination intensified in response to the horror she beheld at Auschwitz. Encountering the scenes of atrocity thirty years after the Holocaust, Klein was especially shaken by the "park-like" neatness of the camps. As she writes in her program note for *Song of Absence*, created over a decade later in 1988, "Neatness remained a priority as thousands upon thousands burned, [while] the Nazis' children played on the well-kept grounds of their parents' camps." Klein likens this brutal contradiction to a social mask that both hides and perpetuates atrocity. She describes "the horrifying way that our social order, our mask, remains intact and perhaps even encourages, and certainly hides, the truth about us as human beings."[20] From this recognition emerged some of Double Edge Theatre's most challenging theatrical work, particularly the Song Trilogy cycle, which extended from 1988 through 2000. So too emerged the company's staunch resolution to "face isolation and erasure; to face despair and pain that can translate into personal incapacity and political paralysis."[21] For in summoning the courage to confront these horrors, Klein maintains, it becomes possible to recognize and uplift the forces of human creativity and the possibilities of cultural life.

This commitment endures into the present. Co-Artistic Director Travis Coe, who has worked with Double Edge since 2016, describes how Klein's "unwavering [...] commitment to envisioning a world of justice and inclusivity" has instilled in him "a profound sense of hope for a world that could survive major crises—especially as a 30-year-old gay Latinx and Black American navigating the complexities of the 21st century." Through her creations, Coe writes, "she empowers others to soar, sing, dance, and dream of freedom, and while I once thought that was incredibly optimistic and utopian, I came to realize that is her way to paint the future she desires."[22] In bearing witness to a world scarred by oppression and injustice, Klein's work with Double Edge seeks to dispel the barriers—emotional and ideological as well as financial and institutional—to accessing radical imagination and hope.

---

[20]Stacy Klein, "Director's Confession: Song of Absence and the Fall of the Ashen Reign" (1988), intra.

[21]From the Double Edge Mission Statement.

[22]Travis Coe, email correspondence with the author, May 10, 2024.

Klein's "relentless pursuit to shape her reality through her art and life," as Coe describes it, dates from her earliest theatrical training, and it was profoundly shaped in turn by her experiences in Poland. The results of this pursuit can be witnessed throughout the writings collected in this book, particularly in tracing Klein's evolving vision of combining the "inner work" of liberatory imagination with the "outer work" of day-to-day training, organization, and care; this combination is as fundamental to artistic creation as it is to ethical existence. The opening texts in Chapters 1 and 3 are excerpted from the earliest of Klein's collected writings, a handbook for teaching theatre to school children she wrote three years after returning to the United States from Poland. Titled *Remodeling Theatre*, the handbook—part of her Master's project in Political Theatre Education—lays out many of the commitments that would later become embodied in and as Double Edge Theatre. Klein recognized that schoolchildren, even at an early age, had already built up defenses against spontaneity and creative expression. Drawing on the participatory tactics of people's theatre, Klein's handbook offers concrete strategies for enabling young students to be "free with their bodies and their voices" as a prerequisite to creative expression. Further, Klein's teaching proposes that art comes from the people and stresses, in particular, that it comes from the genius of the students' own cultures and ethnic backgrounds.

Around the same time as she began *Remodeling Theatre*, Klein's work with Little Flags Theatre and her subsequent academic research further instrumentalized her pursuit of social and artistic transformation in real, practical ways. Klein began a Ph.D. program in Theater at Tufts University in Boston while creating, in collaboration with Susie Chancey, the first two women's theatre festivals in the world, which took place in 1979 and 1980. She completed her Ph.D. in 1988, writing a dissertation on Eugenio Barba and the Odin Teatret, while conducting theatrical research in Poland, Germany, and Scandinavia.

It was during this period that she met the theatre artists with whom she founded Double Edge Theatre in 1982; this included Carroll Durand, who continued as a designer and actor in the Double Edge ensemble until retiring in 2016. Durand recalls their first collaboration, which led to a production of Maureen Duffy's play *Rites* at Tufts University in 1981. The play, a retelling of

Euripides' *Bacchae* set in a women's lavatory in London, became the inaugural performance of Double Edge Theatre a few months later. Here's how Durand, who still lives down the road from Double Edge's farm center in nearby Shelburne, Massachusetts, tells it:

> At the beginning of 1981 I was returning from a semester in Europe where I was doing theatre design, and Stacy had been in classes at the time. I walked into the Acting Head of the Design Department at Tufts, and my first assignment was to design the set for a piece by Lorien Corbelletti. The design was a little radical and very scary for me to do. I don't exactly remember when I met Stacy, but I know she was impressed by the design, and she approached me about getting involved in the Women's Theatre Festival. It didn't work out with my schedule, so I couldn't collaborate on that.
>
> She really needed to show the faculty at Tufts that she was a director, and the program was not going to allow her to do that. We worked out that she could take a slot in what was called the Cup and Saucer theatre series. The people in the design class were given a small budget to present a one-act performance. There was a slot available, and she was allowed to use that slot. The budget allotted for that performance was one hundred dollars.
>
> I think we must have spent at least three times or more of those one hundred dollars. That's part of Stacy: it may not look like it can be done, but it *can* be done, and it *will* be done, and pretty damned magnificently.[23]

Klein's proposal for this initial performance is featured in Chapter 1 of this book; it stands as a testament to Klein's directorial ability to achieve the seemingly impossible, as Durand suggests, as well as to her own steadfast resistance to silencing and erasure. For as Klein notes in her introduction to the proposal for staging *Rites* (see intra), in 1981 there were no women professors on the faculty of the university's theatre program, nor were there any women playwrights on the syllabus.

---

[23]Carroll Durand, conversation with the author, April 5, 2024.

The very name "Double Edge" extends from and commemorates the ensemble's formation around their performance of Duffy's, a modern-dress adaptation of *The Bacchae*. The fledgling theatre company adopted the double-bladed axe used in Bacchic sacrifices—the labrys—as their namesake. While frequently adopted as a feminist symbol throughout the 1970s and 1980s, the labrys stands here less as a weapon, I propose, than as a sacred instrument for combatting "isolation and erasure," part of the ensemble's core artistic and social mission. The company logo reflects this. As explained in the program note for Double Edge's second performance, *Blood Rubies* (1982), the company "transmuted the labrys into a winged woman" for their logo, "to show women's strength inseparable from beauty and truth."[24] Double Edge's iconography has evolved over the decades, much like its intersectional, nonbinary approach to feminism. It's worth noting in this context that the Double Edge mission statement features *three* points, not two: Art, Living Culture, and Art Justice. So too has Klein's career-long pursuit of justice and imagination expanded on the foundational mythos of the Bacchae to prioritize liberation rather than, say, bacchanalian intoxication or madness. In Duffy's *Rites* (a homonymic play on "rights"), the raving women of Euripidean tragedy become a vehicle for the expression of women's political anger. Returning to *The Bacchae* in 2022 for Double Edge's fortieth anniversary Summer Spectacle, Klein centers on the rites of the Bacchae as acts of detoxification and decolonization rather than rage; through these rites the women come to rematriate "their own languages, ritual, ceremony, and story." In this performance, titled *Hidden Territories of the Bacchae*, Klein explains how "we have brought a community of women out of their hidden territories to celebrate the power of their voices, songs, and ultimately, their passionate expression for freedom and a just world."[25]

---

[24]"The Song of the Axe," Program for *Blood Rubies*, 1982, p. 1. Double Edge Theatre Records, UMASS Amherst, Du Bois Library Special Collections, Box 1. A facsimile of "The Song of the Axe" is also visible in Double Edge Theatre's "From Allston to Ashfield: Historical Highlights from 1982-Present," *Medium* (April 24, 2019). https://medium.com/@DoubleEdgeTheatre/from-allston-to-ashfield-historical-highlights-from-1982-present-931c35c0714d, last accessed May 27, 2024.
[25]Stacy Klein, "Program Note for the *Hidden Territories of the Bacchae*," intra.

Hidden Territories of the Bacchae is in many ways an allegory for Double Edge Theatre itself: although the ensemble has included men and nonbinary artists since 1985, it has always remained "feminist to the core of its being," as Klein once put it.[26] This means working actively to counter sexism, oppression, and racism in all its forms. And like *Hidden Territories,* Double Edge persists after four decades as a passionate adventure founded on the power of voice, song, and art to create real conditions of possibility for creativity and justice. For Klein, the wisdom of the Bacchae thus amounts to a visionary defiance of hidebound attitudes about what is or is not "realistic."

This is precisely how Cariel Klein, Double Edge Co-Producer and ensemble member, who is also Klein's daughter, describes her mother's stalwart vision for Double Edge:

To cultivate a place like Double Edge, she needed to vision an alternate reality. She eschewed words and realities and created something else. It is not a paradise. This takes a lot of tears and sadness and hard, hard learning. She has crafted a place that she said she couldn't have even imagined when she started, and yet, look where we are now: growing into a place that, like her, defies description.

To describe Stacy Klein as a visionary, in this regard, is no exaggeration. What does it feel like to live in a visionary world? A further anecdote by Cariel speaks volumes:

When I was very young, I asked my mother to describe to me what she did for work. I believe she explained that she has a doctorate in directing, and I'm sure my questioning about the meaning of that provoked a type of response along the lines of "I studied how you see things and make them into reality." Of course, I happily went around telling everyone that my mother was an eye doctor. This moment is a theme in our relationship— conventional descriptions, or even conventional realities, failed Stacy, so she crafted her own description, and we moved beyond

---

[26]Stacy Klein, "Feminist at the Core of Its Being," intra.

words. This would be the ethos of Stacy: understand the words, listen, but go farther. Don't wait for them. When the reality fails us, exist in a place of dreaming, but let that dreaming be accompanied by determination and drive.[27]

✳✳✳

An Alchemy of Living Culture contains five chapters, in addition to Klein's introductory "Address to the Reader" and a conclusion. The first chapter, "Search Determines Form: Foundational Writings," addresses the history and development of Double Edge Theatre. It traces the origins of Klein's theatre practice and the formation of the Double Edge ensemble in the early 1980s, in response to the underrepresentation of women artists in contemporary theatre. The materials on this chapter trace how Klein articulated the purpose and exigency of her theatrical work as Double Edge evolved. The chapter also includes a sequence of artist's statements written ten, twenty, and thirty years after the formation of the company, reflecting on the core commitments of her work as a collaborative artist.

Chapter 2, "An Artists' Ensemble: On Autonomy and Collectivity," features short essays Klein wrote directly to the Double Edge ensemble and its community, articulating the working principles of the ensemble. Beginning with "Letter from Sardinia" (1985), which documents the powerful lessons of a residency in Italy with Klein's mentor Rena Mirecka, the texts in this section express the ideas about radical creativity, the work of collective experimental artistry, and the ethical commitment to lived experience that have come to exemplify the work of Double Edge.

The book's third chapter, "'Each Person Must Ask Why They Are Here': Training and Performance Creation," shifts its focus from the organization of the Double Edge ensemble to one of the core elements of its artistic practice, highlighting the intensive sphere of daily physical training. Consisting of embodied movement work and collective improvisation, physical training amplifies an artist's capacity for psycho-physical expression, enabling theatrical

---

[27]Cariel Klein, email correspondence with the author, May 14, 2024.

co-creation to draw on bodily as well as cognitive experience. To train, Klein explains, is to work on developing the capacity for physical dialogue; it means becoming adept at *not* succumbing to the pressures and demands of everyday life that stifle creativity. It thus also means learning to experience oneself beyond those restrictions. Incorporating excerpts from the journals Klein kept as she trained with Mirecka and Grotowski's Teatr Laboratorium as well as later interviews, training speeches, and other journals, this chapter highlights the core insistence of Klein's artistic ethos: never to impose a method, but instead to evoke each artist's unique process of searching and questioning, to foster their investigations into the recesses, as well as the limits, of bodily and imaginative possibility.

Chapter 4, "Art, Living Culture, Art Justice," turns to the social and political universe in which Klein's work has evolved; it traces how the lessons of Klein's work in the 1980s and 1990s have expanded into Double Edge's three-part mission in the present. The texts in this section address how Klein championed the social function of experimental art through the so-called Culture Wars of the late 1980s and 1990s, broadening the ensemble's feminist vision to redress racial and ethnic injustice. Galvanized by the company's relocation to rural Western Massachusetts and an immersive tour of Poland and Ukraine, texts in this section address the social and individual meaning of collective art in the face of genocide and atrocity as well as de-funding and privatization.

The final chapter of the book, "A Hidden Secret: Double Edge in and as Theatre History," presents Klein's research on the history of experimental theatre alongside her reflections on Double Edge's place in that history. Beginning with excerpts from her training diaries and journals from her early apprenticeship with Mirecka, it features the illuminating preface to her Ph.D. thesis on Eugenio Barba, as well as essays reflecting on Klein's approach to devised theatre.

Suggested Further Reading

Akeret, Julie (director). *Theatre on the Edge: Growing Art and Community at Double Edge Theatre* (2012); 38 minutes. https://www.akeretfilms.com/theater-on-the-edge.

Anderson, Rhonda; Spotted Crow Mann, Larry; Eburne, Jonathan P.; Klein, Stacy; Uriona, Carlos. "Where's Decolonization? The Ohketeau Cultural Center, Indigenous Sovereignty, and Arts Institutions." *The Routledge Companion to Decolonizing Art History*, ed. Tatiana Flores, Florencia San Martin, and Charlene Villaseñor Black. Routledge, 2023; 185–95.

Eburne, Jonathan P. "Worldmaking 101: Imagination and Reparation at Double Edge Theatre and Ohketeau Cultural Center." *HowlRound Theatre Commons* (November 14, 2022). https://howlround.com/worldmaking-101-imagination-and-reparation-double-edge-theatre-and-ohketeau-cultural-center.

Eburne, Jonathan P. "The Silences of Double Edge Theatre," *Theatre Magazine* 54:2 (2024), 134–7.

Fairley, Brian. "The Illuminated City of Memory: Double Edge Theatre in Jamaica Plain." *Ethnomusicology Review* (June 26, 2016). https://ethnomusicologyreview.ucla.edu/content/illuminated-city-memory-double-edge-theatre-jamaica-plain-0.

Glassman, Matthew. "Growing a Living Culture." *HowlRound Theatre Commons* (October 17, 2012). https://howlround.com/growing-living-culture.

Illakowicz, Krystyna Lipinska. "The Double Edge Theatre: Eastern European Allegiances, Resonances, and Alliances." *Slavic and East European Performance* 30:1 (Winter 2010), 24–32, 92.

Jimeno, Margarita (director). *American Theatre Wing—Working in the Theatre: Double Edge Theatre* (2016). https://vimeo.com/159814798.

Johnson, Jennifer. "'All Artwork Is a Magical Act': An Interview with Susan Aberth and Stacy Klein." *ASAP/J* (October 10, 2019). https://asapjournal.com/feature/all-artwork-is-a-magical-act-an-interview-with-susan-aberth-and-stacy-klein-jennifer-johnson/.

Klein, Stacy. "A Brief Talk about a Long Friendship in Theatre—Stacy Klein of Double Edge Theatre and Geddy Aniksdal of Grenland Friteater." *Medium* (September 11, 2019). https://medium.com/@DoubleEdgeTheatre/a-brief-talk-about-a-long-friendship-in-theatre-stacy-klein-of-double-edge-theatre-and-geddy-ffa298549783.

Klein, Stacy and Baraka Sele. *Double Edge Theatre: A Case Statement* (2021). https://doubleedgetheatre.org/wp-content/uploads/2021/04/DE-Case-Statement-April-2021.pdf.

Klein, Stacy and Baraka Sele. "The Radical and The Revolutionary: Stacy Klein and Baraka Sele on their Experiences in Theatre and Life as part of Double Edge Theatre's Fortieth Anniversary." *HowlRound Theatre Commons* (October 16, 2022). https://howlround.com/happenings/radical-and-revolutionary.

Landis, Kevin. "Dreaming in Place: For Double Edge and Its Audiences, an Old New England Dairy Farm Is a Living Theatrical Laboratory." *American Theatre* 26:6 (July–Aug., 2009), 28.

Martin, Carol. "Double Edge's 'Grand Paradise' Rushes the Gates of Heaven," *American Theatre* (April 1, 2013). https://www.americantheatre.org/2013/04/01/double-edges-grand-paradise-rushes-the-gates-of-heaven.

McAra, Catriona. *The Medium of Leonora Carrington: A Feminist Haunting in the Contemporary Arts.* Manchester, UK: Manchester University Press, 2022.

Miller, David. "Songs at the Well: Double Edge Theatre." *TDR* 39:2 (Summer, 1995), 115–46.

Schechner, Richard. "Double Edge Theatre in Its Ashfield Community: An Interview with Stacy Klein." *TDR/The Drama Review* 64:(4 (248)) (2020), 44–71.

Shea, Megan. "Transmogrifying Bruno Schulz's Universe: Double Edge Theatre's *Republic of Dreams.*" *TheatreForum* 32 (Winter/Spring 2008), 65–74.

Short, April M. "The Double Edge Theater's Project to 'Rematriate Land'." *Counterpunch* (March 22, 2024). https://www.counterpunch.org/2024/03/22/the-double-edge-theaters-project-to-rematriate-land/.

Williamson, Telory. "Rebuilding the Ruins: Intercultural Theatre Alliances between the U.S. and Eastern-Central Europe." *Slavic and East European Performance* 17:3 (Fall 1997), 76–83.

STACY KLEIN AND DOUBLE EDGE THEATRE: A TIMELINE

1956, November 16	Stacy Klein is born in Baltimore, Maryland. From the age of seven, she attends Ethel Rocklyn Drama Studio, Center Stage, with teachers Dwight Bowes and Vivienne Shub, and attends performances at the experimental international Baltimore Theatre Project.
1974, September	Moves to Boston to attend the Boston University School for the Arts and remains in Boston until 1997.
1975	Directs a performance on James Joyce, conceived by Colin Lane.
1975	Winter–Summer: Attends Tel Aviv University and spends a month in the desert.
1976 and 1977	During the summers, Klein studies theatre in Poland with a variety of theatrical artists, such as Tadeusz Kanto at the Cricot Theatre; Henryk Tomaszewski's Mime Theatre; and Jerzy Grotowski's Teatr Laboratorium, where she is trained by Rena Mirecka, Ludwig Flaszen, Antoni Jaholkowski, and Zygmunt Molik.

1977–9	Klein works as Assistant Director to Maxine Klein (no relation) of Little Flags Theatre, a political theatre for the 98 percent.
1978	Klein receives a BFA in directing from Boston University School for the Arts.
1980	Klein receives an MA in Political Theatre Education from Goddard College and writes *Remodeling Theatre: A Workbook on Teaching Children's Theatre* after working at the O.H. Perry Elementary School as an instructor and consultant.
1980	Klein enters the Ph.D. program in Theatre History and Criticism at Tufts University.
1980 and 1981	Klein co-produces, with Susie Chancey, the Womyn's Theatre Festival, the first international women's festival.
1981, September	Klein proposes to direct a production of Maureen Duffy's *Rites* at Tufts, with Carroll Durand as designer.
1981, November	Performance of *Rites* at the Arena Theatre, Tufts University.
1982, April	Double Edge Theatre founded by Stacy Klein, with Carroll Durand, Daina Robins, Lorien Corbelletti, and others featured in DE's first performances (including Lynn Bailey, Madeleine McNamara, Kayla Black, and Andrea Dishy).

The Women's Cycle (1982–6)

1982, April	Double Edge's first production, *Rites,* premiers at the Institute of Contemporary Art in Boston.
1982, October–November	*Blood Rubies*, adapted from Michael McDowell's novel by the author, with the ensemble; Old Cambridge Baptist Church, Cambridge, MA.
1983, July–August	*My Sister in this House*, by Wendy Kesselman; Overland Theater, Massachusetts College of Art, Boston, MA.
1983–4	Double Edge adds men to the ensemble, and in all aspects of the theatre, including David Flaxman and Nachum Cohen, who later become core creators of the Song Trilogy.
1984, January–February	*The Hunger Artist*, by Tadeusz Rozewicz, after Franz Kafka; adapted by Michael McDowell for Double Edge Theatre; Actor's Workshop, Boston.
1984, August	*Electra,* by Socrates; Arena Theatre, Tufts University; the performance culminates a Double Edge summer residency at Tufts. Bonnie Cordon, core creator of the Song Trilogy, joins DE.
1984, November–December	*Had She Spoken.* Translated by Daina Robins from pieces excerpted by Klein from Christine Brueckner's *If You Had Spoken, Desdemon*a; Church

	of St. Luke and St. Margaret, Allston, MA.
1984, December	The Parish Hall at the Episcopal Church of Saints Luke and Margaret, an unused 30' × 60' space next to the Church, becomes Double Edge's home for the next twelve years. After renovations, the permanent site enables the Ensemble to develop its intensive training practice and create original performances.
1985, March–May	Double Edge immersive workshops for the ensemble in Allston and for a group in Beckett, MA led by Rena Mirecka, with Mariusz Socha.
1985, April–May	*Bold Stroke for a Wife*, by Susanna Centlivre; Church of St. Luke and St. Margaret, Allston, MA.
1985, Summer–Fall	Klein, joined by David Flaxman, travels to Odin Teatret in Denmark to research her Ph.D. dissertation, and to Sardinia, Italy, to continue training with Mirecka. Out of this journey, the Song Trilogy Cycle is born (1987–98). During the visit Eugenio Barba takes Klein to see Poland's Gardzienice theatre, leading to a longstanding exchange between DE and Gardzienice that includes the production of each other's work, conversations, friendship, and the first phase of the "extra-

	theatrical" *Republic of Dreams* project (1985–2000).
1986, January–February	*Chehov Project*, adapted by Jacques Chwat from *Three Sisters*, by Anton Chekhov. Guest director, Jacques Chwat, is a mentor of Klein's (Allston). Although Klein is the lead trainer for the ensemble, this is the only performance in DE history in which she takes part as an actor.
1986, May–June	*Request Concert*, by Franz Xaver Kroetz (Allston).
1986, August	Klein, Bonnie Cordon, and Andrea Dishy attend the first Magdalena Festival, led by Jill Greenhalgh, during which Klein meets Grenland Friteatr's Geddy Aniksdal, a lifelong friend and collaborator.
1986, September	Max Palar, Silat Master, begins public seminars on the White Crane System of Indonesian Kung Fu. Pilar subsequently becomes a resident artist and collaborator with Double Edge, particularly in working with Klein.
1986–7	First versions of *Song of Absence and the Fall of the Ashen Reign* presented.
1986–8	Research begins in Poland, in Germany with Ludger Schnieder of Pumpenhaus Theater (later a contributor to *Song of Absence*), and in Scandinavia with Grenland Friteater, Norway.

Later the entire company conducts a research visit to the Lubavitch community, New York City. This research initiates the "Republic of Dreams" project, which continues through 2000.

The Song Trilogy (1987–98)

1987–8	Guest Artists: Zygmunt Molik of Teatr Laboratorium, Poland; Ludger Schnieder, a dramaturg for *Song of Absence* (Theater im Pumpenhaus, Germany).
1988, January	Electra '88, an international festival of experimental solo performances by women, co-produced by Double Edge and the Women in Theatre Festival (Allston). The Festival collaborates with DE until it closes in the 1990s. As part of this, The Theater Offensive, who later become a partner of DE in the 2020s, premiere their first performance at Allston DE space.
1988, May	Klein receives Ph.D. in Drama from Tufts University, completing a dissertation, "Eugenio Barba, Master Craftsman and the Odin Teatret's *Oxyrhynchus Evangeliet*."
1988, September–October	*Song of Absence*, third and final version, premieres on tour of Poland. Directed and conceived by Klein, *Song of Absence* is co-

created with Cordon, Flaxman, and Cohen. The role of Bruno Schulz passes from Corbelletti to Dishy, then to Diane Edgecomb, then to Gwido Zlatkes, whom the company meets on Polish tour. Durand also plays an acting role in *Song of Absence*.

1988–9

Guest performances of Gardzienice's *Avakuum* and *Gusla*. Guest Artist: Jacek Ostaszewski (OSJAN, Poland), composer of pieces of DE performances *Song of Absence*, *Song of Songs* (1993), and the performance *Republic of Dreams* (2007).

1989 Winter

Back from the Polish tour, without funds, company members take full-time jobs. Further performances of *Songs of Absence*. DE hosts intensives and undertakes research for *Song of Songs*.

1989–90

Klein and Zlatkes begin research on *Song of Songs* in Poland. Flaxman, Klein, Cordon, and Nachum Cohen conduct research in Israel.

1990

Group work begins on *Song of Songs* on a retreat in Maine.

1990, December

Klein takes research trip to Norway, continuing her association with Grenland Friteater.

1990–1

Klein is introduced to the Trust for Mutual Understanding, a

	Central European-US exchange foundation, which begins an over thirty-year relationship that continues through the present day. Includes funding for Conversations, touring, and research on projects such as the "Republic of Dreams," led by their then program director Wendy Newton and, more recently, Executive Director Barbara Lanciers, who also becomes a Board member of DE.
1991	Double Edge's internship program begins.
1991	Klein's daughter Tadea Isa is born, the first child born to a current member of the company.
1991–2	Public Training Program: Theatrical Vision (training program ongoing).
December 1991–January 1992	*Song of Absence* performed during a six-week residency at Philip Arnoult's Baltimore Theatre Project.
1992	Work on "extratheatrical Republic of Dreams," with sessions between Klein and Włodzimierz Staniewski of Gardzienice, with Philip Arnoult, in Boston and New York.
1992, February	First preview performances of *Song of Songs*. Felicia Shpall becomes an intern, then a performer, in Double Edge for *Song of Songs*.

1992, September	Klein's mother, Carole Sollins Klein, dies.
1993, March	Theatre Culture meeting. Double Edge's association with the Charlestown Working Theater dates from this meeting; CTW company members Jennifer Johnson and John Peitso become associates of DE, joining the Ensemble for *Keter* (1997).
1993	In May, Klein's daughter Cariel is born.
1993, September	Flaxman, Shpall, and Zlatkes travel to Ukraine for the first exploration of "Republic of Dreams" with Staniewski and Gardzienice.
1993, November	Charlestown Working Theater apprenticeship/collaboration begins.
1993, November	Final version of *Song of Songs* premieres (Allston).
1994, January–April	After obtaining permit to house a theatre company there, DE purchases 101-acre former dairy farm in the rural town of Ashfield, MA. This decision is precipitated by the absolute economic impossibility of paying exorbitant Boston rents and housing overseas guest artists for long periods. Having witnessed examples of rural theatre outside of major urban hubs in Central Europe and Scandinavia, the Ensemble determines

	that sustainability might be found more readily in a rural environment.
1994, February	Klein and ensemble travel to Germany, Belgium, Poland, Ukraine, Bulgaria, and Israel for development of "Republic of Dreams" and other projects.
1994, April	Klein and her children move to the Farm. This begins a three-year period of overlap between Boston and Ashfield. The dream of living in Ashfield and maintaining performance space in Boston dissolves by 1997—after three years of traveling three hours back and forth to Boston with young children in the car.
1994, June	Flaxman, Cordon, Cohen, and Durand move to the Farm, joining Klein. Johnson and Peitso split their time between the Charlestown Working Theater in Boston and DE in Ashfield.

Training begins on the Farm

Work begins on creating a center for international performance and research in Ashfield. Between 1994 and 1997, Klein and DE find local support from Gene LaValley, who manages and renovates the farm for eight years; as well as from Ray Gray, an excavator, and Kevin Purinton, a plumber, who continue to support DE through the present with renovations of fifteen buildings and four separate properties.

1994, August	Training workshop led by Klein at the Portland (Oregon) Theater Festival.
1994, Fall	DE makes full company expedition to Ukraine for the final part of "Republic of Dreams: Hidden Territories," now independently from Gardzienice. The company performs *Song of Songs* in Ukraine, and later at Portland International Festival in Oregon.
1995	Continued renovation and development of the Farm; Klein and ensemble begin developing *Keter: The Crowning Song*.
1996	Carlos Uriona arrives from Argentina with his own company, Diablomundo, and soon becomes a leader in the Double Edge ensemble, bringing with him a unique view on alternative economic systems. Uriona's work grows out of Diablomundo's response to the Dirty War in Argentina, which involves holding large-scale actions of music, dance, and spectacle in Plazas across Argentina, as creative protest. Uriona partners with Stacy Klein to bring together his own grassroots work with Double Edge's training and performance process, as well as the cultural research from Central Europe.
1996	While Klein works on the final piece of the Song Trilogy, *Keter,*

in a still uninsulated barn in Western Massachusetts, her father, Belman Klein, dies, leaving a gift to the theatre that enables renovations of the barn and its substructure. Ceceile Klein, Stacy's sister, becomes a patron and Board Member of the theatre and has remained so through the present.

1997, March

Keter, The Crowning Song premieres in Boston.

1997, May–June

"Republic of Dreams" project continues in Romania; perform *Keter* at the Sibiu International Theatre Festival, Romania.

1997, June

Renovations to the barn completed; Double Edge opens first performance space in Ashfield—the Barn—with a staging of *Keter.* Conversations series, co-presented with Arnoult, begins with TMU and other Central European artists. Series includes programs on "International Theatre Training," "Laboratory Theaters," "Art and Place," "Local, National, International," and "Bold Women," featuring guest artists from around the world.

Group kitchen built in former farming workshop attached to barn, and living spaces for Ensemble created under barn. These rooms go through many transformations but are now

	dressing rooms for ensemble and company.
1997, July	DE hosts first Training Intensive for students at the Farm, lasting a full month.
1997, September	Final version of *Keter* premieres at the Farm.
1997, October	DE performs *Keter* in Poland at Lublin Festival.
1997, December	Open rehearsal for DE/Diablomundo collaboration, "The Spiral Mirror" (Carlos Uriona, Perla Logarzo, and Manuel Uriona, then a fifteen-year-old percussionist, who continues to perform with DE through the present day).
1998, Spring	Expedition to Argentina.
1998, Summer	Premiere of the Song Trilogy in its entirety (Farm Center). Uriona takes over the roles David Flaxman co-created, and Johnson takes over Shpall's role in *Song of Songs*. Flaxman and Shpall leave performing to raise their children, Zack and Anna, while continuing in other roles with DE; Felicia dies in 2004. Final performance of Bonnie Cordon and Nachum Cohen after fifteen years in the Ensemble.
1999–2002	Klein and Uriona work together, continuing research on Kabbalah, magic realism, and explorations of Jewish and Latin American

	(and Latin@) cultures, under the name of The Spiral Mirror project. During this period Eugenio Uriona (born in 1994) moves back to the DE Farm. This begins Klein and Uriona's work-life family merging, with the Klein-Uriona family consisting of Tadea, Cariel, Eugenio, and Manuel Uriona (the latter living most of the time in Argentina).
1999–2001	Formation of The Consortium of Theatre Practices, a US-Poland theatre exchange involving Gardzienice, Kadmus Theatre Studio, and DE.
2000	DE converts third barn at DE into an indoor Pavilion, a second space for training and a lobby for audiences. Due to all the barns being used as theatre, the only new building on Farm Center is built as an animal barn.
2000–3	*Relentless*, created with Johnson, Peitso, and Uriona and directed by Klein, is researched and performed in the barn and on tour in Poland, Burlington, VT, and Boston, MA. This begins the Garden of Intimacy and Desire Cycle, although Johnson and Peitso do not appear in the rest of the Cycle, as they suspend indoor performance creation with DE to raise their son Eliot and attend to the Charlestown Working Theater.

2002–Present: Summer Spectacles

The first outdoor Spectacle draws an audience of forty people to three outdoor settings on the Farm (the barn, the field, and the pond); the Summer Spectacle now has a six-week season that draws an audience of thousands, and the performances take place all throughout the Farm. This special event comes to define the Living Culture of Double Edge and the town of Ashfield, which, over the course of these creative years together, become a community. The Summer Spectacle is a clear manifestation of the merging of Klein's vision with that of Uriona's popular and street theatre. From *Don Quixote* through *Arabian Nights*, DE welcomes new Ensemble members Matthew Glassman, Hayley Brown, Jeremy Louise Eaton, Adam Bright, Hannah Jarrell, and Milena Dabova, among others. Richard Newman later performs in several pieces in the Garden Cycle. Brian Fairley takes over from Justin Handley as Music Director during the Garden Cycle.

2002, Summer   *The Saragossa Manuscripts* (Summer Spectacle).

The Garden of Intimacy and Desire (2001–10)

Beginning with *Relentless*, the Garden Cycle continues with three performances exploring distinctive visions of magic realism in Jewish and Hispanic culture, created by Klein with Uriona and Matthew Glassman. With the exception of the first piece, *Relentless*, the Cycle—*The UnPOSSESSED*, *Republic of Dreams*, and *The Disappearance*—is presented in its entirety in 2010, with performances featuring shared meals, Conversations, and other offerings.

2003, Summer   *Don Quixote* (Summer Spectacle).

2003   Preview of indoor version of *The UnPOSSESSED*.

2003, Fall   Tour of Central Europe with the *UnPOSSESSED* with Carlos

	Uriona as Quixote and Matthew Glassman as Sancho.
2004, Summer	*Master and Margarita* (Summer Spectacle). Includes international students from Poland, two of whom Michal Kuriata (designer) and Ewa Timingeriu (carpenter and musician), return as collaborators and company members through today.
2004, October–November	Inspired by *Don Quixote, The UnPOSSESSED* premiers at La MaMa in New York City. Performance then tours to Spain, Poland, ART in Boston, Hartford Austin Arts Center. Performances (2005–10).
2005, Summer	*The Three Musketeers* (Summer Spectacle).
2006, Summer	*The Magician of Avalon* (Summer Spectacle).
2007	DE purchases second property in Ashfield as a residence for students and guest artists.
2007	*Republic of Dreams*, performance based on the life and stories of Bruno Schulz, created with Uriona as the Father and Glassman as Bruno Schulz, with the DE ensemble.
2008, Summer	*The Illustrious Return of Don Quixote* (Summer Spectacle) Klein co-directs with Matthew Glassman.
2008–10	*The Disappearance* (2008–10), final piece in the Garden Cycle.

	Written by collaborator Ilan Stavans, from his book *The Disappearance*, and interspersed with scenes from *The Merchant of Venice*. Directed by Klein, co-created with Ensemble.
2009	For "Bold Women of Theatre," in Conversations series, Rena Mirecka makes her first trip to the Farm, enabling her to teach a new generation of DE artists. She returns two additional times during her lifetime, overseeing the construction of a meditation pavilion called Temple of the Sun. (Klein, Uriona, and Cariel Klein visit Mirecka in Poland on multiple occasions.)
2009, Summer	*The Arabian Nights* (Summer Spectacle).
2009	Tadea Klein, age seventeen, begins designing costumes for the theatre and, through many transformations, remains the costume designer for DE. All the children of DE—Tadea, Cariel, Eugenio, and later Eliot—take part in performances as children, mostly because the ensemble works outside all summer and needs to include them. As of *Shaharazad* (2013) we leave this behind as the work become more complicated and the kids no longer want to participate. One continuing outcome is that Cariel becomes interested in flying acrobatics and circus, goes

to circus school, and has been flying and choreographing aerial work with DE ever since.

The Chagall Cycle (2010–15)

Performances in Chagall Cycle conceived and directed by Klein. All are Summer Spectacles based on Marc Chagall's paintings, with the exception of *Grand Parade*, which is based instead on Chagall's life throughout the twentieth century. In *Grand Parade* the actors do not speak, although they sing. Media from the beginning to the end of the century designed by Brian Fairley. For *Grand Parade* the Ensemble includes Uriona, Glassman, Hayley Brown, Jeremy Eaton, Adam Bright, Milena Dabova, Jennifer Johnson, and Hannah Jarrell. Our collaboration with Alexander Bakshi (composer) and Liudmila Bakshi (musical director) begins during this period and continues through all group indoor performances directed by Klein to this day.

2010, Summer	*Firebird* (Summer Spectacle).
2011, Summer	*The Odyssey* (Summer Spectacle); performances at College of the Atlantic, Amherst College, and in Norway. Morgan Jenness comes on a site visit for New England Foundation for the Arts, and becomes a dramaturg for DE. She remains dramaturg and creative consultant until her death in Novmber 2024.
2012, Summer	*The Odyssey* (Summer Spectacle).
2012	*Theatre on the Edge: Growing Art and Community at Double Edge Theatre* Directed by Julie Akeret, documentary.
2013	Klein receives the Doris Duke Artist Award.

2013, Summer	*Shahrazad, A Tale of Love and Magic* (Summer Spectacle). Amanda Miller and Andrew Todd join DE during this period. While both begin by performing, Amanda becomes costumiere and then co-musical director in 2022 and Andrew becomes Production and Facilities Manager in 2023. Walton Wilson begins vocal coaching for DE and continues through today, eventually acting in *The Bacchae* as Cadmus.
2013–16	*The Grand Parade*. Touring includes Arena Stage; CityStage (Springfield, MA); PEAK Performances (Montclair, NJ); Baltimore Theatre Project; Colombia College, Chicago (where we meet Travis Coe); Norway; and Russia. Amrita Ramanan meets DE at Arena Stage, and soon after becomes Associate Producer. After an absence of several years Ramanan later returns as Board member and dramaturg.
2014, Summer	*Shahrazad, A Tale of Love and Magic*.
2014	The Conversations Series, including "Art and Place" and "Art of the Rural," transforms into the biennial Art and Survival Convening, working at the intersection of art, community, and climate. Led by Matthew Glassman with Nick Slie (Mondo

Bizarro), Art and Survival is later led by Ebony Noelle Golden as it becomes a three-year BIPOC fellowship, leading to a final Convening and Festival in 2023, hosting six performances and forty international artists, as well as a visit from Little Amal.

The Latin American Cycle (2015–18)

Performances in this cycle conceived and directed by Klein, with story by Klein based on Uriona's history during the Argentine military dictatorship. Text adapted by Glassman. Ensemble led by Uriona, Johnson, Glassman, Dabova, Jarrell, Peitso, Bright, and Eaton (this is Eaton's final performance role, who decides to become a designer and director). Music by Manuel Uriona and Mica Farias Gomez. Ebony Noelle Golden visits the Farm for the first time in 2016.

During these years, Bob Carlton, now Chef and Musician, joins the Company; Johnson and Peitso move permanently to Ashfield; Dylan Young, now Business Manager and musician, begins in 2018; Silas Riemer applies for a cooking job and becomes the greatest outdoor designer I have ever worked with, partnering with me on all landscaping and stonework, designing labyrinths, and moving DE's environmental work forward. In 2017–18, Victor Figueroa arrives as a fifteen-year-old student to take part in a Summer Spectacle, returning as a professional dancer and aerialist in 2023 to become a Company Member. Michael Fitzgerald, who grew up on the Farm as the son of the farmers who preceded DE for forty-five years, becomes Operations Manager for five years beginning in 2018.

2015–16	*Once a Blue Moon—Cada Luna Azul.*
2016	*American Theatre Wing— Working in the Theatre: Double Edge Theatre.* Director/

	Producer Margarita Jimeno (documentary).
2016	*The Latin American Spectacle*; tours to the streets of Jamaica Plain and a public park in Springfield, working with community members and high school students. These events use abandoned churches, streets, and underutilized parks to bring the community together.
2017, May	Ashfield Town Spectacle & Culture Fair. The town spectacle is a gift back from DE to the town. Researched for a full year, with community groups, townspeople, and the Historical Society. Collaboration begins with Rhonda Anderson, Jasmine Rochelle Goodspeed, and Larry Spotted Crow Mann, who found the Ohketeau Cultural Center, DE's first official partnership. In 2024, Anderson leaves Ohketeau and Mann became sole director. The town spectacle takes place throughout the town and involves eighty local community members and artists, with scenes/stories/events by Johnson, Glassman, and Eaton. Performances are followed by a community dance on town commons (the first of many) choreographed by Dabova; a parade to the Lake, with music led by Peitso, Miller, Manuel Uriona, and Mica Farias Gomez; and an aerial flight over the Lake

by Cariel Klein, with costumes by Tadea Klein. Ray Gray, neighbor and friend, provides the equipment—historical and contemporary—for the Town Spectacle. Produced and created by Klein, with Uriona and Adam Bright. Bright has been producing outdoor spectacles with Klein, along with overseeing all production, for years. This partnership expandes the possibilities of outdoor theatre, and later the theatre itself. This is the first appearance by Travis Coe in a DE performance, and the first associate producing by Cariel Klein.

This is an important time at DE. Yulia Dabova Bright, daughter of Dabova and Bright, is born three days before the Town Spectacle, followed in October 2017 by Davi Glassman, son of Eaton and Glassman. Tadea, already costume designer, learns farming from Adamah Farm in CT and starts developing the Farm vision and implements DE's working farm, which today includes large vegetable gardens, a hoop house, orchards, and some animals.

2017, Summer

We the People (summer spectacle). Based on the Town Spectacle, *We the People* centers on five historical figures from the region who were instrumental to social transformation in Massachusetts.

The Surrealist Cycle (2017–present)

Performances conceived and directed by Klein, with *Leonora: La Maga y la Maestra* and *Leonora's World* co-created with Johnson and Uriona. *SUGA* is solo performance created and performed by Coe and directed by Klein

2017–present	*Leonora: La Maga y la Maestra.* While researching Leonora Carrington (British-born, Mexican refugee) we meet Susan Aberth, a foremost Carrington art historian, who becomes instrumental with this and all our work on Surrealism. The Bakshis return from Russia to compose the music, and Manuel Uriona continues to play percussion. The performance evolves from a large-scale production to a core company performance led by Jennifer and Carlos, with Milena, Travis, Amanda, Hannah, Cariel, and John as lead musician. A variety of people, including Mica, Matthew, Adam, and Tomantha, have played roles in this series. Desire Graham, DE artist-in-residence, takes a role in *Leonora* as well. Tours include the Pitt Festival in Norway and Teatr Brama in Poland.
2018	DE becomes part of Barr Foundation cohort and develops an exchange based on rural community art building.

2018, March	Anger / Appetite / Ambition / ART—a Symposium on Women Innovators in the Arts: Montclair State University. One of three panelists, Klein meets Baraka Sele, the Facilitator, who becomes DE's consultant through 2024.
2018, March	*Leonora: La Maga y la Maestra* performed at Peak Performances at Montclair State University (Montclair, NJ). This performance premieres under the leadership of Jedediah Wheeler, and is later filmed for public television.
2018, Summer	*We the People* (summer spectacle). The Farm is developed to include seven outdoor performance sites.
2018, Fall	*Leonora's World* (fall spectacle). A three-day event using imagery from the world of Leonora Carrington. The DE Ensemble works with several groups in the Consortium such as Open Flame and alumni from student trainings, who came back to create professionally.
2019, March	Preview of *SUGA*, solo performance by Travis Coe, directed by Klein.
2019, April	*Leonora's World* performed at the Farm Center.
2019, Summer	*I Am the Baron* (Summer Spectacle), directed by Glassman

	and Eaton and written by Glassman, this is the first Summer Spectacle not directed by Klein. Glassman, like Eaton, decides to focus on directing, and although he continues to perform for another year, begins his move toward creating his own children's theatre project.
2019, Fall	*Leonora's World* (fall spectacle).
2019, November	Premiere of *SUGA*, performed at the Farm Center. Ritual performance inspired by James Baldwin, SUGA delves into the life and ancestry of Travis Coe, with an exhibit before the performance and followed by "respondency" with audience.
2020, February	*Leonora: La Maga y la Maestra* performed at the Farm Center and during Technical Residency at ArtsEmerson (Boston, MA).
2020, March	*SUGA* performed at CRASHBOX by Rude Mechs (Austin, TX).
2020, March	*Leonora: La Maga y la Maestra* performed at the Revolutions Festival (Albuquerque, NM); this is intended as the first stop of a US tour, but the Covid-19 pandemic forces Double Edge to cancel tour.
2019–22	During the Covid-19 pandemic, there is much building at the Farm, including renovated kitchen with views of fields and Farm; four-season wood

shop in original 1700s barn; music room; the Ohketeau Cultural Center and kitchen; artist studio renovation; a hoop house; and arbors. Renovations to the farmhouse (which begin when Klein and Uriona move to a house in Ashfield in 2011) continue with office conversions, and creation of two apartments for guests and company members. Some of this work is funded by Art Place and the Mass Cultural Council Cultural Facilities Fund.

Covid Spectacles

In order to keep working during Covid, Klein and DE create outdoor-only work held in small groups for our community; we hold safe residencies, particularly with Ebony Golden; continue building our partnerships; and we introduce the "Living Presence of Our History" series with Ohketeau Cultural Center and host artist immersions, out of which Tomantha Sylvester, now part of the Ensemble, first comes to DE. Growing out of Ohketeau and their work with Andre Strongbearheart Gaines is another partner organization, No Loose Braids. Harold Steward comes for a residency and brings The Theatre Offensive, who have now become another DE partner, led by Tonasia Jones.

During this period, Adam Bright, who has transitioned from actor and technical director/rigger to executive director, and Cariel Klein, who moves quickly from associate producer to co-producer, and now to producing director, begin producing frequent events with Klein and other Ensemble members. Events include community days, conversations, and continuing open trainings.

2020, Summer   *Six Feet Apart, All Together*, performed outdoors at the Farm, attendance limited to masked

	groups of thirty (Summer Spectacle).
2021, June	*Howling at the Moon*, directed by Klein with Coe, Uriona, Johnson, and Dabova, featuring Larry Spotted Crow Mann.
2021, Summer	*Memories and Dreams*, directed by Klein, co-directed with Jeremy Louise Eaton (summer spectacle).
2021, October	Klein and Baraka Sele participate in "The Radical and the Revolutionary," a public conversation about their work.
2022	**40th Anniversary Celebration.**
2022, April	Double Edge hosts RITES: A Magdalena Festival, in collaboration with the Magdalena Project. Five-day festival features performances from worldwide women, non-binary, and trans artists, as well as symposia; includes work by longstanding collaborators Jill Greenhalgh (*Daughters*), Geddy Aniksdal (*No Doctor for the Dead*), Ebony Noelle Golden/ Jupiter Performance Studio (*Spectre of Sunlight*), and Open Flame (*The Garden*); also includes Tomantha Sylvester's *Something Else* (the first of two performances at DE, co-produced with Ohketeau and Anishinaabe Theater Exchange) and Eaton's *Lightning* (the first of three presentations of this performance at DE).

2022, May–June

Constellations, An Outdoor Festival, highlights DE's partnerships with Ohketeau Cultural Center, The Hinterlands, and Jupiter Performance Studio. Performances include *In the Name of the Mother Tree* (JPS); *Will You Miss Me?* (Hinterlands); and *Freedom in Season,* by Larry Spotted Crow Mann (Ohketeau/DE co-production).

2022, Summer

Hidden Territories of the Bacchae (Summer Spectacle). Performance directed and conceived and designed by Klein, bringing DE full circle from its first performance, *Rites,* also based on *The Bacchae. Hidden Territories* centers on the women's chorus rather than the patriarchal society of Euripides's classical tragedy. Co-created by Johnson and Dabova, with DE's ensemble, plus collaborators from throughout the history of DE (including Daina Robins, co-founder, and Desiré Graham, who performed in *Cada Luna Azul* and now an artist-in-residence of DE).

The indoor performance of *The Bacchae* includes artists-in-resident Desirée Graham, Mica Farias Gomez, and Tricia Trinh, with score composed by Alexander Bakshi and Liudmila Bakshi, to premiere in 2026.

2022–4	Coe directs new Company member Karol Matuszak in *Rainbow Exodus*, about Karol's history of growing up in Poland as a young gay man. Carlton creates solo performance, *My Soul Is in Command*. Artists-in-residence include Sage Crump and Muhti Reed. Klein initiates the Living Culture and Art Justice Village project, a vision of the theatre that includes housing, design spaces, Indigenous crafts, and climate justice work. Bright and Klein are Producers of this project and the four properties at DE start expanding to fulfill this vision. Bright is now working to combine municipality and town and to create a model of climate reparation at DE's site.
2023, June	*Leonora: La Maga y la Maestra* tours to Teatr Brama (Poland) & Porsgrunn Internasjonale Teaterfestival (Norway).
2023, Summer	*Hidden Territories of the Bacchae* (Summer Spectacle).
2023, October	Klein and Carlos Uriona step away from daily artistic direction and become Vision Strategist (Klein) and Cultural Strategist (Uriona). Klein continues to direct; Uriona continues to act; both continue their work with DE partners, as well as Living Culture Village project. Travis Coe, Milena

	Dabova, and Jennifer Johnson become Double Edge's Artistic Directors; Adam Bright becomes Executive Director and Cariel Klein becomes Producer. Other ensemble members are John Peitso, Hannah Jarrell, Amanda Miller, and Tomantha Sylvester. This group represents over two hundred years of combined work experience at DE.
2024, January–February	Intensive work period on converting *Hidden Territories of the Bacchae* to indoor performance with Dabova, Johnson, Uriona, Coe, Miller, Sylvester, Desiré Graham, and Mica Farias Gomez. Bakshi returns as composer and Ludimila Bakshi as Music Director.
2024, May	Klein attends Doris Duke Artist retreat as council member. Kim Pevia joins Ohketeau Cultural Center as Leadership Consultant. Pevia also works directly with Klein and Uriona on developing connective partnerships and community vision.
2024, July	Klein attends LaMama Umbria Director Symposium in Spoleto, Italy, as teaching artist, with colleagues Amrita Ramanan and Barbara Lanciers.
2024, Summer	*The Heron's Flight* (Summer Spectacle), directed by Johnson and Coe.

2025

Cultural and Survival Strategies developed for facing the US leadership crisis and its destructive effect on DE Community and larger populations. Among other actions include performing *Leonora* in March, hosting community gatherings, addressing housing and food security, organizing environmental work, and supporting our community, working particularly with under-represented populations.

2025, January–March

Second intensive work period on *Hidden Territories of the Bacchae*, with premiere in 2026.

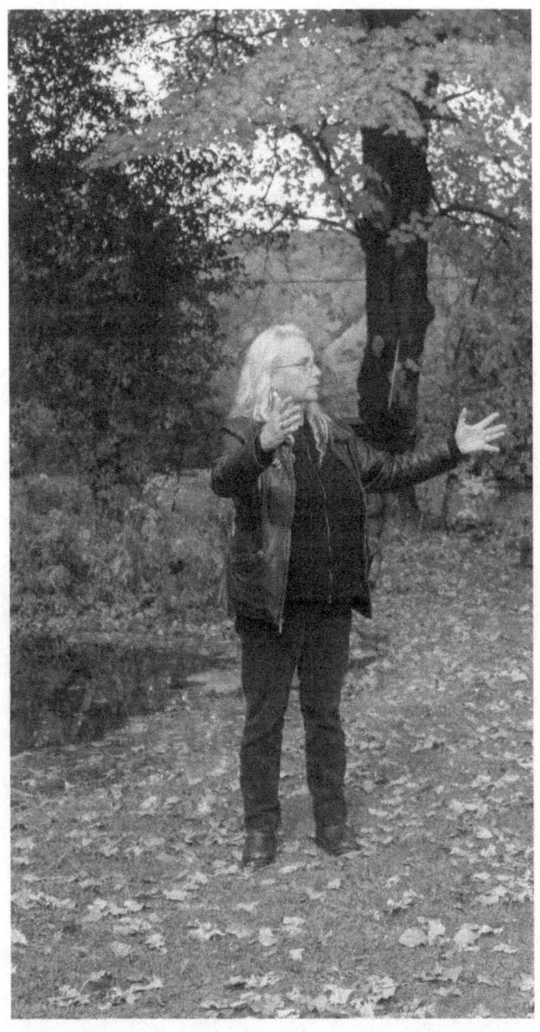

FIGURE 1 *Stacy Klein directing* Leonora's World, *2018. Photo by Kim-Chin Gibbons.*

Introduction: An Address to the Reader

Dear Reader,

It has taken me many years to write a book about my work, and as you will see, this is a book about a book: it compiles writing that dates from even before the very beginning of Double Edge, and it includes a lot of reflection on the words I have written over the span of my career. One reason for the delay in publishing these words has been that it is unusual for me, and therefore for Double Edge, to use words as the starting point in any creative process. We have historically begun our work—our creative process, our training, and our student training—in silence. Today, too, we start our work in silence, yet we recognize today that the power of the voice is required. We are living in an historically impossible moment, when we must not only acknowledge the many voices that are shut down, but also fight with all that is available for our survival. I, therefore, want to share my words and embrace and uplift the power of the voice. I hope to lift the shared experience in front of us, so that we can all be part of it.

First, I want to take you on a short walk through the world of Double Edge and offer some words about how we understand the spaces where we train and create—particularly the barn, which has been our central space for the thirty years we have lived and worked in Ashfield. My company was located in Boston for twelve years before we moved to this region. We have tried to make our theatrical home a sacred space. When we enter it, we want to remove ourselves from the tumult of our daily lives, the noise in our heads, the things that distract us. I ask myself, and anyone who joins us in this space, to leave that noise behind as we attempt to summon the quiet within us. Concretely, this means that the barn and the nearby pavilion (when used as a creative training space) are not spaces for daily conversation or chatter, but for attempting to find that peace of mind—for holding space for oneself and others beyond the daily, the daily answers to stress.

Double Edge was founded as a feminist theatre, and as a training theatre. From the beginning, we have sought ways to achieve a balance between our political selves—which include our belief systems about the world we live in—and our inner experiences. As political beings, it was extremely hard for us to focus on inner experience, and we had to insist or force ourselves to do so. Maybe you find, as we did in 1982, that it is difficult today to dwell on the inside while living under extreme circumstances. We often faced the expectation that we would be performing social theatre, or that we would go out and fight in the streets. And we were, and we did— but what we really wanted was to work on ourselves at the same time as we fought for our beliefs. This is what we have been doing ever since. It is challenging to find balance between the external needs, necessities, and limits of our lives, and the internal desires one finds through the vulnerability of questioning and the discovery of unknown possibilities.

I won't give you a history lesson right now, because my words are particular to this moment. During the time we share as you read this book, you can learn about how my group and I have approached the project we set out to undertake over forty years ago, and also how this project has continued to evolve. If you were visiting Double Edge in person today, you'd have an opportunity to talk to the people who have been here for many years, as well as to look around and experience what Double Edge is and has become since the days when the company consisted of five women moving from temporary space to temporary space, while trying to train and create a new sense of autonomy. Each member of our group invites visitors to speak with them, and we always invite audience members and visiting artists to congregate with us after performances, to share wine and water, to gather in artistic collectivity in silence or in dialogue.

We are and have always been an ensemble of individuals, and each person holds a unique place at Double Edge. At the same time, our group is united in a collective desire to replace cultural imperialism with *art justice*. This informs how we deal with even the most mundane aspects of our work, such as the ways we source food for our company meals, and the ways we respect each other and the land—even, for example, how we ask our audiences and students to refrain from using single-use plastics on our properties. We work out all these positions together. While recognizing that we operate within a capitalist system, we seek to create alternative economic practices for the exchange of goods and services, barter, and local food exchange. Some of these bartered goods can be found on the table whenever we share meals together or with our many guests.

For hundreds of years—for thousands of years—and certainly of late, there has been trauma, personal hardship, and political and social pain. And this is taking its toll. We all share in holding this situation to task, so at Double Edge we want to be sensitive about how we move from this outside context to our inside work at the theatre, reaching into the hidden territories of our training journey. We are sensitive to the fact that we are inviting people to a new and unfamiliar place, and that it is a rural place. This is a rural place that we love, and which Double Edge chose. We chose it over thirty years ago, knowing absolutely nothing—and perhaps we would not have chosen it if we had known some of the things we have since learned. It may be a very different world than the one you live in; some of the visiting artists who train with us have never stepped out of the city before. We consider living in this environment to be incredible; it's incredible to be in a relatively unspoiled environment, where we haven't yet utterly ravaged the land. And we're trying to continue that. But on the other hand, the farm is remote. So far there is no cell phone service here. We are in the wilderness. Ashfield is not simply a farming community; our environment includes untamed wild animals: coyotes, bears, bobcats, moose. This is where we are located, and this location is connected to how we want to access ourselves: the wilderness within. And yet we, you and I, are strangers; we must *seek* a connection. We live in a community you may not be familiar with, but we have worked for all these years to help it become a welcoming place for our group and for all the many people who have joined us over the years. Most people in this town of 1,700 know each other, and most of them know Double Edge; if not they know someone who knows us. We are constantly working on our relationship with the town, the people, and this is what we call community.

I am sensitive to the fact that you, dear reader, may not have trained with Double Edge; perhaps you haven't yet seen any of the performances we've created. Either way, this book will hopefully inspire a journey, and journeys usually involve the unknown. Training is the basis of Double Edge's work: it is a performance practice; it is an artistic practice, and, let's say, it is a practice of connection between all of us. Our training proceeds from bodily movement and physical improvisation. I cannot possibly reach out to engage you in the physicality and touch essential to our way of communicating. But you can still participate in it. I want to share with you, the reader, what I say to people who come to our training, as if you were right here with me. I want to share the quiet that is so difficult to find today. The first principle of training is that every day is a beginning, for each one of us. So, let's begin together. Starting now.

Our training is physical; it necessarily involves touch and physicality. But even more importantly, our training is about choice. And so too, I hope, is this writing. I offer a strong plea for you to push past the trappings we are all subject to, and the constraints around us, and discover how you will dedicate yourself to your own artistic expression and cultural dialogue. If there is discomfort with anything presented here, you can choose to step back. You don't need to engage when you cannot. That's not the purpose of our ensemble culture. But if I ask you to go a little further with yourself, it is an invitation to try. Let's go further. We are all here to go further. Our training is quiet, as we try to achieve a point of stillness. We may use text. We may offer some instruction, some needful talking; but our training is ultimately an attempt to find the still point that has been getting really, really, really (and many thousands of reallys) lost in our contemporary world, a world with so much stimulus and input.

Our method is based on *search*; it's not based on *form*. The work is not prescriptive. After a training program, or a visit, or even a performance, you wouldn't be able to say, "I've got the Double Edge method." Rather, you will be invited, for the rest of your life, to call upon this moment as a means for searching yourself and for asking essential questions. We are asking you to ask essential questions in a new way: Who are you? What do you want to believe? Who do you want to be? How do you want to live your complete self? I think it's important to believe that we *can* remove the things that block us from living as we choose to live. We can choose to do that externally or internally. Those are the questions here each day, and those are the questions Double Edge brings to performance creation.

We acknowledge that the process is a vulnerable and intimate one. One moment you might be crying, and the next you might be joyful, and then you might be screaming. It is a genuine process. We see you. We want you to understand that we respect the challenges, as well as the incredible joys, of the process we have developed, and we will support both of those aspects, as well as everything in between. That is our work in the training period. Relating to the personal nature of this search and the vulnerability it demands, I offer in this book selections from my journals, to share a writing process rooted in my own internal, non-linear wanderings.

We believe that building trust is a daily practice. We believe in the hard work of building the daily courage our imaginations, our selves, our students, and our audiences all require. Let's think about that for a minute. We understand this work as an artistic process that is also a spiritual process, a creative process, a political process, and a social process sustained by courage and trust. And we build trust and courage together, every day, as a daily practice.

Our vision is to prioritize imagination in times of creative, emotional, spiritual, and political uncertainty.

Our mission is a journey that holds space for authenticity, interaction, identity, for whoever is seeking creative, emotional, spiritual, and political clarity.

Our art is grounded in a rigorous, ensemble aesthetic that unfolds in dream imagery, metaphor, mystery, and symbolism.

Our work is created and sustained in an open, honest, meaningful, relevant, shared experience. We call this living culture. Our dedication is to face isolation and erasure, to face the despair and pain that can translate into personal incapacity and political paralysis. To uplift. We call this Art Justice. Art + Living Culture + Art Justice = Double Edge.

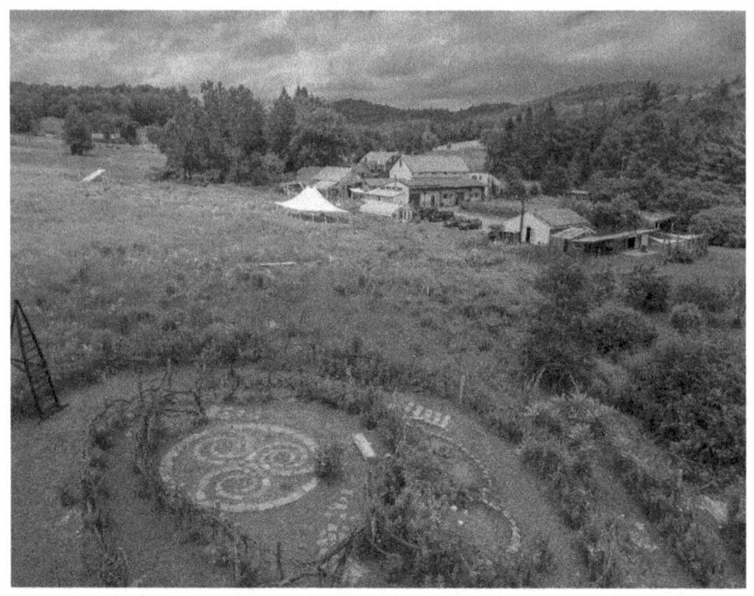

FIGURE 2 *The Double Edge Farm Center, featuring the living labyrinth, designed by Silas Riemer, and the Farm Center property, 2023. Photo by David Weiland.*

EXCERPT FROM A JOURNAL: *GRAND PARADE, c. 2013*

My way of working on the personal is to keep the pain without cutting it off—to accept it, to walk with it.

But I will not relinquish myself.

You and all of you rejoice in your lives.

I rejoice in my choice,

Even if I don't understand the priority in this moment.

1

Search Determines Form: Foundational Writings

Introduction

There is always something we can do to change and improve our circumstances. During my time at Tufts University in the 1980s, it did not escape me (nor did it escape any of my teachers) that I was more focused on directing theatre than I was on conducting scholarship. I studied living directors when most teaching was rooted in the theatre of past times. I fought hard to write my dissertation on Eugenio Barba, founder of Odin Teatret, largely so I could go and learn from him how to create my own theatre ensemble in a country that still thought that repertory theatre was experimental.

I yearned to create an autonomous theatre, similar to that of my mentors at Jerzy Grotowski's Teatr Laboratorium, in which all the artists participate in the work of inventing. I yearned to create a theatre that included women and drew on cultural identity as its leading creative forces. In spite of these yearnings I became a graduate student at Tufts, where, at the time, ensemble theatre was all but absent from the curriculum—not to mention the very existence of women directors, playwrights, and teachers, as well as the presence of non-Western cultures.

In its absence, I had no choice but to create the first performance of what became Double Edge Theatre. Called *Rites*, the performance was a modern interpretation of *The Bacchae* set in a women's bathroom in London. This was the starting point not only of Double Edge, but also of my ensemble, which celebrated its fortieth anniversary in 2022.

The group of eight women that formed at Tufts inaugurated Double Edge's ongoing effort to understand and manifest itself as an ensemble, and thus as a community. The idea of building a group and a community, for which Double Edge's work has become renowned, began with the simple need to work with women and to create a necessary cultural life.

There were eight people in the founding group of Double Edge: Daina Robins, Lorien Corbelletti, Carroll Durand, Madeleine McNamara, Lynn Bailey, Kayla Black, Andrea Dishy, and me. That was a time when women's groups were starting to form and develop collective visions throughout the United States, as around the world. We started with a collective model of how we planned to operate and make decisions. We had hours of conversations, to the point where we said, "we're actually not going to talk so much, because we are talking more than we're doing." We would have to discuss every aspect of our lives together, even the stationery we planned to use. I think most of us remember long, drawn-out meetings, where we would talk about everything. And yet, in the end, it was always a couple of people who would do most of the work. Maybe it's the same today. There might always be a collective desire, yet there tend to be specific people who do the work or, let's say, who do the leading work. This has always been a kind of theme for me. I've always been on the side of arguing that if you're a doer-laborer, then this work is just as important as the work of a leader or decision-maker, but it's a muddy and complicated issue, and remains so. It will always be so, because we are immersed in a capitalist system that reinforces, for anything that we try to do, how we end up *reacting* rather than seeing how to create.

Let's take the example of a collective. On the one hand, nobody has the authority to say how a collective should be run. Each collective, each new experiment in working collectively, might be completely different from others that came before. But so often we come to understand the idea of collectivity in a restricted way. Over the years, some people have challenged the notion that Double Edge is a collective, because we have a hierarchy. But there is a substantial difference between, let's say, a corporate hierarchy and the leadership at Double Edge. In Double Edge, each person has a voice in the artistic as well as organizational direction of the theatre.

It is hard to abandon the systems we've been forced into, but it is necessary to transform those systems, and their injustices, from the inside out. That's been true since the beginning of Double Edge, and maybe from the beginning of theatre. We were *very* reactive at the beginning and we talked about *every* single thing for hours, and when it turned out that there were a couple of people who seemed to be doing most of the work, then the question became: "well, let's talk about *that.*" Did those couple of people have the authority to make all the decisions, even if others were working with them? What does the amount of sleep you get (or don't get) have to do with your decision-making power? These questions will always exist for collective work under capitalism; they exist for us to this day.

We recently held a series of ensemble meetings about the role of the ensemble in the overall leadership of Double Edge. We have a producing wing, and the producing wing seems to be leading a lot these days. My position was: the producing wing is handling production duties, because nobody else is producing, and we have a lot to produce, since we need a lot of money these days (or what seems like a lot to us). We want living wages, and we want to keep up the seventeen buildings that comprise the physical environment of Double Edge Theatre. But the production wing was not asking for artistic leadership. So how do we sort through the processes of collective decision-making? Our answer is that we're always working on this; it's not a foregone conclusion, but a necessary part of the creative work we do as a collective.

Double Edge always works to move from an ethical philosophy toward an ethical *action*, and this is something that always needs to be founded in reality, in practice, and thus not only in principle, as a topic for discussion.

In 1994, Double Edge relocated from Boston to its current home in Ashfield, Massachusetts, to create a center for the development of living culture. This experience was similar to my arrival at Tufts as a radical Jewish woman a decade earlier. There was little to be seen of Jewish culture in Ashfield, or any real ethnic diversity; there wasn't even that much of a town. Looking deeper, we found people willing to help us survive, to help us build, and even to watch us perform. Eventually we grew together, and today the Farm Center, with its multiple landscapes, theatres, living spaces, and goats and cows, not only thrives but also provides us with a local base for our international travels.

When we moved to the Farm Center in Ashfield in 1994, the words "sustainable" and "autonomous" were of the utmost importance to us. We were sick of the alienation of the city, and we were sick of being forced to uphold a standard model of what theatre represented: "you're a theatre, so you perform, and the audience arrives, then leaves." Even basic steps toward an alternative—such as sharing a drink with our audience members after a performance and distributing materials outlining our artistic process—struck people as incredible and different. We couldn't go any further with this kind of participation without access to land and the natural environment. The idea was ultimately that we would grow, prepare, and eat our own food, and that we would no longer be dependent on grants and donors and the preconceived ideas of financial supporters. We would be self-sustaining.

We also had no idea of what we were really getting into. Small-scale farming is just as bad as theatre, or the restaurant industry, when it comes to the sheer difficulty of surviving. You can work yourself to the bone, but the profit margins remain small, especially when the value of food, as of art, is so limited in our consumer-oriented society. That's one reason why there is so much food injustice. Ironically, in trying to become autonomous, Double Edge ended up combining three equally precarious industries, rather than settling on just one. We have attempted to make the most of this combination, while unraveling the built-in models of alienation and exploitation. This has meant attending to the needs of our human and environmental resources, rather than concentrating on money alone.

We did immediately start a garden, and that felt good. But then every time we would enter into a performance-heavy period, we had to set that aside. With all our dreams of autonomy, it was clear that we could not grow into our desires without incorporating professionals into our ensemble of artists. Eventually, and I would say organically, this led to Double Edge becoming a company. The ensemble can't do it all. As of 2024, Double Edge includes a farmer-orchard keeper-landscaper, an operations director, a company manager and administrative coordinator, two carpenters, and a food systems director. Each of these people participates in design, music, and other aspects of our artistic production. All of this has required growth as well as adjustment. We wouldn't have been able to do all this work with just the ensemble, although the ensemble still leads the daily business of Double Edge, in conjunction with our roles as creators. We never want to stop growing as artists.

Likewise, we must never become insular; rather, we must try to increase our awareness of the world we live in. In our striving, we can move toward our dreams, for ourselves and for others.

1. From *Remodeling Theatre* (Excerpt) (1980)

*What follows are several sections of the practical handbook
I wrote as part of my Master's project in Theatre for Social
Change at Goddard College in Cambridge, MA. It represents the
beginnings of my lifelong passion for creative research. It was also
the first articulation of how my mind was working to combine a
psycho-physical approach to theatre-making with a fervent belief
in changing the social and economic structures that were holding
back a majority of our population from full self-realization. The
experience of working with young people caught in the horrors
of Boston's bussing crisis forced this thinking to emerge from the
domain of pure concepts into the stark reality of the third-grade
classroom.*

*In retrospect, my perspective was naive. The issues facing the
students at the school were far more complicated than anything
a theatre class could possibly unravel. Systemic social change
and alternative structures—including a truth and reconciliation
process—are necessary as a starting-point for true change. And
yet, to encourage autonomy in creativity and thought, from the
beginning of the educational mandate, still seems a fundamental
necessity toward these goals. As more and more restrictions are
placed on public education, and as the possibilities for teaching
history within this education system evaporate, this idea—to open
the gates of the hearts and minds of our young, through theatre,
music, and writing—can still contribute to transforming our living
culture. As in 1980, art justice may very well be one provocative
action we can take toward our survival.*

✳✳✳

Imbued with the idea that the public thinks first of all with its
senses and that to address oneself first to its understanding as
the ordinary psychological theatre does is absurd, the Theatre
of Cruelty proposes to resort to a mass spectacle; to see in the
agitation of tremendous masses, convulsed and hurled against

each other, a little of the poetry of festivals and crowds when, all too rarely nowadays, the people pour out into the streets.

The theatre must give us everything that is in crime, love, war, or madness, if it wants to recover its necessity.

Everyday love, personal ambition, struggles for status, all have value only in proportion to their relation to the terrible lyricism of the Myths to which the great mass of men (and women) have assented.

—Antonin Artaud, *Theatre of Cruelty*

Introduction: Remodeling Theatre

Throughout history, theatre has not been recognized as a legitimate art form in education. It has not been included as a structured part of the curriculum in the same way as other art forms such as painting, drawing, and music, but rather as an afterthought, a "playtime," an "icing on the cake." The reason for this is that theatre has never been considered a "high" art form, due to its historic roots as a people's art, created in the streets. Although painting and music began from the same roots, they were raised in their status by the simple fact that they could be recorded and thus glorified in retrospect, largely by the church and other powerful patrons.

As a people's art, theatre does not fit into the classical definition of education which holds that art in the schools should be used as a tool for teaching discipline rather than as a means to express creativity. It is my belief that the teaching of the classical art forms should be used only for those students who have already chosen a particular discipline to pursue. In early education the purpose of art should be to open the child up to her/his own creative potential. Thus theatre, as a people's art, is the most appropriate form to use. It is born from within, from the scope of one's imagination and experience, and does not require, in the beginning, any learned skills such as are necessary for drawing or music. Every child, regardless of economic and class background, imagines, pretends, role-plays, desires. There is no prerequisite of private music lessons or sophisticated parents who provide an exposure to the arts in the home. Every child can create theatre.

It is often suggested that only the "talented" can sing, dance, or act. This notion stems from the traditional attitude of "art for art's sake." There are those "chosen ones" amongst us who by education, environment, or accident are considered to have special talent in the arts. They are selected out, processed, and prepared to become part of that group designated as "gifted." I believe that there is no God-given quality called "talent" in theatre or in any of the arts. The talented are seldom the innovative. What is often put forward as "talent" is a reinforcement of already established criteria for "good art," i.e., those who reflect the qualities of the status quo. The reasons for this stem from the fact that new forms are a threat to established forms, they are unfamiliar and therefore unpalatable, and they often deal with a subject matter that is critical of the establishment. Even on the elementary school level, when children try to express themselves in a new way, experiment, or introduce subject matter that is not considered the "proper topic" for the realm of art, they are shunned and told they are untalented. The suppression of creativity begins here; a child is told that s/he must draw straight lines or that s/he must sing "in tune," rather than trying to find her/his own tune. People's theatre allows for experimentation and therefore can break down the stereotype of the "talented child." It functions from the premise that every child is gifted and has a unique contribution to make toward the artistic product—the play.

The notion of talent has a carryover to the "star system." Society picks and chooses the "sexy," the "talented," the "white," the "macho," the "brilliant," and packages them for stardom. They are sold as products to be marketed and aped. This mythologizing of the stereotype, of the ultra-conventional, imposes upon people's art an unrealistic Madison Avenue image. The advent of television has propagated these images, particularly in young people. When elementary school children are told that they are going to do theatre, they immediately begin to try to imitate Donny and Marie, Farrah Fawcett, Laverne and Shirley, the Fonz, or rock groups such as the Bee Gees. Unfortunately, most programs for arts in the schools do not provide an environment which will encourage the students to deal with ethnic, cultural, or spiritual issues with which the children can create images from their own heritage. Rather the goals set for them demand a regurgitation of images from the media or from the teacher.

Aside from dealing with important contextual matter, theatre is also an invaluable tool for teaching a standard classroom curriculum. It involves much more than dramatic skills. It introduces song, music, dance, and the visual arts. Theatre can be used in English, creative writing, speech, and history classes, as well as in introducing vocations such as electricity or carpentry. Teaching the children to act, to write, and to produce plays becomes a vehicle for a much more holistic way of learning.

In the Boston public schools, particularly at this time of desegregation and recession, theatre could be used as a creative outlet for the anger and frustration of both students and teachers. Not to dispel this anger and frustration, but to help express it. It was with this intent in mind that the theatre workshop at the Perry Elementary School in South Boston was created. Under a grant from Try/Arts (a program which gives funds to arts groups to teach in the public schools) several people from Little Flags Theatre, a Boston-based people's theatre, designed a program for the children at the Perry School. This booklet, a documentation of that project, is dedicated to those children in the hopes that other academics will take notice and discover the value of theatre in their own classrooms.

Theatre in the United States and Around the World

The concept propelling the theatre arts program at the Perry Elementary School was threefold:

1   To introduce children to the real world of theatre, and to counteract the notion that theatre is composed only of stars and famous directors, by delving into all the different jobs needed to produce a play.

2   To introduce children to different ethnic cultures around the world through the theatre.

3   To inspire the children to tap into their own creativity and therefore allow them to express the genius of their own ethnic backgrounds.

Opening Talk: A Child's Concept of Theatre

The first step toward introducing the classes to theatre was to have a discussion with the children about their own concept of theatre. Here are some of their "pre-" and "mis-" conceptions:

> stars on the stage
> > a director
> > > a cameraman
> > > > ticket takers

An Introduction to People's Theatre

The second step in introducing children to theatre was for the teachers to help the students understand the difference between television and theatre by explaining that theatre is a live art and does not require video equipment, such as cameras. After this explanation the teachers and the students together determined the following list of jobs involved in the theatre:

> actors and actresses   playwright
> director   producers   audience
> publicity   lighting technicians   set and prop crew designers
>   front of house   stage manager
> business manager   bookkeeper
> singers   dancers   musicians

Evaluation of the Discussion

The purpose of the entire discussion was to open the students up to the notion that theatre is down-to-earth work and that it is dependent for its life on numerous creative workers.

Cultural Workers

The structuring principle of each class was (1) to learn one distinct task of the many facets of the theatre and (2) to learn one craft or technique or art from an ethnic group, i.e., a dance, a song, a story, etc.

WORKSHOP, SECTION I:

The Program: Dancers and Choreographers

One of the teachers was an educator from South America and thus chose to teach the group about traditional Latin dance. Using tango music, the group was taught a folk dance from Guatemala.

1 We invited the students to listen to a recording of the music and feel the rhythm.

2 We demonstrated the dance using the two teachers who were familiar with it.

3 We invited the students to get up and walk to the rhythm of the music. This was necessary because the most important thing about dance is to be able to coordinate the body to the rhythm of the music; without this, the steps are meaningless.

4 We asked the children to walk to the music while clapping hands to the beat.

5 We turned off the music and taught the dance steps in their sequential order.

6 We invited the children to do the dance steps along with the music.

7 We taught the hand motions that occur simultaneously with the dance steps.

8 The students put all this together with the music.

This entire process was achieved during a period of two weeks, and after this the dance was used as a warm-up at the beginning of each class period.

Problems during the Dance/Choreography Section of this workshop included the following:

A Shyness among the children. Many of the children were afraid to dance in front of other people for fear of criticism. Two methods were used to combat this problem:

1 The first was to divide the class into small groups, with each of the theatre teachers and each of the regular teachers taking a group. The children were asked to form their own groups so that they would feel free to move in front of others.

2   A criticism style was created whereby, at the end of each run of the dance, the children would be asked to evaluate for themselves what they were doing wrong and what they could do to change it. In this way, the children started to learn about the meaning of constructive criticism without feeling the pressure of an authority figure standing over them.

B   Cooperation. There were signs of gender-based tension and racism among the children. The white children tended to exclude the Black children. (This is a bussed school.) They would not allow the Black children into their groups. Girls and boys were not comfortable with each other as partners for fear of humiliation by the other children. These problems are deep-rooted and cannot be solved over a short period of time. The teachers felt that the only way to handle this problem was by example. Whenever there was a demonstration, it was always done with a gender and racial mixture. This attitude was not a denial of the fact that there are many times when one would like to share with one's own ethnic group or gender, but since the attitudes were totally separatist, there was a need for some cross-participation. When it seemed appropriate, the teachers also tried to encourage the children to integrate themselves in their choosing of partners. The other attempt to solve this problem was in the concept of the workshop itself: to learn and understand different cultures.

At first the children's attitudes were hostile toward the South American dance; they could not understand why they should learn a Latin dance. However, once they became involved in it, the joy of the dance made them forget their former feelings.

The difficulty in dealing with the above-mentioned problems was made greater by the attitudes of the regular classroom teachers. One of these teachers was fond of making sexist jokes to his male students and demeaning the Black students in front of others. If he felt that a student was interfering with the class, he kicked them out of the room. One day, when we were practicing the dance, three Black students started to do a take-off of the dance in their own style. They were thrown out of the room before the theatre teachers could object. The problems this created were the following:

1   The children interpreted this as a sign that they could not
    use their spontaneous creativity, but instead must learn by
    rote what they were being taught; this automation acted in
    direct opposition to the goal of the program.

2   The children were being denied the chance to be able to
    appreciate another ethnic group's interpretation of the
    dance; this was another lesson in shunning Black culture.

Henceforth the theatre teachers asked the regular teachers not to
share in the discipline of the class, but rather to think of themselves
as students.

C   Discipline. Many times the children were noisy and
    disrespectful of work their peers were performing. This
    mayhem occurred largely because they thought that a
    theatre workshop meant a play period. The children's
    prior concept of learning was to sit at a desk quietly and
    memorize the material their teachers dictated. The theatre
    teachers attempted to show them that they could learn how
    to balance spontaneity and discipline in the theatre class.
    If someone was disruptive, they were given the choice of
    not participating. However, they were never dismissed from
    the room. When the choice was presented to the child, s/he
    would usually decide to stay in the program. It took a long
    time for the class to understand that just because they were
    not behind a desk didn't mean that they were not learning.

D   Mixture of Special Education and regular classes. During
    the class period in which this project took place, the
    children from Special Education and the regular classes
    were taught together in the same space for the first time.
    The problems with mixing the Chapter 766 classes and the
    regular classes came mostly from the fears of the teachers.
    Each time one of the children was loud or ran around, their
    teacher would apologize for them and exclude them from
    the next class. In actuality, they were not as well "trained"
    in their behavior as the other children, but they had an
    amazingly free attitude toward creativity. The theatre
    teachers felt that the mixture was balanced, as the 766
    classes could teach the other children about free expression
    and the third, fourth, and fifth graders could teach the 766
    classes about how to fit into society. It was also apparent

that if the 766 class became involved in an activity, they would concentrate totally on it, as would all of the children. This was an inspiration for the teachers, as they were forced to make the activities interesting and exciting at all times. Unfortunately, this was the only time in which the classes were combined, a great disservice to all the students.

The Program: Mime

The second step in the program was to teach a more abstract form of movement to the class; this form is mime.

One teacher put her hand behind her back and pretended to take something out. When the teacher's hand came forth, it was in the shape of a small ball. She then simulated throwing the ball across the room to one of the children and the child, without thinking, tried to catch it. When the children realized that the ball was not real, they were quite surprised and began to laugh. It was then explained that mime or pantomime is using the body to imagine certain actions.

The children were asked to find the ball that was thrown and look at it. They replied that there was no ball. One of the teachers created a new ball and threw it again. One of the children caught it and threw it to someone else. As the children continued to throw it, the ball changed shape and kept getting bigger. The children were then asked to remember the shape and size of the ball so that when they did the mime, it would have a sense of reality.

The next step after the children began to understand the concept of mime was to teach them how to use it in order to express different actions or emotions. The teacher threw the ball again and allowed the students to play "ball." After a little while they were told that the ball was getting heavier and heavier. The children started to have difficulty lifting the ball because of its weight. Then they started lifting it up with two people at a time.

Next, the teacher said that the ball was starting to fill the room and there wasn't any room left for the children. They ran into all the corners trying to find hiding places. The teacher said that the ball was returning to its original size, but that it was hot. The children bounced the ball up and down because it was too hot to hold.

The next step was to change the ball into a different object. The children created

        hot dogs
                dogs
                        lions
                                trees

The final step was to show the children how to use the mime in skits. They were divided into groups and asked to recreate something they do in normal life. The children then performed the following skits in mime:

        a football game
        jumping rope
        a party
        a disco
        a basketball game
        a swimming pool

After the skits were presented, there was a criticism section in which the actors explained what they thought of their own work, followed by feedback from the rest of the class.

Problems during the Mime Section included the following:

A   Consistency. The children had a problem maintaining the sizes and shapes of the equipment they were using. The teachers had to remind them repeatedly to be consistent. They also forgot that they had the equipment; the balls suddenly disappeared, and they would walk through the pool after they had gone swimming. This was mainly a problem to be solved by practice.

B   Criticism. The class had a problem with the criticism section because they tended to look upon it as something insulting and negative. In response, they were told not to say that something was good or bad but rather to say, "I think that worked," or "I think that did not work, because you …" In this way they learned that criticism was not a punishment but rather was something to help them.

In this part of the workshop, there was no problem with imagining. Children are very creative because they have not yet been exposed to a lot of the fears that adults have about expression and rejection and therefore they are free. They never had a problem in the abstract of imagining that something was there when they could not see it before their faces.

[...]

WORKSHOP, SECTION II

This part of the workshop originated from the same general concepts as in Section I: To teach the classes about theatre that draw from the students' own experience and to share theatre from other cultures.

The difference in the following workshop is that it is designed for a shorter period of time and a younger age group.

Warm-UP

Each class began with a physical and vocal warm-up.

This warm-up was facilitated by the use of a familiar game: Simon Says. The purpose of using a game that the children already knew was to make them feel less threatened when they were asked to do movements with their bodies that they had not done before in a group.

By the second week of the program, the children began leading the warm-up themselves in order to give them responsibility for their work and to instill in them cooperative means of working together.

The idea of playing a game without competition, and under their own leadership, was a new process for the students and took a while to work successfully. At first, the children wanted to play in the usual, "competitive" way: if someone made a mistake, s/he must leave the game. Since the purpose of the game was to increase their bodily movement language, this style of playing, with people being called "out," would defeat the purpose. Divested of competition, the children must learn to play the game for its own sake; hence the activity must be interesting enough to keep their attention. One way of accomplishing this is to change the leader often, so no one person would run out of ideas.

Benefits of the warm-up included:

- Increased physical ability
- Cooperation and respect for peers
- Playing games without competition

Introduction to Theatre History

At the end of the music, dance, and mime section, it was explained to the children that dance, mime, and music were not created as "art" forms but rather as a way for people to express themselves. Just as they had written songs, created dances, and mimed actions in order to express a feeling or to relate an idea, people all over the world use these mediums for the same purpose. They were told about the New Song Movement in Chile and about the way Victor Jara used his music to teach the people about their political situation and to give them strength. They were told about how mime is used in Poland, Africa, and America (minstrels), among other places, to show people that the use of ritual ceremonies is another way of expressing their particular struggles. After each discussion, an example was demonstrated by the teachers: a song from Chile, a mime from Poland, etc. This section was created in order to show the children that true art comes from the people and is representative of their own cultures.

Evaluation of the Workshops; Including Dancers, Choreographers, Mime, Singers, Composers, and Musicians.

The first objective of this section was to teach the children to be free with their bodies and their voices. This is a prerequisite to creative expression. This goal was met to a certain extent; they did become relatively free in both areas as the work progressed. However, the theatre teachers did notice that the children, even at this early age, had already built up defenses to the work. This is caused by parents and teachers (and society at large) trying to inhibit the children from being spontaneous. One child told us that her parents told her that she had a rotten voice. A second child told us that he had been told he was uncoordinated. The teachers tried to emphasize that no one was naturally uncoordinated, or had a bad voice, but rather that anyone could learn to sing, dance, and create music. *And they did!*

The second objective was to teach the children the beauty of other cultures and to help them understand it through the arts. Encompassed in this objective was the desire of the teachers to fight the racism and sexism that occurred during the classes, and to try to help the young people gain consciousness about the problems of our society. The children learned to enjoy the South American dances and the African American songs. They also learned about some European and Eastern European cultures through the mime demonstrations. The students were very thoughtful after the discussion on slavery. This discussion led to their writing some very provoking lyrics about other injustices such as pollution, police brutality, and class problems. (Most of the students came from working-class backgrounds.) A significant by-product of the work was that the teachers also noticed the students starting to abandon their racial and gender-based cliques and begin to intermingle.

The final objective of the section was to begin to introduce different theatre jobs and to rid the class of the mass-media notion that theatre is just for the stars. They learned about different jobs and were ready to move forward. It should be noted that a warm-up for all ensuing classes consisted of a review of the songs and dances the children had learned [...].

2. Proposal for the Staging of Maureen Duffy's *Rites* (September 25, 1981)

In rereading the document that follows, which I see in retrospect as the conception, pregnancy, and subsequent birth of Double Edge, I immediately reflect on how far we have come in these forty years, as well as on how far we still have to go. I arrived at Tufts University as a Ph.D. candidate after a three-year embrace with the radical women who created the first women's theatre festivals in the world (produced by visionary Susie Chancey and me). Before that I had worked with another radical woman director, Maxine Klein (no relation), at her theatre, Little Flags. Although she had been one of the few women directors on Broadway, she spurned that career to create a theatre ensemble which, among other actions, toured striking coal mines in Stearns, Kentucky, and performed an ode to Chilean martyr Victor Jara. I still remember the two exercises she taught me during that time, one called "living newspaper" and the other called "childhood story." "Living newspaper" involved choosing something from a newspaper considered factual at the time and creating a short scene; mine came from an article I read in the South where a heterosexual couple was jailed (this was in the late 1970s) for living together without marriage. "Childhood story" involved creating a scene based on something important that happened to you when you were a child (my sister laughing at my piano playing, after which I never played again). I still use these concepts in my work today.

I had also been working with Rena Mirecka, a founder of Grotowski's Laboratorium, who had been mentoring me since 1976. Imagine my shock when I matriculated at Tufts and found that I did not have any women teachers or directors, nor were there any women included in the curriculum! One particularly fierce argument took place in the theatre history class for which I was employed as a teaching assistant. After I took issue with the fact that there were no women on the syllabus, the teacher "allowed" me to teach the final class and I chose Ntozake Shange's For Colored Girls. *I remember that years later one of the students was still upset that Shange had replaced his hero, Sam Shepard ...*

And here is the sad part. In subsequent years I did begin to see more women, and women of color, move into the theatre world and the teaching community. This seemed to be happening regularly enough that by the early 2010s I had all but stopped shouting out about this subject, both in my work and in the theatre world. Maybe this was out of fatigue—I was tired of fighting—and maybe it was false hope. But then the lead-up to the 2016 election happened. I realized that from the cradle of my experimental theatre, I had become immersed in a world of my own making, with partners of my own making, and I had forgotten (or avoided) my responsibility to see the external reality. It was shocking to witness again, just as I had at Tufts, that the mainstream was still so anti-woman, and that a struggle I considered to have been already won was instead on the frontlines, along with violence against Black and Indigenous people and the LGBTQ communities in particular. I realized that Double Edge always needed to continue our struggle from the inside and out, for identity in art culture and justice.

***

In order to practically demonstrate the skills I have acquired in my previous theatre experience as they are augmented by the knowledge I have gained from Tufts, I propose that I mount a production of Maureen Duffy's *Rites*.

Due to the fact that I already have a master's degree in theatre, it is not possible for me to take a directing class for credit, and in consideration of the fact that I have already had six semesters of directing classes, it would not be advisable for me to audit the class.

However, I have discovered that the first slot for a Cup and Saucer is open and I would like the faculty to consider a production of *Rites* in that slot.

Several members of the faculty have suggested that I demonstrate my directing abilities at Tufts and I feel that this would be a perfect opportunity to do so. I do not think that this production will conflict with my studies; last year my work outside of Tufts as the producer of the 1981 Women's Theatre Festival provided no interference, and since I have now discontinued this work I am able to take on new theatre opportunities.

I understand that this proposal is late; however, as *Rites* was scheduled to be mounted last spring at the Festival, all of the preparatory work has been completed and I am prepared to begin rehearsing immediately.

As well as benefiting me personally, this play would be an asset to the Tufts season. As in most theatre departments, and indeed theatre in general, the number of women who wish to participate far exceeds the number of roles available. Although this year there has been an attempt to address this problem, *Rites*, by virtue of its twelve-woman cast, will provide welcome additional opportunities for actresses.

Similarly, women playwrights, with the exception of Lillian Hellman, have been largely overlooked, and a production of *Rites* would serve in the interest of rectifying his situation.

From any perspective *Rites* is a challenging theatre piece. Based on Euripides' *The Bacchae*, the metaphor for *Rites* is a woman's lavatory in Britain. The play begins in a naturalistic mode and moves toward a ritual ending. The twelve roles provide excellent acting opportunities because of the specificity of the characterizations, each being from a different class and walk of life. *Rites* also provides a directing challenge, due to the necessity for a detailed and intricately woven orchestration of the play.

Rites is not a feminist polemic—it has none of the shrill and divisive qualities that many people associate with feminist theatre. It is a carefully constructed dramatic work which is open to very exciting theatrical interpretations. Maureen Duffy wrote in her introduction to the play that *The Bacchae* is Pentheus's story and *Rites* is Agave's. The play is about people who stereotype others (and themselves) to such an extent that they lose sight of what humanity is. In their denial of life, they are destroyed.

In terms of practical considerations for the production, I have spoken to Carroll Durand and she has agreed to give me technical support in the Arena, as well as to design the show, if the proposal is accepted. I am waiting for your answer before pursuing the other designers I have in mind.

Obviously, my rehearsal needs would come after those of the students taking the course, but the nature of the play makes it possible to use other rehearsal spaces. I would like to request the money for a Cup and Saucer, as this would help a great deal in fulfilling the technical requirements of the play. If, however, this is not available, I would still be interested in doing the play.

The running time for *Rites* is approximately forty-five minutes.

3. To Tremble with Wonder and Dismay: Program Note from *My Sister in This House* (1983)

My Sister in This House is an extraordinary play by Wendy Kesselman, based on the original news article about two maids who murdered their employer and her daughter. Genet also wrote The Maids, a very different play, about this case. I worked on this play with Daina Robins, Lorien Corbelletti, Kayla Black, and Madeline McNamara, all extraordinary core actors of Double Edge's Women's Cycle. It was a perfect container for marrying the intensity of training and ritual with a contemporary theatre piece.

✳✳✳

After one and a half years of existence, Double Edge Theatre Productions has already made a "Best of" and a "Worst of" list.

Rites, our first play, presented in April 1982, was cited by the *Boston Phoenix* as one of the ten best small theatre productions of 1982. Our second production, *Blood Rubies,* presented in the fall, was named as one of the worst 1982 productions.

Perhaps the second "honor" should mortify us—and indeed, we aren't necessarily thrilled with the citation.

However, we are a company who truly want to be challenged by our audiences and who are open to honest, concerned criticism. We view our work as *an ongoing process* and are determined to remain suspicious of stagnancy, complacency, and self-congratulation.

Consequently, we invite all of those who choose to work with us and all of those who see our work to join us in our "climb up the mountain."

Reaching the summit is not the main point.

Continually climbing is.

Double Edge Theatre Productions is based on two major commitments:

1 The pursuit of artistic integrity and excellence in its productions.

2   The search for and the expression of a theatre that is
      feminist.

The producers of Double Edge are bound together by the priority
we've each individually given to these two commitments.

However, we're all very diverse people—from different
backgrounds, with varying ideas and methods. No completely
unanimous definitions of theatrical excellence or feminism exist
between us.

That is, we are on a *search*—both individually and collectively—
to discover what these words mean to us and how we can put our
ideals into practice, both through the theatrical pieces we present
and through the way in which our ensemble functions.

Such a search demands great trust from us all, as we strive to
listen to and *work with* each other and the world around us.

Certainly, we *do* share some very definite goals.

In Double Edge, we are committed to working with *women*.
Our company was founded by women, and it is our great pleasure
to work principally with women, on shows which in some direct
manner illuminate women in society. We feel that for many of the
crucial issues of our society, women's concerns are both *metaphor*
and *reality*.

At the same time, we realize that by the very nature of life and
society, men must be a part of this process at nearly every level.
Life, Theatre, and Art are too complex and paradoxical to resort to
exclusion. We remain committed, however, to the presentation of an
unabashedly female perspective in what we present to our audience.

Our artistic goal—lofty and unattainable as it may be—is
to present *Truth,* naked and searing, complex and paradoxical,
unexpected and often uncomfortable for ourselves and for our
audiences.

We are trying to build an *ensemble,* a group individually and
collectively determined:

—to *break* artistic *boundaries*

—*to give* ourselves *in full* rather than in measured doses

—*to render* ourselves *vulnerable* rather than impregnable

—*to break* down established *hierarchies* so often present in the
    rehearsal process and *not to hide* behind our titles of Actor,
    Designer, Director, and Playwright

—*to rid* ourselves and our productions of *glibness* of form, message, or presentation

—*to enliven* our audiences, by indulging and intensifying the *paradoxes* that are inherent in the theatre

—*to go* beyond the obvious, the superficial, and the facile *to the extraordinary* and *the essential*

—*to stun* with whatever means are at our disposal—*to shock* with laughter, *to terrify* with pity, and *to make* our audience *tremble* with wonder and dismay.

We cannot allow ourselves to dilute ourselves, the theatre's language, or its reality. Our measures must be *full strength*. Our respect for the audience drives us to present shows which can't be reduced to headlines, but which make audiences quiver with an overwhelming *complexity of response*.

Our members share these same goals with us, having demonstrated both artistic talent and dedication to the company. With every new production, we recruit new women and men to work with us and seek to encourage them to contribute to our development as much as possible. We are *not a closed company*—we are continually open to people who are interested in our goals and can bring new insights to our "climb."

Our advisory board of directors consists of individuals chosen for their experience, artistic integrity, and their sympathy with the goals of the company. With their assistance and by dint of our dedication and hard work, we expect to achieve our long-term goals—a permanent site and staff for our productions, the ability to pay both staff and actors, and the establishment of classes and a tour schedule for our productions.

4. Director's Confession: *Song of Absence in the Fall of the Ashen Reign* (1988)

The past is not past. The past is not fixed or inalterable. All my understanding has come through the lens of my Jewish culture and its near extinction. The following describes the moment where all the autobiographical underpinnings of my work begin, and from which they continue to extend. It is the force and com/passion of my world view.

The text below is a program note for the first theatrical piece in the Song Trilogy Cycle, Song of Absence. *The Cycle began in 1986 and ended in 1998, and included three performances and a range of extra-theatrical work throughout five countries in Eastern Europe as well as throughout the United States.*

✳✳✳

In 1976, during a theatre trip to Poland, I visited the Auschwitz concentration camp for the first time. I was profoundly moved as I came face to face with the actual grounds upon which thousands of people, my people, were butchered with less compassion than that bestowed on a lamb taken to the slaughterhouse. For ten years, I tried to make sense of this horrifying era, trying to rationalize how the human being was capable of committing such atrocity, and how the human being could allow himself to become the ultimate victim. Over the past ten years, I tried three times to create a theatre production based on this event, and each time I was forced to give up because I could not find the necessary understanding. I thought of the massive piles of hair shaved off the victims' heads, the ghastly ovens of burning bodies, and the proximity of the farmhouses to the camps. I could not understand. I could not create.

There are two factors that have since given me the audacity to create a performance about the Holocaust. The first is my discovery of the art of the victims of the Holocaust—the music, visual art, and theatre which was created during this period, in the ghettos and the camps themselves. Sometimes this art was produced at the insistence of the Nazis, as a reflection of fascism's distorted value system, and sometimes it was created out of the desperation of the Jews and other victims to continue to express their own humanity, even in the most horrible circumstance possible. As the people were stripped of their humanity, the voice of life still expressed itself through the notes of the songs, through the lines of the drawings. I felt, as I studied the surviving work, that if these people, in their suffering, still had the courage to create, to affirm life, then I must also find some courage. The attempt was as important as the result. The urge to create.

The second factor which forced my hand was the image that continued to haunt me from Auschwitz. To my surprise, it was not the hair, the countless possessions of a thousand people, or even the ashes, but rather the tidiness of the camp in its present state. The well-kept lawns, the glass-enclosed relics, the picket fences separating the tourists from the attractions. For me, the horror of Auschwitz today is its sterility. This contradiction—the burial ground of the twentieth century, turned into a park—seemed like the ultimate joke, the deepest mockery of the sufferings of people. But what did I want: the skeletons strewn on the lawns, the hair thrown about the floor, the chambers of death still functional? In one sense, this is truly what I want: a recognition/admittance of the brutality of which we as humans are capable.

Many people who watch Double Edge productions have said that the suffering is too much, that death is too present in them. For years I rejected this judgment as the result of people's own inability to face themselves. But this answer is too simplistic. The question of the suffering and the ways it gets masked goes deeper than this. The park-like quality of Auschwitz today is not a modern invention, but extends from the camps in the time of their activities. Neatness remained a priority as thousands upon thousands burned. Beds were made in the morning in exemplary fashion, bodies swept into ditches and covered compactly; the Nazis' children played on the well-kept grounds of their parents' camps.

The contradiction of the Holocaust for me is not in the brutality of the action, but rather in the horrifying way that our social order, our mask, remains intact, and perhaps even encourages, and certainly hides, the truth about us as human beings. Yet, in Auschwitz, the brutality and the humanity existed and, indeed, still exist underneath the pretty green grass. The stench of the bodies, echoing the final cries of a slaughtered people, still screams out its song of life. The stench is not death; it is life. How many of us are willing to smell the smell of life, behind the iron-clad social mask we so desperately need? And who among us can even see the life, the death, the brutality, the horror from within the walls of our social order?

I have been asked why I had to do a play about the Holocaust. "The suffering is past."—Why did I have to do theatre which suffers? I didn't know. I kept trying to find the rationality, the reason. The sterility of the camps is the reason. The mask, while completely dangerous, is also the only way for people to accept their relation to reality. If people saw the truth behind the mask—that is, the utter lack of morality, the unbelievable atrocity, the capacity of one person to hurt another with a complete lack of feeling—not only would they not believe it, but if they did, there would be utter despair. We are so comfortable with the mask of thousands of years of rules and social order that we have forgotten what people really are. In art we have an obligation to the audience to help them accept what is underneath the mask, to help find a way in. Even in the art of the Holocaust, the mask still exists, although it is frail. Yet this same mask, in art and in life, also promotes and allows atrocity to be committed. Hiding behind this mask, we no longer recognize what lies beneath it and, therefore, are no longer responsible. We ignore the smell which is carefully disguised. We do not need to face the cruelty in each of us, because it is carefully groomed. Responsibility can be taken care of by reading newspapers and watching TV news. We have read, therefore, we need not think. Feel. Face.

The mask, so important and so dangerous. When it allows itself to exist unfettered, we lose sight of what is underneath, in ourselves, in society. No longer do we take responsibility for our actions, our world's actions, our neighbors' actions—we are removed, living lifelessly in the sterile, uncaring mask. No responsibility. No choice.

It is the balance between the mask of acceptance and the mask of hiding responsibility that I seek. At the same time, I want to rip off the grass and let the bodies be seen; I also want to face the horrible mask and the beautiful mask. This is my question as a Jew, and it is my question as an American. What is buried under our parks, behind our fashionable attire, inside our computers? Is the coldness of our world an unacknowledged signal of the disguising of humanity, or perhaps even the loss of humanity? Is it so entrenched that we do not even care about this question? Do we have the courage to rip it off and face our history, our future, and ourselves?

It is undeniable that we exist on top of a burial ground, a slaughterhouse. My search is to discover whether we have truly faced this fact, whether the human spirit ever really has a chance to shout, or whether we kill it, even before we commit our atrocities, with our tightly fitted mask? If we as a species have no morality, shouldn't we admit it so that we can at least have responsibility and choice?

EXCERPT FROM A JOURNAL:
SONG OF ABSENCE, 1988

The work is curative, but we are here to find artistic expression, not therapeutic expression. Good to deal with energy but I'm more interested to use energy, not just to change it. Why not use existing energy? Changing the energy doesn't create art, it creates people.

I must live in order to create; if I can't create, I die. I must have purpose, there is no reason to live in this world without purpose. Who cares for happiness when there can be beauty? I must live for a purpose. When it comes to the choice I choose the theatre, even my heart says with all of its pumping says my soul is for a purpose if not myself then there must be a reason. Stacy—have courage with your soul, your heart. You would love to fly but never come back.

You insist on your space; even you know that I need it. I cannot insist with energy, it has to be banal. You take your right to do nothing, feel sorry for yourself, self-medicate. Where is the work? I have responsibility, I can't just be free. No freedom in banal, no freedom in energy. This is the luxury of man. (you pig)

It is my responsibility to get through, to share my beauty, wonder, pain. Am I yet the director or have I lost it again, afraid of what I've become. Should I return to the human or should I plunge into the director?

Last weekend the audience reaction was quite exciting; it made me see what we have truly become.

5. Four Vision Statements (1992, 2002, 2012)

As the fortieth anniversary of Double Edge passes by, I keep thinking of the time I began making the stationary for the ensemble's first performance, Rites. *Having named the theatre "Double Edge," after the two-headed labrys axe used by women in sacrifices to Dionysus in the ancient precursors to theatre in Greece, our iconography reflected a sacrifice and a matriarchy that had been hidden away for so many years.*

Looking at these other anniversaries—1992, 2002, 2012, our tenth, twentieth, and thirtieth anniversaries—I am acutely aware that I always tend to write and think the same, or very similar, things. As the Polish director Tadeusz Kantor said, "each director only has one play/story done many different ways." My own story, and the story of Double Edge, involves the journey between the "external nightmare that we have created (or live in) and the impossible dream we must risk creating," as I put it in one of the pieces below. While those who accompany us in these hidden territories of creation may change over the course of several generations, and while external circumstances may pose different challenges, what does not change is the fight for each one of us, in Double Edge and in communion with Double Edge, to access their human potential. I hope to see that same story unfold in every decade of my work.

***

i. A Living Culture

December 9, 1992

Double Edge often assumes the label of an "experimental theatre." It is a label that is at the same time uncomfortable for us and incomprehensible in the context of our work. The members of our group consider theatre to be an experiment as much as life itself is an experiment—"We were born without practice, we will die without routine," wrote the Polish poet Wislawa Szymborska. So experimenting, or attempting to create everything anew at each moment of our lives, is our common destiny. This is what Double Edge means by the title "Center for the Development of Living Culture."

We do not embody any ready-made outside works, plays, books, etc., but instead we create from scratch an entirely new piece of work in an elaborate and time-consuming process of recognizing ourselves in the world around us and naming both the world and ourselves anew. The actors do not portray or represent characters from outside the world of the work, and scenes are not reconstructions of events that took place elsewhere. Names in performance programs are simply references that give the audience dimensions for the world on stage—much as the quote "to be or not to be" evokes the world of Hamlet in conversation.

In the very essence of our work lies the fundamental conviction, so obvious that it is usually forgotten, that people have souls. Every human being is ultimately individual, unrepeatable, and irreplaceable, and this individuality is the most important subject of our art. We make the pursuit of this individuality the central core and goal of our work, and we believe it can be expressed in a way that is comprehensible and relevant to other people. This is distinct from the traditional theatre, which silently assumes that art communicates primarily what we have in common, whereas our individuality is expressed only as a supplement, i.e., that the essence of theatre is an everlasting Hamlet character which the individual actor may enhance by adding a personal touch.

The process of creation in Double Edge is the quest for knowledge about one's own soul, the truth inside of ourselves. We pursue this through dialogue and exchange with the world outside us; through gatherings and projects with diverse groups; through books, music, and art; through social concerns and problems; and also through our everyday lives. Such a pursuit demands that we persistently strip away the schematic and the casual through constant self-examination. This is why our performance creation takes years, and why it involve our entire lives, not only in their holy and glorious moments, but also in their flaws, stupidities, and weaknesses. This is why our performances are at once tightly fixed and precise, and also totally alive, and why each presentation is an exact repetition as well as the creation of something entirely new—a living culture. The late actor Ryszard Cieslak compared this process to making love, which is always confined to relatively few gestures and situations, but, when true, it is always a new and penultimate experience.

The fact that our theatre extends into our "civil" lives does not only mean that during a substantial part of our private time we look for and gather material for our performance work, while the rest of our lives are totally separate. This relationship works in both directions: our theatre helps to shape our everyday lives, often informing our actions in concrete situations. Through our theatrical work of self-recognition we learn what to improve and change in our existence, how to become better and fuller people. It is this that moves us far away from the common notion of the artist, who, in order to nourish his art, pushes life to the limits of excess. It is not a paradox that in our "experimental" theatre the exploration of tradition and the past is so important, that in some strange way we can call ourselves conservative or old-fashioned people.

To change and fix the world, to make it more human, was for centuries the dream of the theatre artist. Even as we embrace this dream, we admit that it lies beyond the realm of possibility for art, which may be able to make a revolution but immediately after loses control and eats its own children. We have unfortunately been recent witnesses to this phenomenon. On the other side of the spectrum lies an even more disturbing conviction, ever present in America, that theatre and art aren't *real* parts of life, but rather available to serve us in our spare time as one of many forms of relaxation—a sophisticated aerobics to follow our serious work. Ultimately these two views derive from the same source: the opposition of "art" and "life" reflects the fragmentation of contemporary life, which is separated into alienated spheres—time for family, time for God, time for culture. What we attempt to create in our theatre is a living culture, a rebuilding of the fragments into an admittedly utopian *integrity* of human existence. We do this for ourselves, but also with the belief that we can share and transmit this experience to the people we meet.

These people, our community, are actually a reflection of the body of artists who make up the permanent company of Double Edge. Our audience includes the international community of artists and people from the areas we visit to perform and create exchanges, which includes Central and Eastern Europe, Scandinavia, Western Europe, the Middle East, and the United States. We reach this audience primarily through the performances *Song of Absence* and *Song of Songs*, which are focused on the ethnography of Jewish people from around the world in light of the diverse societies that have surrounded them. We involve these communities in the research and development of our performances, in the belief that direct communication between audience, or subject, and artist is key to the lasting resonance and truth of the product.

Double Edge also deals with special projects for special communities represented in the core group of our company—actors who are new immigrants to the United States and actors with disabilities are the center of our present extra-theatrical endeavors. Gatherings of song, dance, and story are held in communities representing immigrants from South America, the former Soviet Union, Asia, and the Middle East. Theatrical Vision trains visually challenged artists to develop their own sensorial performance language guided by Double Edge's core actor Nachum Cohen, who is blind. The theatre's internships allow developing directors the opportunity to create performance based on their own ethnic sources, side by side with the company's work. All of these projects derive from the essence of exchange rather than exploitation—the audience is never objectified and the artist never adopts a persona outside of himself/herself. Our attempt with each community we touch is to identify uniqueness and to overcome isolation and forced assimilation.

Double Edge's success cannot be measured in terms of numbers, finances, or quantity of performances, but rather in the depth and significance of exchange with people in all of the work we do. The few outside criteria we use to measure ourselves include the increasing number of students who work with us and the incredible support of our audience, who have remained loyal despite the infrequency of new performances. The respect of other artists also has meaning to our company. But the most intense scrutiny must always come from the group of people who make up Double Edge. We have the highest standards for our own artistic output, and for our expectation of exchange between the group and the world around us. Our own merciless self-doubt, criticism, and discipline find their response in the silences after a performance, the embraces, tears, laughter, and astounding letters from our audience, and, most importantly, in the extreme intimacy of the experience itself.

While this is subjective and in many ways dangerous to use as the measure of success, it would be more dangerous for Double Edge to allow our work to be measured in terms other than through human contact. Our survival, against all odds, over the past decade—with no money and no social acceptance—has forced us to pursue mutuality and authentic culture as the basis of our art. The greatest risk to our art, and an ever-present fear, is the loss of this humanity with each step into the social and economic environment of acceptance.

Our success will ultimately be measured by the grace and integrity with which we meet this challenge.

ii. "We Realized That Something Had Changed"

March 23, 2002

Double Edge Theatre was founded twenty years ago this April by a group of eight women, including myself. We intended to create a vibrant, passionate, thoroughly original, and permanent ensemble theatre. We sought to redefine theatre for our society, and to reawaken ourselves and our audience to the forces of imagination and spirit which lay dormant within. In short, we believed that art was truly essential and that theatre, with its uniquely human quality, could evoke the most moving of all art, if we dared to explode the boundaries of preconception.

First we created performances about women. Then, as new members joined the ensemble, we began to look to culture as the source of our work. In the beginning, research focused on the Jewish culture, but again, new members came, and the focus broadened to include the variety of cultures reflected in the group. Four years ago, we began work on our third cycle, The Garden of Intimacy and Desire. It moved beyond external concepts and definitions to delve into the hidden territories of our inner beings. Through this search, we came full circle to the issue of women and culture, this time from the inside out.

As we began to reflect upon the last four years of this new work in light of the original mission of Double Edge, we realized that something had changed. Survival, which had always taken the back burner to all artistic work for the theatre, had slowly taken over, creeping toward the front, as the group, now between the ages of thirty-three and sixty-five, had needs for family, daily life, and at least a certain amount of security. And, approaching twenty years, Double Edge had become a "real theatre," with a unique and very thorough methodology. We have a home, even a theatre center, and we have to meet the needs of artists, students, and audiences from around the world. We are no longer, or simply, a band of artistic rebels.

We insisted on facing the question, even with despair, about the contradictions between being a seasoned (and responsible) group creating excellent work, and a group whose purpose was to rip the seams off of convention and to prove that artistic creation was even more important than our own lives. This query has led us to embrace a new generation of young artists into the theatre.

They came as students two years ago, fully accepting the ways and methods of an established and recognized theatre. We struggled with their lack of knowledge, and they struggled to identify themselves. We began to understand that we did not want to repeat ourselves, even if the repetition had its brilliance. We chose to continue the true journey of Double Edge, "to redefine theatre and reawaken ourselves to the forces of imagination," and for this path, the new generation, with their lack of knowledge, and therefore total artistic freedom, is essential to us.

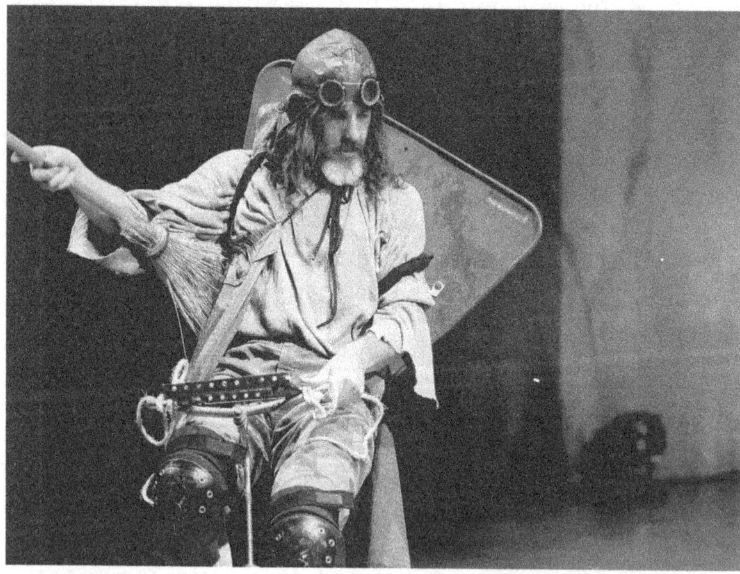

FIGURE 3 The UnPOSSESSED, *conceived and directed by Stacy Klein, with Carlos Uriona (pictured) as don Quixote de la Mancha, 2004. Photo courtesy of Double Edge Theatre Archive.*

The UnPOSSESSED is the very difficult process and result of addressing this question. It is a performance about individuals, about cultures, but most of all, it is about generations. It is about the immense value and the inherent flaws of tradition and institution, and the reckless dangers and absolute necessity of youthful risk and rebellion. In this, it is not only about the reawakening and rebirth of Double Edge Theatre, on the eve of its twentieth anniversary, but it also speaks deeply to the schism of our fractured world in the twenty-first century.

iii. "To Dream Another World"

March 27, 2002
Artist Statement for *The UnPOSSESSED*

I write on the eve of celebrating the twentieth anniversary of Double Edge Theatre, the ensemble theatre company I founded, and which I have directed since 1982. I did not have the capacity twenty years ago to imagine that this ensemble, much less my own artistic work, would still be valid, or even alive, in another generation. This awesome personal reality should bring with it a certain satisfaction, if not joy.

Yet I find myself incapable of accepting this joy, and certainly unable to be satisfied. Like many of the characters in my performances, I am faced with an incomprehensible reality, one in which people would rather shoot than talk, imprison victims rather than heal them. It is a reality that has replaced the human potential with catatonic isolation.

I have spent my career dedicated to the investigation of this human potential. I have pushed myself, and my ensemble, to go to the ends of ourselves to uncover the vast possibilities of our hearts, minds, and souls. We have worked—physically, vocally, and imaginatively—to break all boundaries that exist, in ourselves, and with our audience. Throughout the world of our work, which has taken place primarily in the United States, Central Europe, and South America, we have attempted to create an intense dialogue between cultures, and between individuals.

This dialogue was never verbal. This dialogue was never rational. This dialogue was never about form.

This was always an artistic dialogue, one that could and would use any means, whether it be movement, song, object, or image, to tell the story of the human being.

This story, although complex, dark, and incomprehensible, is certainly one of hope. I have witnessed this hope in the eyes of my collaborators and my audience, from strangers in Central Europe who dared to move beyond their anti-Semitic beliefs and embrace our theatre, to young people in Ashfield who abandoned their daily despair in the face of the creative act of performance.

The UnPOSSESSED, like all of my work, exists in the juxtaposition between the external nightmare that we have created and the impossible dream that we must risk creating. Although I have spent my life trumpeting the necessity of art, never before have I felt so convinced that without it, our descent into chaos is inevitable. For it seems clear that hope lies beyond our frail attempt to "understand," and art is one of the few realms that deals with the world beyond this "understanding."

Perhaps I am Don Quixote, the leading figure of *The UnPOSSESSED*, who in the face of horror chooses, quite simplistically, to dream another world. But with this project, I will risk becoming the fool who actually believes I can contribute to that possibility.

iv. Imagination, Memory, and Mythology of the Twentieth Century

2012
Artist Statement for *The Grand Parade of the Twentieth Century*

It all started with a question. How would we write a mythology for our time? We began with the recent past—the twentieth century—and the paintings of Marc Chagall.

We encountered a brutal and chaotic century, one in which cataclysm and destruction branded the times. This is how we chose to walk alongside Chagall. For the better part of the twentieth century, he chose the flight of the imagination, folk tradition, and the juxtaposition of dreams as his portal of memory, as a means of passage through the war and revolution and exile he painted.

In Chagall, the bride flies over the ravaged village, the rooster and cow play their cellos, and masses of people flee or dance. As we confronted the extreme conflicts of the century, we also understood that vivid imagination must be at the crux of building a mythology for our time. How do we dream, how do we dance, how do we invent, and how do we love? For Chagall, "color is love." What is it for us?

As we worked, we identified events and figures that were important to us. The actors donned and shed different personas, and we found ourselves rooted in the midst of the "American Century." That American lens of history informed our choices about what to include and gave focus to the multiplicity of perspectives in our group. We soon realized that reflecting history through our own eyes was the only way to speak to our desires for the future.

Memory, as an essential component of our lives, seems to have faded. We cling to a limited sense of reality (Whether "reality TV" or mundane materialism) and have exiled memory and imagination. Dreams are things of the past, beauty is seen from the media's vantage point, and quiet is drowned out by insistent sound and the seduction of belongings. We lose ourselves amid accumulating piles of bodies and trash.

How, then, will we write the future? We offer intimacy and the sounds and dances and inventions of history, the beauty of flight, and the choice of a forgotten world of dreams. Together we enter a simple yet profound dialogue with the future—destruction or creation?

EXCERPT FROM A JOURNAL: EARLY *GRAND PARADE*, 2010

"In life, just as in art, there is but one single color that gives meaning to life and art—the color of love."—M. Chagall

Training transformation. How to use the problems or challenges of the time to see your art. Don't be right or wrong, Archetypes. Create your own myth of the 20th Century.

Theatre is moral—how do you live through it and how do you live through things you will never experience?

A story or thought that enamors with magic and wonder calls to people with its parallels to our own lives.

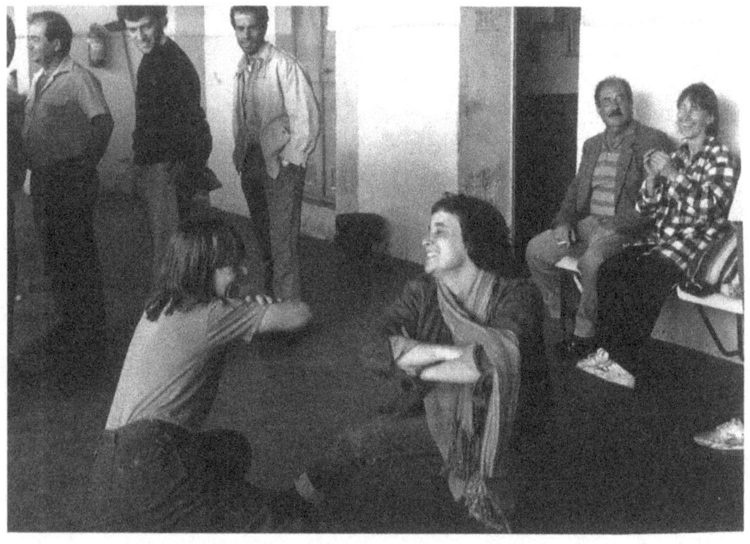

FIGURE 4 *Stacy Klein (bottom right) and Eva Benesz (bottom left) dancing at a bus station in Sardinia, with Rena Mirecka (far right, seated) looking on, 1985. Photo courtesy of Double Edge Theatre Archive.*

2

An Artists' Ensemble: On Autonomy and Collectivity

Introduction

There's a photograph [Figure 4] of me dancing in Sardinia with Rena Mirecka, my teacher, who is now among the ancestors. I started working with her in Poland in 1976. I arrived there on a kind of whim, through a competition at my college; at the time I didn't really know anything about her or even who she was, but I ended up working with her for the next forty-five years.

Rena Mirecka was a founding artist in Grotowski's Laboratory Theatre, and she was a major part of the work they developed, although this fact has not been properly acknowledged in the history books, even in the history of the Laboratory Theatre. She has been acknowledged as the only woman to have appeared in every one of their performances, but she has not yet been recognized as one of the leading motivators of the work itself. Recently, because she died in 2022, something of a reassessment of her legacy is finally underway. One of the other actors in the Laboratory Theatre named her as one of the leaders of the group's creative process: that is, as a creator of the work, and as the person motivating the work among the actors. This was ignored during her lifetime.

I bring this up to suggest a number of points. The first is that from the beginning, when I started working with Rena and several others from the Laboratory Theatre, it was Rena to whom I was immediately drawn. She and I had a special bond right away. I understood her training as an intense dialogue that wasn't based on words, but on visual, visceral, spiritual, emotional, and physical practice.

I had never encountered anything like that before. I'd always been told I should just talk, or memorize scripts. These could be interesting scripts, but the message was that dramatic theatre was confined to talking. That was in the 1970s. If you wanted to do something else, the logic went, you should do dance theatre.

This was astonishing to me, and I kept going back to Poland and trying to work with Rena, wherever she was in residence. Sometimes I was successful in this, and sometimes less so. During the first days I started training with Rena, I thought that pushing my body to the edge was the way to achieve artistic totality. When I broke my collarbone after leaping through the air, however, I realized that giving my all did not mean that I had to be reckless. To push against our limits and the barriers we create against our potential requires a carefully grounded awareness that risk and safety go hand in hand. In one of my journals soon after that time, I quote Rena as telling me, "No, no, no, you can't come now." She knew that I wasn't ready to take that type of risk again so soon after my injury. Even such refusals were part of the training.

That was a beginning. At the same time I started working with Rena, I was also in Poland for the first time, the place where my family came from and where many of my family had been murdered. It was a shocking place to be, from all kinds of different perspectives. I wrote something about this when I first visited Auschwitz on the same trip. This encounter with inhumanity and horror has haunted all the work I have done ever since—and it forever will. Practically speaking, it determined the manifest content of my work with Double Edge through our Garden Cycle (2001–2010). My experience of the dichotomy between the external and the internal, which has exemplified my work, began in Poland. Here was a land that had rejected and helped, in large part, to eradicate my people; and yet at the same time, here was a person that I could identify with more than I'd identified with anybody else in my life. It is worth noting that many of my deepest connections were found in Poland, which helps me understand that I should fight any unilateral conclusions I may draw. This remains so moving to me, that my Jewish soul could be so intertwined with people who are so deeply rooted in the spirit of Catholicism.

The photograph dates from a crucial moment that took place a few years later, when I went to work with Rena in Italy in 1985.

I'm on one side of the image. Rena is sitting on a bench, and I'm dancing with her assistant, Eva Benesz, who is now a teacher in her own right. We're in the bus station in Sardinia and acting crazy. I'm sure the other people in the bus station thought we were nuts. We were in our own reality.

The project we were working on together in Sardinia left a deep and lasting imprint on my work with Double Edge, as I write in "Letter from Sardinia" below, which recounts the experience for the Double Edge ensemble and community members who could not participate directly.

My voyage to Sardinia with Rena began as a series of workshops we gave in Cenci. I was there as a leading student, let's say: not really as Rena's assistant but as an ongoing participant in her work. Each workshop lasted five days, starting at sunrise and ending well after sunset. Our practice took place in almost total silence, and included meditation, cooking, yoga, and vigorous physical improvisation. Some of the participants from the Cenci workshop invited Rena to Sardinia to conduct a workshop in an abandoned school. It didn't have electricity or any amenities. There was land around it, and a number of outbuildings. There was a central place where we could do training, and rooms where we could sleep on the floor, as well as a makeshift kitchen.

We would cook together, but we had to call on the people in the community to help because we didn't have electricity. We needed things—we needed food, obviously—so people would venture out and get food. I remember there being a fire. We were vegetarian, because Rena was vegetarian. That was the idea. But at some point men from the town roasted a goat for us as an offering. Or perhaps it was a pig. I can't remember, but I do recall talking about it, and Rena going back and forth with the villagers about our various exchanges. Many of the people involved in the workshop were from the local area or had joined us from elsewhere in Italy. Some were there in search of health solutions, and a few of them were trying to overcome addiction. For me, at the time, the purpose of our work became a question. When we were alone—with Rena, her team, and the people from Double Edge who had come along with me—we were doing incredible things. But when the other people came in, things could get a little out of hand. Rena was trying to find out something about healing. I really wanted to do theatre. In any case, I was pretty wild at this time, and toward the end of our time in Sardinia, she ended up kicking me out.

To Rena's surprise, when I left Sardinia Double Edge ensemble members Carroll Durand and David Flaxman left along with me. Once I was expelled, they weren't about to stay on with Rena. But we didn't have plane tickets back home. We were in the middle of Sardinia, in the Mediterranean. We went back to that same bus station from the photograph and tried to pull ourselves together. It was intense. Once we got back to the mainland, we drove all the way to England to find airline flights back home.

It's important to reflect on why Rena kicked me out of her working group. First, Rena wanted everyone to be celibate throughout all the work, which was definitely not my thing. Not that I could get up to much where we were, because we were all living together under one roof, but I was still full of drive. I was bringing my full reserves of passion to bear on all the improvisations, whereas at the same time many other people were searching for tranquility. I was still learning how to listen.

There was a fundamental divide in the work we were doing in Sardinia, which I could not reconcile. The forms we were using in our work, such as chanting, functioned differently as health care, as Rena insisted, than they did as a means for discovering metaphor and image and ritual through theatre. I couldn't find a way to make these goals compatible, especially because the community working with us were not interested in metaphor. For Rena, this community work was an active research concern at the time; it was what she wanted to do. Since then I've done plenty of trainings with and for the communities I'm involved in, but these have always remained in the realm of art, that is, where any claim to healing happens through art. That's what I feel I have to give. Training is continuous with healing. But they are not reducible to one another. A question that always remains for me thus concerns the boundaries between the creative and the healing processes.

After Sardinia, Rena and I didn't see each other for five years. And then, just like that, the five years were up. I went to visit her in her house in Wroclaw, when Double Edge was on tour premiering *Song of Absence* in Poland. When I walked in the door, she was standing on her head. And I stood on my head, because I didn't know what else to do. After we finished standing on our heads, she said, "So, you understand?" And I said, "Yes." Things don't always move in a straight line.

This I know for certain: Rena knew I needed to find my own work. When I came to Sardinia with her in 1985, I was just beginning my directing career. She had visited Double Edge in Boston, and she had visited the new space we'd acquired, and she had seen that I was finding my way independently. She saw this clearly, and thus I understand our separation as her way of telling me, "This is my thing. You find your thing. And then we'll get back together."

This taught me a lot. It's not always the time for a mentorship or artistic relationship to take root. You might love somebody, and they might be your person, but it might not be the right time. That lesson is one we so often end up learning and relearning over and over.

I think this is true of mentoring more broadly. It's important to know when to hold on to folks and to know when they're not ready, as well as when to push them out of the nest—to let them spread their wings, so to speak. It's a wise person who knows when the time is right. And not only is it wise; it is also courageous. I was an important person for Rena. It took a lot for her to send me away, and I admire that and wish sometimes that I had more of that type of strength.

In terms of her impact on my work, Rena was my artistic and spiritual mother, as well as my friend and mentor. Even our five-year split was a great gift. I *had* to find my own way with Double Edge and step out of her shadow. Serendipitously, Sardinia was a perfect moment to make that leap.

The following writings date from 1985 and 1986 through the 1990s, coinciding with the beginning of a new Cycle of performances—the Song Trilogy—and with Double Edge's first permanent space for creating and developing our process. We could—and did—spend as much as ten hours a day in the unused parish hall of the Church of Saints Luke and Margaret, in Allston, MA. The simple idea of training together, without the need to stop on account of a part-time, rented space or an immediate demonstration of results, but instead with the sole purpose of challenging all our senses and potential into awakening, led to unexpected discoveries.

In each of the following letters and essays, I am especially aware of the discoveries that are still relevant today: I see the work of facing and, hopefully, dismantling the built-up effects of ego. I see our efforts to remove the masks we have learned or have been forced to assume. I see our project of battling form as a rigid supplanter of search and meaning, and our commitment to awakening and igniting ourselves to the possibilities of a vital and magical living theatre.

EXCERPT FROM A JOURNAL:
WITH RENA, JULY 7, 2013

We force too much physically.

Each person needs to understand their individual responsibility and connect authentic action to their inside.

Better yet, not to move ....

Seed of new training.

Love

Quiet

6. A Letter from Sardinia (1985)

From a Double Edge newsletter.

Dear Carroll, Lorien, Daina, Andrea, Humi, and friends in Boston,

We traveled on the ferry from Civitavecchia (near Rome) to Cagliari (on the island of Sardinia). We slept on deck under a bright half moon and awakened to a glorious dawn shining down on the deep blue glistening sea.

We didn't know what to expect in Cagliari, even after working with Rena (Mirecka) several times in Massachusetts—as you know the work is always different and depends on the space, the time, and of course the people involved.

What David and I know was that this was important for our work, our theatre, and our lives—that it would be impossible for either of us to stop pursuing what began with Rena.

Rena asked David upon our arrival to help prepare the work place. I awaited the beginning of the work in Cagliari with Thomas Richards (our friend from the last experience with Rena). There are my usual trepidations—can I go farther with the work? deeper?

Finally we went to the space—an abandoned village that lies between the mountains and the sea in the north of Sardinia. It seemed inconceivable to me that this place could work for us— no running water for toilets or showers, no electricity, and worse, concrete floors all over. Where were the wood floors?

Yet this old village was transformed—its wildness fed into our own wildness which lay dormant. This place became the stimulus for seven days of crucial work for twenty-three people.

Watching the awakening of the sun
Walking ever so slowly in rhythm
Physical training challenging parts of the body that have slept
    too long
Cooking
Cleaning
Eating
Bamboo stick combat

Dancing
Singing
Improvisation
Ceremony
Music
Exchanges with villagers
The sunset
Sleep
A search of silence.

Why have we come so far to work again with Rena? We could stay with each of you and work in Boston. Double Edge has so much going for it now. We are recognized as a company that is highly skilled, that has discipline, precision, and depth. But my dear colleagues and friends, we are only at the beginning of a journey that must never end. Our discipline has led to rigidity, our precision has stopped us from going further in breaking through our limitations, and our search for depth has brought us to walls of horror. But have we truly allowed ourselves to be dirty—have we really gone past the sterility of our lives, our society—have the wild flowers bloomed?

It is clear that Rena cannot give us the answers, cannot fill our loneliness or hand us creativity. Yet certain principles in her work can help us to truly continue to make our work alive.

We begin to recognize that in each moment of life, in every sound, and in each heart-beat we can find fullness. We cannot be impatient, we must not push or say "I must create"—the creative act will happen only as a result of hard work to free our bodies and our inner voices from sleep and allow the flame within us to breathe.

I write to you in metaphor and yet the work must be extremely practical. See the tree, don't just walk past it; watch the rising of the sun, don't sleep through it. The work with the body must not be lazy—push past every barrier in your body—the body has so much potential yet we are usually content to do what we know. We cannot afford to be content with our physical training—if we do not continue to expand our potential at every moment—we will not fly.

When you are ready, start to see other people and the objects around you. Take the time to prepare—what do you need as your stimulus? Approach your creation with a question—*is this truth?* If it is not, do not be afraid to go on. If you find some moment that is more than mundane, repeat it—be precise, don't be afraid that it will die—it will live again in 1,000 different ways. We must no longer be satisfied with relations of the everyday—our true gift and the real search—as artists, as people—is to be able to take people on a journey far beyond what they know—to fly on wings without fear with all who want to travel this path on our backs.

This is the experience with Rena. It is incredibly difficult this time, not only because the physical and inner demands are greater but also because we are away from all that is familiar to us. We work all the time, and do not speak outside of the work. We search for the voice inside of us—we look for the song of silence.

Yet as it becomes more difficult, I begin to expect more from myself and the greatest joy is that is there to be found. You each must trust that the discipline, the repetition, the precision all will lead to a tireless, weightless, unrestricted place that is very real and yet unknown. It is here that we truly communicate with others and with life around us.

Our theatre must not be a choice of ego or an expression of our own problems. The type of theatre we must do demands too much to continue for those reasons. It simply must be vital for your entire being, for your existence itself, that you do this work and share with those who want to see you. This is how we will strip away all the masks, all that is false in our work and make a super-human attempt to find the life, to express the truth. It is essential. We—our world—must no longer sleep.

From my heart,
Stacy

7. Do We Search for Theatre? (1986)

I wrote this piece during the second year of Double Edge's ten-year residency at the Church of Saints Luke and Margaret Parish Hall in Allston, MA. This time period marked the beginning of the transition between the Women's Cycle and the Song Trilogy. The neighborhood surrounding our space was working class and itself in transition from its Irish roots to recent immigrants from a variety of places. We found out that our rehearsal hall was right next to two apartment buildings, and the way people took out the trash was to throw it out the window and try to hit the dumpster. Glass and bottles shattered our precious moments of quiet. At first I was incensed; I couldn't believe it. Then I started to understand that such annoying daily life occurrences were giving us context for our work. It was a reminder that outside our precious room people were living their lives, in this new place they called home. And it was certainly not the same noise as the casual cackles in theatre spaces we had rented, where intentional practice such as ours was viewed by the managers and administrators as some kind of a joke.

✳✳✳

We go to the theatre. Do we have an experience that is necessary for us, or is it just a continuation of our routine? Do we search for theatre—for that part of theatre which takes us beyond the everyday?

Double Edge was created four years ago as a feminist theatre. Yet each time we tried to define this word—feminist—in our work and in our lives, we came up with more questions about its meaning. We realized that there are no answers, no judgments, no statements to make—the truth, the essential, lies beyond these limits. We became a group of mostly women still interested in material about women, but for different reasons. Our label exposed, we were forced to search for something more essential, beyond the words and concepts that didn't fully express who we were, to search for the creative impulse vital to our lives, as women, as men, as members of our theatre.

We train our bodies and our voices each day to help us see that we expect too little from ourselves, physically, emotionally, spiritually—to try to understand that a world exists beyond everyday behavior—to surpass the limitations of our intellect. We work improvisationally to see each other in new ways, to feel the pulsing rhythm of people gathered together sustained in living creative action.

We sometimes have conversations that are vital to our lives, that go beyond the casual, the didactic, the serious, or the rational—conversations that reveal and confront something beyond the words they are made up of. It is not agreeing or disagreeing that is important. But by truly seeing something unspoken, each person experiences his- or herself and the other more deeply.

This is the dialogue of the vital theatre. The actor searches to reveal, by creative actions, that living flame. The search of the spectator, the witness, the other person, is for some REsponding ACTION.

The usual habit following a theatre experience of analyzing or judging becomes meaningless in a theatre that is vital to us, which makes us awaken suddenly to something inside which is beyond explanation. The creative impulse guides us on a search for something vital and true—not a search for an answer, but a search to find the question—the question that keeps the flame alive.

Do we search for theatre?

8. The Living Actor (1986)

From a Double Edge newsletter.

My most recent obsession in the theatre has been about the possibility of the actor actually being alive during a performance—that is, not working to re-create an action or series of responses or trying to simulate a character, but instead being present, in fact, living through each moment on the stage.

This question is not original—it has plagued theatre artists from Stanislavski to Grotowski and still has not been answered. It is not a question of believability or by any means a matter of naturalism or realism, although it is possible to confuse the two issues. An actor may be completely "believable" in the role being portrayed and yet not actually "alive" or in the course of living through the stage experience. As far as realism goes, it may well have been this very search for truth or life that inspired artists to try to re-create life on the stage, but the form itself dangerously encourages attempts to impersonate life, rather than upholding the possibility that the actor's work, in and of itself, is life.

If not believability, and not realism, then what does it mean to be alive in the theatre? Perhaps one can say that at each moment of performing the actor is seeing for the first time, responding to the space, the objects, and most importantly, to the other actors—essentially existing in the process of discovery. The word *process* is most important, for in order to be alive on the stage there can be no fixed emotional responses, nor can the actor have set answers to the many questions posed by the role, the production, or the director. This is not to say that form must be obliterated, but rather that the form, in its precision, becomes a runway for the actor's discoveries.

This process often occurs during improvisation. The first time a question is raised there is an actual search for its meaning, and it becomes more or less easy for the creative, seeing actor, to "live" in the work. The struggle to maintain this active receptivity comes with the attempt to repeat the action. The question is how can one repeat, in a performance, and at the same time be present in the discovery of each moment? In words the answer is simple—there is no repetition. Each time the actor goes on stage s/he enters with a totally different perspective. The form may change only slightly, but the inner life of the actor is in a constant state of exploration. In order to achieve this, the performer must have the freedom and security to give up all preconceptions of the role, all fears of directors' rebukes, and all clinging to answers from previous performances. This is to say that the actor's source must be so strong that s/he has the strength to confront the audience with nothing but the skeleton of a structure and find through the performance, and with the audience, the associations and resonances of the moment.

This process is by no means easy, and I have yet to find a formula for producing such results. I have witnessed only a few performances in my life in which the actors were truly and completely alive and not simply in the act of repetition. The first was Grotowski's Laboratory Theatre performance of *Apocalypsis cum figuris* in 1976, and the second was the Polish Theatre Association Gardzienice's performance of *Avakuum* this past summer. Another was Tadeusz Kantor's *Dead Class*. The profound effect of these theatre productions on my work and my life has forced me to confront the importance of the subtle distinction between "acting" and "living" in performance. As an audience member, I remember that the flame that ignited the actor's birth in performance spread also to me and suddenly I too was re-awakened, or living, through the experience.

Essentially, the significance of becoming the active-actor lies in the enormous effect this process has on the audience. Recently I spoke to an audience member who has had a great deal of difficulty with the work of Double Edge. After our last performance he told me that he had learned to come to our productions without the desire to decide whether they were "good" or "bad" He must come open and allow himself to live through the performance. If he missed something he must not get stuck in figuring it out because then he would not be able to continue—in the moment—his process of discovery with the actor.

The "living" actor makes a proposal to the audience— through the actor's ability to go beyond daily behavior, cut through sentimentality, and sacrifice the self for the moment— to make the choice of life. This extraordinary actor's capability to search beyond norms, gained through much discipline and training, and thus to transcend the theatre within the theatre, taps the desire in the audience to re-awaken the senses. The audience member is no longer watching a re-creation in passivity. S/he is part of the living, breathing organism of theatre. The joy of the performance is born out of the communion of this exciting, active life discovery between the actor and the audience.

This is the magic that is possible in the theatre.
This is the search of DOUBLE EDGE.

9. Director's Decalogue (1991)

The "Director's Decalogue" was an exercise of self-examination I first conceived and then offered to my students and the ensemble, so they could experiment with their own versions. Below is my own Decalogue, with all the flaws and determination of a 34-year-old with a group less than a decade old. Each person in the group, and all of our students, were asked to write one for themselves, whether as a director, an actor, a technician, or a designer. Alongside the Decalogue was an additional exercise: "why is Tadea (my then six-month-old daughter) important to have in rehearsal?" The insight of that writing was to see how authentic interruption, a life *interruption, could actually promote an alertness and presence in the training that could not be manufactured!*

But I want to tell you the hidden story of the Decalogue. For several years I have been talking about including this piece of writing, which I considered fundamental, in the book. My colleagues and I, especially John Peitso, searched everywhere for the document: in our relatively new archive room, through personal papers, on computers (although the original had been typed). The Decalogue started to take on mythic proportions. We just could not locate it. In March 2024, Carlos and I were cleaning out some dusty and forgotten old scripts and other less important files deep in the back of a closet, and the last file we uncovered was the Decalogue. It was meant to be.

Much of what I wrote here remains true. But one thing that has changed, after years of collaboration with my group, is that I consider each of us to be a director in the sense of shared responsibility. We share our "strength, heart, and soul" as one.

✳✳✳✳

1   The director must love and desire PEOPLE. The director must earn the love and respect of the actors by showing them that they have more potential than they expected of themselves, or offered of themselves. This may require

aggression and force, as much as kindness, but always the actor must know your belief in them is eternal. This way they will make *the choice* to be directed by you.

2   To make a group such as Double Edge requires TOTAL BELIEF, TOTAL RISK, AND A TOTAL WORLD. The director must live for the group and force the actor to live for himself/herself. The passion of the director must be felt at every moment, along with the belief that the work is crucial, everlasting, and absolutely necessary. There is no other reason to make this huge effort. If the work is not absolutely necessary and important for you, *forget it!*

3   The director is the interpreter of the actors' language for the audience. The director listens, watches, sees, and finally speaks. Not as a teacher or guide, but in response to the actor's vision.

4   The most difficult work of the director is to keep the group together by making sure that each individual and the group itself is growing, not stagnating, and that the theatre is growing. It requires that the director's defense system is strong enough to withstand attack from the outside, including the press, funders, politicians, and friends who think they understand but do not, as well as from the inside, when the actors have lost their objectivity and need to be manipulated out of stagnation. It means that the individual needs of each member are met, both in the work and outside it. It is better to work with three untrained, undesired people and find a common vision and necessary potential, than with ten stars who are far past any desire to seek or grow.

5   The director needs to know everything in advance of the group, with the exception of the creative work that is the process of the actor. Everything that forms a barrier to this process, from life conditions to human relations to individual and private concerns, must be understood and solved by the director. The creative work of the director is alone and last.

6   The director cannot be self-contradictory, doubtful, or thoughtless. The right to lead and shape the vision of the

work all the time is granted by the actor to any director who truly works with and in response to the actor. Otherwise, there would be no possibility for any progress in the work. However, what the director says is not nearly as important as how the process is built—words which may be true one day would not necessarily be true the next.

7   A real technician is the same as an actor: someone who has curiosity, rhythm, soul, and the desire to perform. The difference is that s/he is also like the director—with no desire to be seen, but rather to make a performance through other means. The director who works with light and sound must make this work as fundamental as the work of the actor. Each person who creates a true part in a group is irreplaceable. Losing anyone after working with such depth not only creates a hole which takes much time to heal but also entirely changes the work. By the same token a group must create according to its members.

8   All of these things are only true because they have been fought for and determined by the group with the director over the long period it takes to establish a group such as Double Edge. No art of quality comes easily or quickly when it is created by human beings.

9   The director must be the strength, the heart, the soul, and the mind of the group. The members of the group should exceed the director in their given area, but the director must be able to lead in all of these directions.

10 In the end and from the beginning, the director is *responsible* for everything and must also instill this sense of responsibility in each actor without any loss of freedom. But when the performance is not to your satisfaction, or if someone gets hurt, you must accept that the answer is only to be found in your work, in your tiredness, in your short-sightedness, in your lack of vision, and nowhere else.

10. On the "Magic Theatre" (1993–7)

Touching Memory. Magic theatre: not for all. Choice of life. Toward the Irreplaceable. Living Culture. From Ruins and Isolation to the Republic of DREAMS.

These words fly out to me as I reread this essay, which combines texts from a four-year period from 1993 to 1997, during which Double Edge created the Song Trilogy and made the move from Boston to rural Ashfield. This writing also reflects our work in Ukraine in 1994, while touring and developing the Song Trilogy. I don't think I understood the full impact of these performances and projects, and even the move, until much later. Yet these words, which you will see unfolding through the writings below, testify to the foundations upon which everything at Double Edge has since been built.

✳✳✳

Double Edge is a permanent ensemble of artists who, for the most part, have worked together for more than twelve years on a daily basis, investigating theatre as a form of art from all perspectives, and demonstrating the results of this research with original performances, theatre training, and special projects that go beyond common interpretations of the form.

The structure and practices of Double Edge are externally conventional—a director and a group of actors rehearse, teach, and perform a body of work. However, the methods, processes, lives, and results of this work hearken back to a much older example of theatre, more similar to that or Molière's group and the King's Men than to either the modern repertory theatre or the avant-garde. And this is, ultimately, the strange dialectic of Double Edge: that we are not easily classified, for we are at the same time quite traditional and yet radically different from the norm.

The uniqueness of Double Edge is the nature of this ensemble as a permanent body seeking to understand and formulate the creative act in the theatre through daily and committed investigation of the necessity of art as a process of self-definition. We take seriously and definitively the notion that the establishment of theatre which fully responds to the individual's complexity of life requires total involvement over a period of years to the development of this life. We see this process through the lens of an ethnic culture whose way of being is built over the course of centuries.

We are in many ways akin to an extended family or clan, which builds its own culture based on belief and the necessity of survival. Each person in the theatre is responsible for creating his/her own work as an actor, and at the same time fulfilling every other necessity of the work. This includes the design and building of sets, costumes, and lighting; the research and rehearsal process of gathering, writing, drawing, composing, and playing; and the daily work of training, teaching, cooking, developing, and maintaining the performance space, as well as managing all of the daily business that any theatre requires.

Every aspect of this often mundane work must be done within the context of the whole—that is, in the sense that the actor must "act" responsible for the creation of the whole world of the theatre and not as a replaceable interpreter of the director, producer, or writer, or as a lofty, yet uninformed "artiste," whose affairs are managed by an outsider. In Double Edge the director is more often the interpreter of the actor's work, and the sculptor of the theatre's vision for the outside world.

The actor as an artist requires a long-term and consistent training process in order to articulate forms, rekindle sources, and develop materials, and often this is a process of years for each performance. This is perhaps the most difficult aspect of Double Edge to understand—the reason and purpose of the lengthy performance process—and herein lie the truth of the actor as an autonomous artist and the essence of the work of Double Edge. It would probably be more comprehensible to name the actor as a composer, or painter, or poet rather than an actor, for in almost every other type of theatre, whether it be spectacle, experimental, or repertory, and no matter how brilliant the actor, s/he can be replaced. The nature of Double Edge is predicated on the complexity and fragility of maintaining a dialogue, and a coherent vision, with seven vibrant (and outspoken) artists. The dichotomy between the group and the individual, in which each artist has the freedom of a creator and also the restrictions of the other members, necessitates endless tolerance and the strictest discipline and commitment, not only to hours of presence, but also to humor, emotion, vision, and endurance. The result of this struggle is a creation which is totally unique to the group and cannot be duplicated. In a very subtle way, it is not a theatre that is made, but rather something living and breathing in itself.

This is the "magic theatre," to quote Hermann Hesse. While "not for all," its magic is a living experience which, no matter what the subject, is an extremely intimate and personal journey, from the entrance into the space, to the performance, to the gathering afterwards. It evokes a memory, often kept in secret, of what can be, and also of what may never be.

Our stories make it possible to break through isolation. It is possible to conduct cultural investigations in a way that appreciates and celebrates vastly differing peoples; and it is possible to create art by choosing the road of knowledgeable respect as creative source, rather than exploitation or imitation.

The work of Double Edge has always been to explode myths and masks, to seek the potential of the artist as a human being, as an actor of choice. Each of us has a memory of our values hidden inside. It is the purpose of Double Edge Theatre to awaken and touch these memories, to trace them for the future, to confront them with modern reality.

11. Director's Mirror: On Collaboration (1997)

*The following text is a meditation on my first partnerships
that developed outside my immediate ensembles of artists.
Reflecting on Max Palar and Carlos Uriona leads me to consider
how Double Edge's present partnerships came about—which,
unlike anything I have seen before or elsewhere, are rooted in
collaboration and dialogue. Max, who left this earth some ten
years ago, exploded every understanding I had previously held.
He provoked a journey into the unknown territories of myself, in
which I was forced to learn how to balance on the tightrope of
mysticism without drowning in its ocean. Max's background was a
harsh one. Born into a broken family as the child of an Indonesian
woman and a Japanese soldier in the midst of the Indo-Japanese
war, he was never able to come to terms with his story, in spite of
the amazing powers of his Silat spiritual and martial arts practice.
Even as he called me brilliant and beautiful, he also fought my
arrogance. It wasn't until I met Carlos that I could even begin to
understand what this arrogance really meant. For over a quarter
of a century now, Carlos and I have gone on to learn, to lead,
and to dialogue. Carlos's difficult background—surviving the
Argentine Military Dictatorship—led him in the opposite direction
from Max. Instead of mysticism, he has used his empathy
and understanding to create pathways for all, for everyone, to
experience the artistic unknown.*

✳✳✳

Collaboration and dialogue are the roots of my artistic soul.
Through this process I am able to envision myself, through the eyes
and ears and mouths of others. I am able to admit things about
myself to which I have been previously blinded. From this territory
of my own unknown I slowly emerge into a state of vulnerable
recognition. It is here that I seek courage for the imperative to
translate my humanity as an offering of art.

This process, which may also be named as my life, occurs in
many layers and on many levels of intensity. As the director of an

ensemble, it occurs on a daily basis with the actors of my group and the individual staff of the theatre. As a mother, it appears in the shape of my children. As a theatre collaborator, it surfaces in relation to the communities who allow my presence and to the other artists and theatre groups who seek to know my art.

As an individual, a human being, the possibilities for expanding this dialogue, beyond the realms of confrontation, literature, or my personal life, are limited. It is difficult, almost impossible, to find the strength proper to a dialogue of two without allowing it to stagnate or disintegrate. But when a dialogue of this nature unfolds, it has the potential to reach the deepest and most profound roots of artistic spirit.

In my artistic life I have been blessed twice by its occurrence. The first time, with the Indonesian Silat Master Max Palar, who is now training master of Double Edge, led to the explosion of my entire artistic being, and, with the ensemble, ultimately translated into my creative journey as director of Double Edge Theatre's ten-year Song Trilogy Cycle.

I recently approached the premiere of the last performance of the trilogy, *Keter, the Crowning Song*, in which one of the sources of my own work was a confrontation with the ghosts in my life who had been disguised as partners in dialogue, but who had instead led to artistic annihilation or personal stagnation. In seeing my fate through this reality, accompanied also by the memory of the recent dead in my life and the dead of my collective consciousness, my performance work echoed the sounds of bleakness, isolation, and aggression.

In September I found a second artistic soulmate, Carlos Uriona, from Argentina, living in Tennessee. This experience did not occur as an explosion, as it did with Max Palar, but rather as a very slow, gentle, carefully balanced, and respectful approach toward the unknown artist in each of us. The results of the collaboration have occurred faster than the speed with which it has been undertaken. Through this dialogue with my artistic twin opposite, I have found what was unknown to me in *Keter*: my own acceptance, my own power of love, and my own desire to heal. I have been able to give my work in *Keter* something totally unexpected, a duality of life which certainly includes pain, but which also looks toward a season of hope.

Carlos and I continue this artistic process. We find ourselves in the realm of the mirror, and we have begun to recognize traces of theatrical metaphor in the literature of the Kabbalah, which in English means receiving, and to explore its translation in my group. I experience in this moment the germ of "receiving" a new performance as a director, perhaps even a new way of working. This involves and demands the meeting of our respective theatre groups—Diablomundo and Double Edge—in the roots of this discovered artistic soul. It is only when we find the possibility for translating this work into the practice of both groups, that we can enable meeting the unknown as individual artists to transform into meeting the unknown in culture. This offers the possibility for discovering the artistic soul of cultural collaboration, a genuine merging of the roots of distinctive trees.

12. "I the Worst of All," An Artist's Statement (2001)

In 1999, two of my closest colleagues left the theatre ensemble for very different reasons. One decided on a more normal life (a life that certainly could not be found at Double Edge, especially then), and the other decided that he needed to focus on Jewish culture rather than on other sources. This was a painful period for me, as a lot of blame was thrown about before the realization came that it was time to separate. Or at least I hope that we all realized it. As I have noted above, I was never as good as Rena at letting go—or rather, I always believed things could be worked out. I still do. When I wrote this artist's statement, the Song Trilogy was over, and I and my three remaining colleagues, Jennifer Johnson, John Peitso, and Carlos Uriona, who are all still with me today, set out together to find another beginning. The piece we created, Relentless, *premiered in 2002 and became this new beginning. The dialogue between two worlds staged in this performance—a woman in prison for child murder and a man staring through a peephole of his Argentine military prison cell—also marked our own transformation as a company.*

✱✱✱

RELENTLESS began as an awakening from a nightmare. The end of the Song Trilogy, the end of twelve years of digging into the graves of ancestors and the roots of culture, left me facing an abyss. Did I have anything more to say? Could I undertake a new creative process, or was I to be stuck forever in the habits, patterns, and repetition of what I had so cleverly created with my colleagues for over ten years? The truth is that no matter how often I protested my desire to move beyond the Song Trilogy, I realized how deeply I was embedded in my own past.

In parallel to my own interior (and for the most part, hidden) struggle, Double Edge was going through a process of renewal, which demanded from me the energy, precision, and creativity of a leader. How was the company to move into the twenty-first century? How were we to develop our own training projects, our touring, our cultural work, our Farm Center? How were we to ensure that recognition did not bring stagnation, that we would maintain our artistic integrity rather than succumb to the bureaucracy of an established theatre?

RELENTLESS became the focal journey toward myself. An exploration: into my inner topography, into my own commotion, into my own desires, and also into my own despair. As I re-entered the dialogue with my hidden territories—a dialogue long postponed by the hardships of accomplishing the Trilogy, building the Farm, "keeping the company alive," and raising my two children—I was once again able to regain my dialogue with the actors.

RELENTLESS speaks of transforming restlessness into work, of insisting even when I want to give up because everything around me is larger than my strength. As Susan Smith, the child murderer, returned to haunt me time after time with her message of horror, I wanted to give up. I became *RELENTLESS* in my efforts to find a way to create new training with the actors, one which could reveal the existence of the mystery of art that is found when we are really together. I have become *RELENTLESS* in confronting the borders of my weakness as well as my power.

The actors brought back a wealth of material in response to my openness: material that mirrored my questions and which opened a new form. The first draft of our future was presented.

RELENTLESS is unfinished. In the next period of its development the dramaturgy needs to be refined. We need to articulate with more precision the discoveries resulting from this search. The actors' work needs to be adjusted and the narrative developed. We want to use what we learned to develop a creative process that does not end, one that is always willing to face the abyss.

RELENTLESS is to be the first installment of the Garden of Intimacy and Desire Cycle. It is the beginning of a new cycle in my own work—one that is deeply personal—and in the work of Double Edge. It has revealed the necessity of humor amidst the overwhelming isolation of our times. It is particularly important that we present it on the Farm, and that we have the opportunity to grow our new cycle in the embrace of this community, which has allowed us to start again.

It is not often that an ensemble reaches maturity. Most theatre companies in America barely achieve their adolescence. Double Edge's twentieth anniversary is coming soon. Although maturity cannot be measured by years, we have entered a period where we can add to the energy of our youth the years of our experience. It is rare that one has the opportunity to reinvent oneself, much less an ensemble. This is a place of privilege, a wonderful opportunity to blossom.

13. Director's Confession: *Republic of Dreams* (2007)

Republic of Dreams was the third piece of the Garden of Intimacy and Desire Cycle. Thinking through the Cycle's title, in the context of the four performances, is curious. Each performance was about the disappeared, imprisoned, oppressed, or isolated. Yet through those lenses, dream, yearning, mystery, and the seemingly impossible shone through. The intimacy and desire was really our desire, as creative artists, to reach our audiences and share this impossible desire for life.

***

Why Bruno Schulz?

My love affair with Bruno Schulz began in 1985 when my mentor Jacques Chwat gave me a copy of the amazing and strangely autobiographical story collection, *Sanatorium Under the Sign of the Hourglass*. From that moment, Schulz's oeuvre, including *Street of Crocodiles*, his letters and his drawings, would appear in my work in obvious and, at times, more mystical ways. In *Song of Absence*, the first performance of Double Edge's Song Trilogy, Bruno Schulz himself, although long gone, made an appearance, and brought along with him his coterie of lively creations. Schulz's visionary courage and inspired presence has continued to guide my dreams in that decades-long journey from my youthful directing to a more mature art.

In the Song Trilogy, I moved from *Song of Absence* to *Song of Songs*, followed by a research exploration entitled *Hidden Territories*, which took place in Schulz's birthplace in Drohobycz (a town that moved back and forth between Poland, Germany, and Ukraine, at the convenience of its occupiers). For this latter project, Double Edge created an exchange with young artists and explored the remnants of the city's surviving Jewish life, which included speaking with some living relatives and students of this profound artist. On this journey, we had the unique opportunity to see the streets and storefronts that Schulz describes with such intimate humor and surreal detail. We were also able to visit his

Synagogue, an enormous monolith that was successively destroyed, first by the Nazis, who turned it into a horse stable, then by the Soviets, who turned it into a furniture factory. Even Schulz could not have imagined this.

Why now?

After twelve years of working on the Song Trilogy, I moved on to the Garden Cycle, thinking that my story with Schulz had reached its end. Through two performances and several Spectacles, Schulz's world remained relegated to the outer reaches of my work, returning only when I gave my copy of *Sanatorium* to my protégé and co-creator, Matthew Glassman. Matthew was quickly consumed by the Schulz inspiration (felt by numerous illustrious artists of the twentieth century, from Cynthia Ozick to Philip Roth, to the Complicité Theatre, to Tadeusz Kantor and his Cricot II). Once again the Schulzian world found enormous resonance with a Double Edge core of actors. Matthew's uncanny resemblance to Schulz himself, embodied in his portrayal of a doubtful young Jewish artist (renamed Joseph in *Sanatorium*), was equally matched by the theatre's lead actor, Argentine Carlos Uriona, and his magnetic grasp of the magic realism and eccentric force of nature embodied in Schulz's other main character, the Father.

The three of us traveled to do research in Poland. We went to Wroclaw, where we spoke to refugees from Drohobycz who had studied under Shulz in high school. Afterwards, we went to Warsaw, where we had the good fortune to view hundreds of Schulz's erotic and fantastic etchings, tucked away in the back room of the National Museum of Literature.

Bruno Schulz lived in a time not dissimilar to our own. Growing up between the wars, a time in which assimilation, fear, and consumerism rose to huge proportions, Schulz saw that life could be more. He envisioned scathing, larger-than-life views of the city as "streets of crocodiles," in which people overconsume with no regard for context or reason. He discloses the depths of the hypocrisy whereby sexuality and religion are fraught with rigid fundamentalism, and framed by ethnic and nationalistic hatred. In his vision we see the undercurrent of horror and indifference that would soon erupt into the Holocaust and, even more disturbingly, we see how the world today bears the same seeds of destruction.

How do you translate dream, image, and metaphor into theatrical narrative?

Schulz was prescient. His etchings of a marching group of gaunt, underwear-clad wax dummies foretold, with shocking accuracy, the story of the millions of souls marching their way into the gas chambers. This unforgettable drawing, created in the early 1930s, provided the explosive core image of our performance, just as Schulz's 1936 essay, "Republic of Dreams," provided its ethos. The essay describes the chaotic world around him while also expressing his desire, as an artist in his chosen place, to live life to its fullest, no matter what. Schulz did not believe in a linear world, and he did not write or draw one. As we attempt to create order from the chaos and uncontrolled events in our lives, we forget that it is not only in the inner regions of our imagination ("regions of heresy" as his dedicated biographer Jerzy Ficowski describes them) that our most joyous and awe-inspiring moments live on.

Like Schulz, I insist on examining life according to a different kind of narrative, on standing firm in my dreams despite the violent conformity and enforced rationality of our world. Circling and spiraling through the imaginative genius of Schulz's creations, I have discovered my own magical theatre—a dynamic layering of events not linked to obvious cause-and-effect. In this way, a deeper truth can be found. The images of Schulz's father flying, inspired by an ink drawing, or the young Joseph mistaking a merchandise catalog for a holy text (from "The Book"), call to mind the fevered imagination of a small child looking in awe at the magnificent grown-ups around him. As Joseph moves the story to his father's death (from the story "Sanatorium"), one simultaneously sees Schulz himself as a grown man in the late 1930s, forced to paint murals for his Nazi protector as his world disintegrates around him. Through these juxtapositions and elaborations, a living reality is built that persists and renews itself, even in the face of the decisive, lethally final acts of history. The truly rare courage of Bruno Schulz lay in his insistence on imagination and freedom. With the strength of that courage I have endeavored to attack all preconceptions—to create an art of vibrancy, provocation, and full engagement.

"We dreamed the region was being threatened by an unknown danger, permeated by a mysterious menace. Against these perils we sought refuge in fortresses of the fantastic. Today, those remote dreams come back, and not without reason. The possibility suggests itself that no dream, however senseless or absurd, goes wasted in the universe."

—Bruno Schulz, "Republic of Dreams," 1936

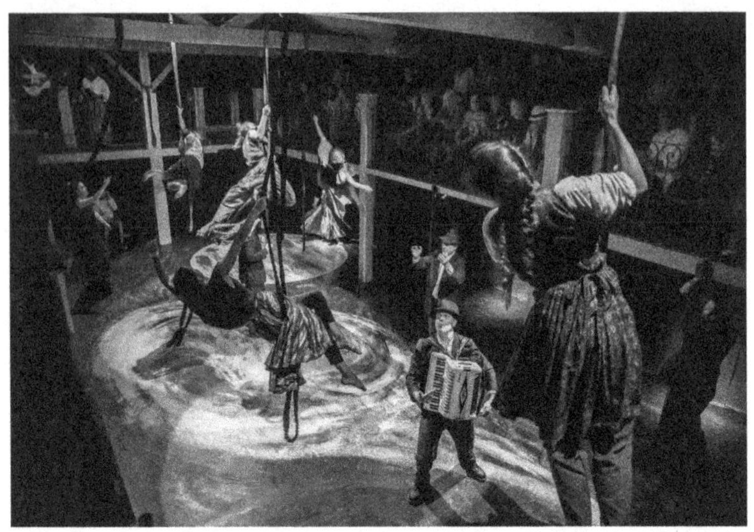

FIGURE 5 Once a Blue Moon—Cada Luna Azul, *conceived and directed by Stacy Klein. Pictured: Carlos Uriona, John Peitso, Jennifer Johnson, Milena Dabova, Hayley Brown, and Hannah Jarrell, 2016. Photo courtesy of the Double Edge Archives.*

EXCERPT FROM A JOURNAL:
CADA LUNA AZUL, 2014

Rehearsal: Where is the animal inside you? Strangeness is external, an idea, not "in being."

Yom Kippur wondering:

There is a training component of the new work related to the creative process rather than the training itself. It is exploration. Separation of creation process from acting!!! Some create individually and some create as a group. Intimacy is in the core, but it does not require external isolation.

I love this new space. Happiness: to fulfill potential, to offer potential to the world.

3

"Each Person Must Ask Why They Are Here": Training and Performance Creation

Introduction

Dear Stacy!
… Call upon the supreme energy in your own heart …
A Wind Will Sing You
My Warm Wishes for your <u>WAY</u>
And Your Friends
Always,
Rena Mirecka

Training is difficult to articulate in words, yet it is the most expressive language I know. When I first went to Poland I was about to step away from theatre, as the emphasis on words and texts could not hold my focus or my understanding of the totality of art. One of my directing classmates found a poster on the bulletin board advertising a Polish theatre summer, which included a workshop with the famous Teatr Laboratorium. I had no idea what that was, but out of a fierce sense of competition with my fellow student, I signed up as if I knew something. In Poland, I found the key to a lifetime of physical language. For years after that I resisted, even rejected, words as a means of communication; the Song Trilogy exclusively used poetry rather than expository prose. For me words, as explanation, could always be twisted into lies or subterfuge. Yet this is not always the case; when Ludwig Flaszen, the dramaturg of the Theatre Lab, spoke it was very similar to the metaphors that I found in the language of training. Later, during the creation of the Song Trilogy, I had a similar experience with Max Palar, the Indonesian White Crane martial arts master. Often, speaking with our group from the end of rehearsal until 3:00 in the morning, he used words to dwell in the unknown. His was a completely metaphorical language, which needed to be interpreted individually by all who listened.

Even as I began to trust words slightly more, I never wanted explanations to invade training. There are very few spaces that aren't based on words, where we engage fully with our senses. Maybe the simplest way to characterize my training—and Double Edge's, as it has now completely been taken over by the actors—is to describe it as a physical, sensorial, inventive language that is always accompanied by a question. This question is yours; it is a demand from yourself, and this is what keeps the training alive. Even if you use the same form of training every day, its nature changes drastically depending on the questions you are confronting.

In outward form, my own training has changed little from what I did with Rena in 1976 and 1977: it involves partner work, plastiques (isolations of different parts of your body, which we then use to lead motion), corporeal body work, running, and the plough (a yoga-based partner exercise). The technical vocabulary of these physical actions is well documented. What has changed enormously in my approach to training, and my colleagues', is the interior content. Both culturally and creatively, the work has expanded as we have continued to respond to it. As the Double Edge ensemble grew, the artists involved brought their own songs, dances, and rituals, and all that has shaped the way we train. When we relocated to Ashfield, the content of training also changed on account of this new environment, as we began to dialogue with our natural surroundings, as well as our physical surroundings, such as the barn. This opened up further possibilities for including large objects in our corporeal work (such as walking on giant cable spools), as well as flying—aerial work that began with leaping, and then progressed into taking flight with bungees, then fabrics, and then up in the trees, soaring over the pond.

Still, for all its physicality, I believe that training starts with a question. It is not a regimen, like going to the gym, although it might use exercises adapted from yoga or conditioning or martial arts or dance. A training session is one of the few places I have found where you can ask your questions, hold intense dialogues, and strip the mask of daily constriction down to the very core of yourself. It is in training that I feel, and am, at my most honest, both in giving and in receiving the responses it yields.

When I first worked with Rena, I wrote every day. Sometimes I tried to translate the language of training into words; sometimes I articulated my emotional responses, of which there were so many. In the *Song of Absence* period, I continued this practice. Slowly, as my work as a director grew, my writing became more specific: it focused on what I needed to remember as a director, or on the intricacies of an Étude (a short, propositional scene created by the actors), or on images that came to me. I no longer journaled about training or about my thoughts or feelings, except in relation to the stories I was building. I believe, or hope, this was because I was putting everything into my performances, and not because I lacked the will. My way of communicating changed to a practice of listening, observing, and, after a long period, responding. I what follows I have included excerpts from journals dating from 1976 through the period when we were creating *Grand Parade of the Twentieth Century* (2012), to share how the training process has progressed.

14. Excerpts from Training Journal (1977)

"Reject what you know and are able to do: cross some barrier in yourself." These words, which I recorded in my journal, date from the seven 12-hour days I spent training with Grotowski's Laboratory Theatre in 1977. During the day we went through eight hours of physical and vocal work and at night we sat for four hours listening to Ludwig Flaszen, the Laboratory Theater dramaturg. The words cited above, which were spoken by Flaszen, have stayed with me throughout my life in the theatre. I believe I am still trying to move through the barriers to my hidden potentials. This may be one reason why the work of Double Edge keeps on evolving.

We are taught from an early age to find answers, to know everything. But I remain far more curious about what I don't know. The unknown, whether external to me or inside of me, is far more vast than the known. We can examine what is going on in the politics of our time, but as to whether it is all part of some great lie or whether it is fueled by a yearning for truth, this is all but impossible to calculate; we can only be clear about the issues. The broader question of how we can all get along, or come to some world-saving agreement, remains part of the unknown. The real work begins here. So too is it from the unknown that the work of arts and culture proceeds. How do we liberate ourselves and our collaborators from the barriers we impose on ourselves, the strictures we are gaslighted into accepting?

Reflecting on this journal entry from so early in my career, I am struck anew by both the dramaturgical treasures it contains and the practical poetics of the actors' offerings. I am convinced that the exercises and ways of thinking recorded below can be put to use today, almost fifty years later. But they necessarily take on new meaning, and new possibilities, with each repetition. This may be how I have come to think of my work as a spiral, with each ascending turn revealing new questions, new unknowns.

***

Teatr Laboratorium Day 1–1977

Group work:

Individual group propositions, including blindfolding half the group and letting them wander. [Ryszard] Cieslak added partner trust exercises.

One person, eyes shut, led by another—open and trusting the person to feel completely safe.

Filling the space, feeling when everyone should rise, build tempo, drop it back to ground positions.

Clay models: two people model each other with eyes closed. Try to copy each other.

Exercise: take a candle into the dark and see people, let it grow from there—if you see someone dance, help them.

Corporeal work—first doing different positions, then relating to others with it. Then rolls, with different paces and different associations. Rolling in positions in red color, in rain, in slow motion, etc.

Working Group A
10:00- 1:00—[Ludwik] Flasen
3:00–5:30—[Zygmunt] Molik
7:00—Rena [Mirecka] and Antek [Jahołkowski]

Flaszen

His role was in dialogue with Grotowski.

He attended all rehearsals (present at the crucial part of creating a piece).

Flaszen did not work with actors.

His job was to formulate Grotowski's instincts, to put them into concrete terms.

In the beginning, 1959, through the process of trying to get away from illustrations of a playwright's ideas, came the Poor Theatre.

Idea of eliminating things to find the seed or essence of theatre.

Spectator—audience relationship—unity—RITUAL.

Actor training development: exercises include yoga, dell'arte. Of special importance: the idea of contradictory vectors in the body.

Transferring the human being into an animal or plant based on associations.

Using the full extent of human range.

The introduction of yoga: very important.

Meyerhold's Biomechanics—doing the smallest gesture—the whole body takes part in it—gives birth to it.

Work by means of very small elements.

Reject what you know and are able to do: cross some barrier in yourself.

Learn courage, how to overcome your own laziness, heaviness. Reject learned gestures which give us security, and then we can face a new sphere, a new world. This new world forces you to undertake risks; call it development, self-fulfillment, realization.

These exercises are not only for performances, but for creating the above conditions.

Rule: when an exercise is mastered, it's then rejected.

Molik—1

Start out by freeing the body, bouncing up and down, running, relaxing, letting tension out.

Relate to the room and recognize the people you are with.

The Plough.

Aim your voice to the ceiling.

Continue moving all the time. Never static, but let movement come naturally.

Let sound come out free—curiosity about how your body can move, but don't move for nothing.

Give or get help, move and make sound freely.

Rena and Antek 1

<u>Part 1—Plastiques</u>
Running and jumping: two legs, one leg, running in place.
Isolations: head, chest, arm, hand.
Find a bird that is in you and go with it.
All the time doing your own dance!
Pretend there is a bell, follow it. Then it is a stone, let it take you around.

<u>Part 2—Corporeal</u>
Mat work: running, dancing, rolling, head stands.
Jump up as high as one can. Body work.

Rena and Antek 2

Plastiques.

> Warm-up—bird: which bird is in you? How does it move? Find your own rhythm for it and go wherever it goes.

> Rolling, leading, dancing to a group dance. Take energy from others when tired. Use all of the positions, but only as your own body discovers them.

Flazsen 3

A director, even if not a dictator, must form, montage, and edit the play, must make final decisions, and put everything into the whole. But still allow the actors to create.

In art, as in life, people and situations are made by manipulation. When you reject this manipulation, you have left the domain called art—you are in another world. What is left when you put aside manipulation? When you abandon the desire to affect the world? [Note from S.K.: It took me a long time to understand the word "manipulation," as he used it, in the context desiring to affect the world. Manipulation as choice with another is not how I learned this word and I remain uncomfortable with it, and in my career I have chosen the word interdependence]. Monk. Vegetable.

Manipulation = progress, but if there is *only* manipulation there is no progress.

The problem of where the food or the rent money will come from doesn't exist in Poland. So they are free to experience this "transcendence." [Note from S.K.: this reflection does not address the extreme poverty connected to the government at that time, and that their giving of food and housing still left the population impoverished.]

To transcend to the other world, one can descend deeply (like Kafka) or ascend and embrace all (like Whitman).

Rena and Antek 4

Begin on your own with Plastiques—whole body isolations. Kicking, running, being pulled from the inside, bird inside.

Corporal positions. Headstands three ways. Shoulder stand, rolls, tiger leaps, cat, handstand, rolling over, crab position. In all of these, find your personal balance and impulses. Next, work with partners. With my partner, it was fulfilling because I used the positions as the basis: we saw each other, changed rhythms, and responded to each other and to our own impulses.

Flazsen 4

Images of mythical creatures, cultures, iconography, were needed in plays—these symbols were understood. When body and mind come together, when all *learned* reaction falls away, when action comes naturally, when all my body is taken, mythic behavior comes naturally. This is when myth appears.

Whatever you are going through—suffering, etc.—push it through to the very end, even if that terrifies you.

What is, is!

Molik 4–7

Physical positions for voice, continuing to try to find vibrations. What positions work, or don't work? What can I do, what can I change to make it open? Do associations help? Words, text, song? Use imagination, but only as a starting point.

Make a dialogue with vocal vibrations. Let your voice come from different parts of your body: shoulder, chest, ears. Point your voice to the walls.

With my partner (Rebecca) I felt energy; people commented that something happened. Problem—there is still no guts to it. Must be rigorous with the body. Molik worked with us, Rebecca pushing into his hand, making her push back. In the end, the sound was open and clear.

The objective was to make yourself sweat—let tones change, the goal to vibrate and to use our full bodies. It was difficult—what is the direction? It is important to have a reason for working. Worked with partners and we found a bug on the ground, which really led us in a direction, inspired us to go on! Zygmunt helped me to open by walking with me and making my body go up from my hips—this is where I found my open sound.

Today it took so much effort to make sound. When you start something, you must finish.

Flazsen 6–7

My life is in expression/art. In the Middle Ages, expression was taken seriously. Books were either canonized or burned. Now art/expression is legal—we call on the artist's imagination. But it is not considered to be an experience, but a mind thing (idea). We look at things and say, "what beautiful poems or plays." It is something objective, rather than being part of one's life. Thus the artist can live in society. So I find a vehicle for imagination.

Actors worked alone without Grotowski's help, and then he would come in and watch and filter through things. Crisis came when we centered the text of the gospels in performance, because the research became so personal. Instead of going farther, there came a gap. They were lost: the relations in the group were worn out. A performance could have been made—a beautiful one—by using the director's image.

Rule at Lab: Save something about to be ruined by artificial means. Tension appeared when (the actors') own personal revelations met with the story given by our culture.

Exercises have nothing to do with work on a performance piece. Exercises are something parallel that go alongside the rehearsals.

The actors were searching for something real. This does not mean everyday life! Behind each gesture, each movement, there is all our life. One must call up everything, for expression.

THIS IS MY DESTINY.

Fragility of human experience. What is my theatrical experience based on? Great pain, great joy. To keep going farther, crossing barriers, growing and surpassing myself.

"I never expected something like this could exist." As long as we can say that, we are still alive.

Rena and Antek 4–7

Develop birds—warm up using the elements. Birds come from your associations; physicalize this bird. This should be a dance of the birds. In the end we were asked to hold a difficult or distorted position—we did that and began our dance with our concrete body.

I worked with Charles trying to get him to respond, but he attacked me. Rena said if I choose to help him I should keep trying, and I think it is a good fear for me to overcome.

Today we were horses. We ran, jumped, and played as horses. Then we used the corporeal positions to dance with each other. We simply tried to relate. We were aware of other people.

People consistently on the floor tackling each other. This was okay for an instant, then onward to surprise somebody by jumping away or anything—SURPRISE.

Today we had a battle because we were still like children, unable to lead ourselves. The work was very general, rushing with no basic element work. So she asked several people to lead the warm-up—it was so rigorous I almost died! After that everybody became strong and gained energy.

Candle experience: the moonlight, do our own dance around the moonlight of the candle. Not too successful today, we did not see each other or dance from ourselves. I tried again to work with Charles and it was even worse—he said "the game is over." I tried to open myself to him but he pushed me away. Afterwards I got very upset partly because of that and partly because I had not really let out in the work all of the guts and emotions I had wanted to. Thus, they came out afterwards.

The session was set up where Wayne was giving a beat, and the mats in the middle were earth and the candle on the side was the moon. People were to work together on the mats and the others were to dance around them. It was obviously not ok; people had many accidents and were not in tune with each other, while the people on the outside were not trying to help the inside people to continue. The dances had no relation.

Lots of anxiety today because of the combining of the two groups. Rena says new things happen all the time, and we simply must deal with them the best we can. We must be aware of the people, as there will be so many.

I was not invited soon, so I invited someone to work. We worked through the elements and only near the end did we get away from them. I felt very strange and then found another partner, and in me was the feeling to make her laugh, since she was drained of energy. And I gave her some. There was a real dance of sharing between us—we just kept responding—giving, taking.

Today I gave all I had and realized that you can have fun, you *can* get new energy from other people, you *can* discover new things in yourself if you keep going and passing the barriers (exhaustion, for one).

We had mats all over the room and we practiced exercises. Headstand, shoulder-to-shoulder headstands, and then into a roll. Try to find your natural balance and try to develop your work. I got mad doing a handstand and Antek told me not to do such heavy things if I simply can't. It makes sense that you try to go past your barriers, but at the same time you need to maintain an awareness of your body.

We worked with partners—I like this work because I can plunge right in and don't have to think. Someone said I did a flip without hands—I don't know—it just happens.

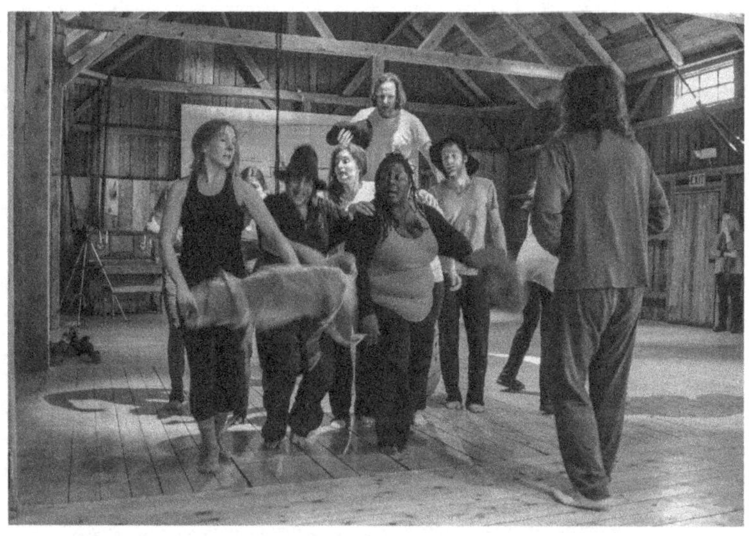

FIGURE 6 *Double Edge training in the barn. From left to right: Hannah Jarrell, Milena Dabova, Matthew Glassman, Jeremy Louise Eaton, Adam Bright, Ebony Noelle Golden, Andrew Todd, and Carlos Uriona (in foreground), Stacy Klein (far right, against wall), c. 2017. Photo by Travis Coe.*

Now I want to work on having the same commitment and awareness but in a quieter, less physically stimulated situation. But this is a step.

Now we are one group, not two. Both physically and spiritually. Today our starting point was the candle at the center of the room. The image, given by Rena, was of constellations moving around the sun. The stars shouldn't touch or they'll explode (countering our problem of constantly touching each other, which is an easy way to relate!). If one wants to touch, simply recognize the reasons and move on. Use your body to say why you wanted to touch.

Elements to partner work. I stayed with my partner for a long time, finding what it meant to be stars in a constellation. Eventually we were drawn to the flame. People were doing strange things at the fire and Rena came up and said to really feel the flame, feel the heat upon your hands. It was a beautiful moment. There was a wild dance and we all collapsed together. Almost religious in a sense.

This was our dance—for the first time, really. Now we must be more alert for everyone, not just our partner, but the whole.

Note: If you find something, you must get past an obstacle in you that bothers you—whether about yourself or others—and fight it!

15. The Impulse to Train (2015)

Jennifer Johnson and I have been working together for over thirty years. Although for a good while she worked in parallel, leading her hometown theatre in Charlestown MA, she is now the Co-Artistic Director of Double Edge and a core creator of Double Edge's work, as well as a singular actor. She is devoted to training, not only for herself but also as part of her mentorship of other actors.

What follows is excerpted from "The Impulse to Train: A Conversation between Stacy Klein of Double Edge Theatre and Jennifer Johnson of The Charlestown Working Theater,"published in HowlRound Theatre Commons *in 2015.*

✳✳✳

Jennifer: Securing your space, a church hall in Allston, gave you the capacity to work in a new way.

Stacy: Right, we didn't just have to work from 7 to 11 in a rented space. We worked from 9 a.m. until 1 o'clock in the morning and so that space gave us Double Edge and Double Edge's training. Before that all we could do is run around and do some minimal plastiques, and maybe a little bit of corporeal work I had learned from Rena. When we got our space, we could play. Not only could we play, but we could play with things; we could play with large objects, like spools or cement blocks; we could incorporate balancing and other movements that were very enticing for me, and which I saw as part of training. This was the big change that transformed the training I had learned into my own training practice.

But there was development as well. It wasn't just a matter of having all that stuff, but of having the space, and therefore the time, to be able to develop something. In my mind the possibility for research really began with the space, the real research. You can't really develop something in four hours a day when you have to make a performance in a three-week time period. In that case you have to use the objects, the play, only as the immediate tools for making the performance; you can't use them as a way to research.

Jennifer: Can you talk about what partner work is?

Stacy: It is very similar to working with objects. It is work with *the other*. I find it very hard to conjure up the other when I'm by myself, particularly in theatre. It's a little different when you're writing, but in theatre you want to be engaged. So partner work is your audience or your mirror. Maybe it starts with certain exercises, but it develops into a whole relationship. My training and my teaching are all based on partner work, and the relationships that emerge in and between partner work and object work. These are places where the human being is very engaged. You have, first of all, the resistance of your partner. You can't simply make your partner do what you want; you have to invite your partner to do what you want, and you have to convince them to do what you want, and they have to convince you to do what they want, so there's a sense of real engagement and play. And then this resistance can be developed to create a sense of risk. Not a dangerous risk, but the potential for surprise, so maybe you jump on someone's back, or you walk on someone's back, or you throw someone into the air, or to the ground. I find partner work to be exhilarating, and also very moving.

Jennifer: I'm jumping now to the more recent work at Double Edge's Farm. I think it's easy to think of training as preparation for something: you're preparing yourself. Obviously that is part of it. However, it could be said that at Double Edge the training itself is the thing, the creative act. I find this approach to training to be earth shattering. It is so freeing, so focused on being present, that it develops a demand for presence that is rare in a theatrical experience.

Stacy: Yes! Depending on the people involved or the location, the training will be different, even though nothing basically needs to change. I think that is a key. I remember once when we did this great work with Rena in Poland. She was blown away, really happy. And the next day she said, "Do it again." We couldn't even begin. We had no idea. So we tried to repeat the things that we were doing, and it totally didn't work.

Jennifer: And that's what the discipline really is: a redefinition
   of repetition.

Stacy: Yes, and it means asking: what's your take-away from
   the great improvisation? What are you remembering? For
   instance, I remember I had my brown skirt on, and I'm
   holding it, maybe like a baby, or maybe like chains or
   something, and all I wanted to do was repeat that action. But
   it wasn't a matter of repeating certain actions, because you
   can never repeat an action. You have to repeat the process
   underneath, the essence. That was the problem Double
   Edge was encountering at that time. A big question about
   our approach to training thus became: how is it related
   to yourself? If you're transporting an action, how do you
   transport yourself within that action, without having the
   whole score?

Jennifer: There is a foundational, elemental aspect of Double
   Edge training. What can you say about the training of
   the company today, and the training of students, both at
   the Farm and away?

Stacy: We really believe in training as a process that is essential
   to theatre.

It's a very collaborative process. Matthew's [Glassman, Double
   Edge Co-Artistic Director] training definitely hails from my
   original training, as does Carlos's [Uriona, Double Edge
   Co-Artistic Director], but Matthew's training is unique to
   Matthew and Carlos's training is unique to Carlos, and we
   have an ongoing dialogue about that. I had a really good
   time with them when we trained with Anne [Bogart] and
   SITI Company because we were working together in the
   room as we created an improvisation. After thirty-three
   years with the ensemble I think we are finding a new kind of
   training, a new way of working.

Jennifer: I would like you to say something about the vast
   number of students that Double Edge has mentored. The
   training model is not just about developing the company; the
   model is also about reaching out, as in the case of the open
   trainings Double Edge regularly hosts.

Stacy: We run open trainings at the Farm and we also offer
   them on tour. We host open trainings of various kinds,
   such as family trainings, where little kids are coming in

and training with their parents. We want everybody to understand theatre as a creative practice that engages the whole. We have year-round training programs; we have hundreds of alumni. There are at least four groups that have spawned from Double Edge, and there are a lot of other young groups emerging. We want people to find their own training. Training exists to help you find your uniqueness and your voice, and so we expect, and want, that people will leave here with some means to develop their own voices. That's why there are so many groups doing very different work than we are; that's also why students from other artistic disciplines, like visual artists and musicians, have benefited from this approach to training, and I feel really good about that.

Training is creativity. In today's world, where the imagination is neither respected nor employed, it's essential that we do our part in ensuring that people can imagine. Even people who won't ever train can still share in the imagination of that training, in so many ways.

16. Excerpt from *Song of Absence* Training Journals (1988)

Song of Absence was Double Edge's first completely devised and original performance, which I conceived and directed, and which I co-created with Nachum Cohen, Bonnie Cordon, and David Flaxman. We worked on it from 1985 until the performance opened in Poland in Fall 1988, and we continued working on it well after that. By 1985 the company had moved into its own space in Allston, so we were able to train every day for up to six hours or more. Then we rehearsed. We were looking to explode any stereotypes inherent in our subject matter, as well as in ourselves. The journal entry below documents my thought process as a director, which remains integral to the process of the ensemble. Even at this late phase in the creation of Song of Absence, *you can see my thoughts jumping between the physical and the metaphorical, jumping between worlds and realities, with the known facts of history juxtaposed with the feeling of present history in the making, with dream worlds and nightmare worlds juxtaposed with the ordinariness of daily life, and with moments of love engulfed in fires of indifference. The stories overlap; the archetypal fuses with the personal; and at this moment in the process all the intellectual research involved in creating the performance is given up to the very, very present moment of creation.*

✷✷✷

SONG OF ABSENCE
Physical movement style + individual content
Objects
Ramp to stage
Piano on stage
Boiler—fire, Sodom and Gomorrah, cart, bath, crematorium
The train—transportation. Where are you coming from, where are you going? Train transforms to Ark.

Cement blocks—Work. Bricks to build set and world,
Suitcases
The Ark—Bible; refugee boats; pleasure cruise. Death wagon
Sand—ashes, desert, food
Trunk—luggage, coffin, magic trick
Image
Stadium—Chile—field lights
(cement blocks)
Auschwitz—oven
Detention camps—Native Americans, Palestinians, South Africa
Homeless—U.S.
Refugees—always moving
Wailing Wall
Vaudeville, orchestra
The set is a world; actors build it and tear it down. No home;
even as home is built, it is destroyed. Objects move, everyone
on Ark, moving. Legs on slide that fold in.
Ladder or steps on boiler.
Holocaust is framework for whole work. Structure includes:
Set/world
Lights
Gesture
Rhythm
Text
Images.
Actions
Physical object training—The language of the performance—
violence, impulse, rising/falling
Fighting/dancing. Running
Carrying/throwing—blocks, bodies. What is the Dance of Death
of our time?
Freeze
Rising/falling
Opposition
Repetition—The train: walking (through the desert); working
(transport camps; distortion)
Lines—selection lines, strip showers
Contradictions

***

David and Dermot—boxing match, Herod and slave, friends/ lovers. David on boiler, Dermot at wall. Develop work through language of the Body. Blocks passed through boiler, carried. Create stepping stones

David—rabbi/hangman. The spoiled child

Bonnie—Hassid/cabaret/male impersonator, Kol Nidre.

Dermot—criminal

Andrea—neurotic city bourgeois

Wedding—up stairs to top of boiler. Marriage bed is a trap. People dancing below.

Actors breaking down ramp, boiler—moving—then put up to create roof-lodging.

Auschwitz—everyone crowded at gates to watch, at last moment a gallows is erected.

David working in oven with rope/noose; crazy dance around him. David building with cement blocks, Dermot in tub. Chaos surrounds—the action is chaotic with David in center. Wailing, sacrifice. Dance to Tanttz, Andrea on knees and up again.

Very strong building of space. Each coming in from a different place: Andrea—brewing, Nachum waving and hitting with stick, David bringing a horse to temple, Dermot circling with cement block. Suddenly the blind man climbs up the blocks, dancing on them.

Playground—playground of atrocities.

The Wedding

The Battle

The corpse

Andrea burying Carroll in the sand. Our rituals are on dirty soil—can we clean the Earth?

Dermot on boiler, Lorien through legs. David carries Lorien to ramp, lifts her, dumps her into oven.

Cement blocks—banging, throwing. Brick dancing. Crawling out of rubble. Abraham and Issac chopping on blocks.

Everyone walking on wall. Kissing through wall. Clothes off, walking in different rhythms. Balcony rail, Image— townspeople outside camps. Using suitcases for jumping over. Jumping contests of prisoners organized by SS. Traveling with all possessions.

Bonnie on balcony—light on Bonnie, Kol Nidre, everyone

watching. Someone dropped from roof? After hanging, everyone dancing. Beauty from horror?

Puppets in show? Shadow puppets? Roof on balcony the whole time? Consider Baal Shem Tov and Bruno Schulz story.

Shekinah

Rape on ark, repetition of ramp sequence. Andrea with suitcases, thrown off ark. We see showers in back of curtains.

With Max Palar, Silat Master

Opposition—legs = thunder, arms = waves; legs make loud noise, arms are quiet

The last fall, the last stand

Impact = repair

Trance with movement. Movement = subconscious

Stand—back down, feet fall, somersault, up again

Twelve Wise men movement—Drunken Gods—North Star comes to earth as a beggar.

Garden of flower—deadly movement.

Monkey movement?

17. "Our Work Requires Awareness": Student Training at Worcester College (2000)

Awareness is a core component of training and must remain a focus from the first day onward, throughout the life of one's training. This means an awareness of the environment around you, an awareness of the people in your proximity, and an awareness of your own breath and body. We can run around in a room full of people, jump onto a spool, grab the fabrics, and swing onto the balcony. Or we can fly from one tree to the next, and dive into a pond. Yet all of this demands awareness. The risk that accompanies our trainings can only be undertaken if you fully understand this demand; otherwise the risk becomes danger, akin to driving a car without noticing a fallen tree or a car speeding next to you. Risk-taking requires an awareness of danger. Pushing yourself to jump higher than you thought possible means knowing how to fall. In the end, the risk is all about listening to yourself and trying: pushing yourself to move beyond what you thought was possible, whether physically or emotionally.

In a patriarchal and white-supremacist society, awareness must take on other dimensions as well. There must be a sensitivity to touch and to relations, such as the relation to your own sense of vulnerability as well as your relation to that of others. This is the only means to build trust and allow for the intensity of this type of expression. Awareness extends to the audience in the same manner, offering intimacy and the space for questions.

What follows is excerpted from a group conversation with Carlos Uriona, Jennifer Johnson, John Peitso, and students at Worcester College. The conversation was filmed and transcribed; this excerpt has been edited for clarity.

✱✱✱

Our work requires awareness. It should be like that in our lives, too, but it's not. It's dangerous work. It's just as dangerous as walking across the street: it is *that* dangerous. We're not removed from life in this space. We pose a metaphor physically to ourselves, representing the kind of involvement that is necessary to be full and present and involved.

Even so, I noticed some people's embarrassment during our training demonstration, and I was thinking about how strange it is that people consider this work—which, for us, is fairly simple—to be so intense. It's strange how we've developed to the point where, if we call on our involvement in any way—or our imagination, or if we touch somebody, or if we love—then this is what seems intense to us. By contrast, things like corruption and war and rape and murder don't seem to really matter all that much.

It was a strong experience for me when I realized how common this tendency is. It seems that as a society we are moving toward that lack of involvement our theatre is trying to confront in an artistic way. But involvement is also at the core of how Double Edge works as a company. Every day we exercise our creativity in order to work together while maintaining our individual identities. It's always evolving; it changes all the time. The life and the work cycle together: sometimes they are the same, and sometimes they're different, but they always have a cause and effect relationship to each other.

Here's something that might clarify what this involvement means: even though we name John, Jennifer, and Carlos as actors, this doesn't mean "actor" in the regular sense of the word. They are creators. In our work, each of the participants is a major force in the creation of a performance, not someone who merely fulfills a role.

Likewise, in our text and in our song, we're trying to be as involved as we can be in our bodies and in the music. The first part of this involvement is instinctive. It has to do with what is important and relevant to each one of us individually; and if it is really essential to us, then it will be essential to the audience in turn.

The second part of this involvement has to do with asking, as we go: how do we manifest the words of a performance for the audience?

Sometimes this is a very literal matter of deciding whether to translate a text into English or keep it in the original language. When we drew on Jacobo Timmerman's *Prisoner without a Name, Cell without a Number* (Preso sin nombre, celda sin número), which was written in Spanish, we decided to use text from the English translation. But when Carlos cites Lorca, he's doing this in Spanish. It depends on where the meaning develops, whether it's more sound-based or visceral, or whether we need the words. If we need the words in the moment, then we need to translate it to English, but otherwise, the audience can read about it.

It's the same with the music. Also, it's largely a cultural issue. We don't perform texts in languages that aren't languages the company speaks. Our current performance uses Spanish and English. Other performances drew from Hebrew and Polish.

Coincidentally with training, each artist in the company does their own research, and this comes more and more into the co-creation of the work. If somebody reads twenty books, for instance, we may end up with two in the final work. The same goes with physical actions: we work through hundreds of them, but there may be two that feature in the final performance. And it's the same with the music.

18. "A Dialogue with Space and Time": Consortium of Theatre Practices (2000)

The Consortium of Theater Practices was led by Double Edge, Gardzienice Theater Association, and Kadmus Theater; it took place at Gardzienice's home center near Lublin, Poland. Later, students traveled from Poland to Double Edge's Farm Center. After the Consortium finished two years later, Double Edge continued bringing emerging artists from Poland, Hungary, and Romania for training and performance. Double Edge has led two other major collaborative theatre projects—the Spiral Mirror, with Diablomundo from Argentina; and the Consortium of Training and Place-Based Theatres, which included Jupiter Performance Studio (Harlem); Pangea World Theater (Minneapolis); Mondo Bizarro (New Orleans); the Hinterlands (Detroit); Open Flame (Oceola/ Minneapolis); and q Staff (Albuquerque). These collaborative efforts, among many other short-term or individual residencies, have been a principle of Double Edge's adherence to exchange as necessary for building theatre culture.

What follows is transcribed and edited from a taped training demonstration and discussion at the Consortium of Theatre Practices, 2000.

***

In terms of artistic dialogue, the materials that we can give you serve as facilitators, in order to make a dialogue with space and time. What you do with anything that you gain here, in the future, is up to you. I hope you do everything. What I can ask for now is that you find your presence here, through the training, which is all of the training. And this is going to create the dialogue that you find today. That will not be anybody's work. That will be everybody's work.

I can break this down. One of the components of Double Edge's practice is individual work. This is often tricky for people who come to us to negotiate, since whereas there is a deep need for each person to create their own work, at the same time there's a choice involed to find that work with and through challenge and dialogue with the other people you've chosen to work with. So it's not as free as it apparently looks. At the same time, over the course of the process, it should become intimately you. That *you* is coming from the work that you're doing with other people. That's the first step, at least.

What we plan for the first week is engage in a huge amount of physical training, which will be led primarily by Jennifer and by John. This will encompass our different ways of training. There will also be a talk and a demonstration about working with objects, and then you will have a chance to work with the objects yourselves. Each element that is important to our training, we will throw at you during this first week. At the same time, we will work on creating a five-minute Étude, which will be in response to a theme. You need to meet that theme with your own question, what you are asking of yourself; and through the week we will share with you our ways of working on that project. Jennifer and I will also work with you and help you build your individual Études.

What is an Étude? It's not a performance. Rather, it is an individual moment to express and articulate a theme, an image, or story without interruption and with few words. Improvisation, by contrast, is all about dialogue and interruption. To me, the important thing about improvisations is that you don't get stuck trying to make *the* improvisation to get fixated on an idea; rather, this is the place where we need people, the other people. If you've already formed it in your mind, then there's nothing left to do in this space. What do you find when you are challenged to give up your rigid view of self? When the boxes you make are torn down and you discover a self you never imagined? What do you find when someone's speaking to you, and they interrupt your train of thought? That is the creative place.

The first component is the training. This will involve a variety of physical practices. One is related to embodiment. One is related to creating action. And one is related to dialogue. After that point, and in conjunction with you starting your own work, the training begins to create what we call character. This is very personal, working with the meaning of character. Character can be expressed in movement or action; character can speak to a story—either your story, or an outside story, which may be a motivating point of departure. And through that character one begins to merge the elements: the training, the Étude, the improvisation, and the group that exists. In the group work that we've created at Double Edge, each person makes a character, and with each character they create a world. The world of the performance is created through the juxtaposition of the individual worlds of the artists.

So, let's say that five people are working on a training together in energy, and then people start making characters in their own individual way. And then there is a reality created by the interaction between those characters. That reality could be called "medieval" for us, or it could be called an insane asylum. But it is a reality that everyone shares because the creation of that reality is everyone's. The world is more complex now because there is a reality that everyone shares, but in addition to that, each person is still creating their own world. The shared reality is happening as a result of each person's own reality, and as a result of the ensuing partnership. We are not working traditionally on roles. There are no traditional roles here, because we're not an interpretive theatre. We call it character, we can call it a role, but really we are creating our own world, or a telescope to another reality.

We are working on the principle that each person takes responsibility for the manifestation of their own reality. That is their mystery, their ecstacy. This can be discovered only in a process of mutuality.

If you stop inventing, which means you stop being open to yourself, and to other people, it's the end. We need to keep very focused on this word, invention.

Another key word is imagination. This is why our research includes so many other artistic and cultural mediums. These materials help us invent, rather than getting so wrapped up in what we already know that we become hermetic. The personal is essential to our work. What's the opposite of personal ... the universal? That's essential too. It's extremely important for us to create through the kind of intimacy that is only possible with other people—in mutuality rather than privacy or isolation. So much of our work relates to that issue.

19. Approaches to Training (Excerpt) (2009)

What follows is excerpted from a recording of a public conversation titled "Approaches to Training," convened by Philip Arnoult and me, with the ensemble, at the Farm in Ashfield, on November 15, 2009. For me, the most interesting part of the conversation was the distinction that emerged between Double Edge's training—which is not based on form—and almost all the other training propositions from the other theatre groups, which included world leaders in the field (including Gennady Abramov, from Class of Expressive Plastic Movement, Russia; Jarek Fret, director of Teatr Zar, Poland; Joan Schirle, director of Dell'Arte International; Peter Van Heerden, performance artist, South Africa; Carlos Uriona, Double Edge; and commentators Steve Nunns, director of MFA at Towson, Maryland, and Maria Shevtsova, Editor of New Theatre Quarterly, *London, England).*

As I mentioned in my Address to the Reader at the beginning of this book, we at Double Edge do not teach form. Rather, our focus is on awareness, energy, capacity, dialogue, flight, and questioning. Below I offer an overview of our approach to training.

✳✳✳

We just spent the last week talking about how we don't have a language to describe our training, and how we are now trying to develop this language. I don't know if this is a shared issue for all the theatre companies here, but it is certainly one for Double Edge. I've been thinking about why this is. The reason is because the purpose of Double Edge's training is to take an individual into someplace that's unknown, and to tap the resources of the individual, whatever those resources and the potential of the artist may be.

Each element of our training, each step in the process, involves an intensive physical dynamic, one that always tries to identify the *other* that is, let's say, arguing with the individual. The role of that confrontation is to take an artist further in their exploration or to not let themselves indulge. That other could be a partner, or it could be an object. We like objects a lot in our training. That other could be anything the artist finds to work with in this dialogic way.

This process goes from purely physical work to improvisational work as soon as it can. The improvisation remains physical for a while, and then it needs to be layered with something else, which we call research. This could involve reading, dramaturgical work, stories, history, or whatever somebody's theme might be, their archetypes. This research then becomes the other for the artist to argue or dialogue with.

Alongside that, we've become particularly interested in sound: in music, instruments, and vocal singing, as one of the layers of the work we do. All of these layers of training have the goal of identifying oneself, whether it's a student undertaking their very first training, or whether it's Carlos training after twelve years of experience. There's an endless capacity for wonder.

Here on the farm we hold three-month intensive immersions for students and visiting artists—they're intense; they're not 24/7, but they're pretty close to 16/7 or maybe 18/6 ½. This includes about four hours a day of physical training at the beginning; it's much more intensive at the beginning, in order to get past the physical barriers against getting fully involved. Then there are a couple of hours of musical training. It then moves on to incorporate improvisation. A parallel thread has to do with a person's individual work. Our work goes between the individual and the group, and those are very important parallel factors. We don't believe that the individual can work in a group without also becoming authentically themselves. It's the same thing even in a couple. So the student will try to make their own work; we call these Études. These are two-to-five-minute gems that identify different elements, different ideas, depending on where you are with your work.

We also hold summer intensives which are a month long, which actually are 24/7. We are not necessarily working on performances with our students until a second round of involvement, an advanced immersion. The students and emerging artists do work on our performances with us, either interacting with our audiences or supporting the performance, which they've been doing so wonderfully in the Garden Cycle.

Generally it goes on from there for a number of years. We've recently found that it takes three or four years of training before you can really take part in this process of performing. And then it continues for the rest of your life.

Double Edge does not just train actors. We train whoever wants to participate in a creative process. This can be a writer, for instance; the person can be anything at all. Training involves much more than preparing a performance, for the artists as well as for the audience. It's about the creative process.

20. Excerpt from a Journal (1988)

What follows is another entry from my journal from the period when we were creating Song of Absence. *My reflection here takes a broader view of the training process and its role in the co-creation of an original performance, which we had been exploring for the past three years.*

***

SONG OF ABSENCE JOURNALS:

Joining together of training philosophy and practice—training, philosophy, form. Question of CHOICE—INTELLECTUAL, EMOTIONAL, PHYSICAL. Training is a meeting of individuals who make the group. Individual work/responsibility is development of character, group work is creation of structure. We are conceivers of work, creating understructure and superstructure, using text, sound, action. We find different stories within a structure—nuances, change. What do you want training to be? Only to be alive at each moment, but also in search. Each person enters with an answer—for another, for themself. The universal issue is CHOICE.

Ask—how to develop research into concrete work? This is a time when people ask: what is training? It's easy to meet the challenge of experience, but experience cannot be understood if there is no repetition. Finding true repetition equals work, not the high of improvisation. If you make work alive, you have found a process. How do we keep it alive? Find more depth. The solution is in action—this is why the group was formed—not as an escape, but searching together in loneliness. This is the life of humans—cultural identity—group as collective differentiation. No indifference! No submission! Each time is a sign of life, not death. Everything can be seen with curiosity as a whole, not limited vision.

21. "What Are You Investigating?" A Discussion with Students (2014)

Sometimes in my talks with students I end up learning more about myself and my work than they do. So maybe the title here should be "What am I investigating?" In this particular talk I was reflecting on how I have built performances with my core creators, and on the role of training in that building process. Since I speak a lot about objects, as you will see below, I wanted to mention two performances I saw in Poland back in the 1970s that I still dream about today: Anna Livia, *directed by Kazimierz Braun and co-directed by Zbygniew Cynkutis (from the Lab Theatre); and* Dante's Inferno, *directed by Josef Szajna. I had never seen such physical vitality in repertory theatre. In one scene of* Anna Livia, *the bed flew into the air with the actors in it, and this breathtaking metaphor has stayed with me ever since, and has perhaps even influenced my use of bed-spinning dream sequences in several Double Edge performances. Szajna's immense globe with actors on it and in it, revolving around a third of the proscenium stage, jarred me into a realization of how the actor can use the object as a site of dialogue and metaphor. Our experiences, and our witnessing, can and should be part of developing our creative life.*

The following is edited from a transcription of a recorded discussion with Double Edge students in February 2014, representing the Question and Answer portion of the conversation.

✳✳✳

The early stage of Double Edge's process belongs to the actor: this includes training and the process of developing an imaginative world. There is either some agreement beforehand as to what the subject or material is, or this comes shortly after the beginning. For instance, with *The Grand Parade,* we started with material from *The Firebird* and were thinking about doing some sort of indoor version of that performance. At some point we started working with the twentieth century as a historical period. That brought us to the middle point of the process, which is not about improvisation, but about creating material.

It is very much the actor's work to create the material. I would say that my work as a director is to define what material we end up working with. For instance, I proposed that we divide the twentieth century up by decade and work decade by decade; the other artists brought in the historical or imaginative figures they wanted to work on and what events they wanted to focus on. In our case, there's a process through which I take what has been made and edit it together, while also asking for material that's not there yet. Even after it gets incorporated an artist's material remains their material, although they might be performing it in a very different context than their original ideas. I would be the holder of the context.

The Summer Spectacle is a little different because it's a short process; instead of developing over several years it begins and ends over the course of a single season. In *The Grand Parade* and in an indoor world, I'm writing the performance with the actors who are involved. So there are two processes—one is the playwriting, let's say, and the other is the performance. In the playwriting section, we are all the same—we work in teams. In the performance work, I'm the leader and people have to hold on to what they wrote. In the summer, there is much more of the second part. There's a team of four to five people involved in the playwriting—and everyone else fills out the sketch of the visual and narrative aspects. Also, the summer is different because there is a book from which we derive the performance. For *Shahrazad*, we used a book [The 1001 Nights] in certain respects, although in this case our "book" consisted of Chagall's drawings responding to the book, which was important. But the main idea was altogether different: we wanted to work with the women's power in that book. All of the magic involved working with the women's magic. Shahrazad is a powerful woman and the singing was all led by women, so the idea was to do the opposite of what we did with *The Odyssey*, which presented a male world. The world we create in *Shahrazad* is an investigation of beauty and power: what would a world look like if it was led by women? These were the overarching ideas we were working with, but when people were developing, say, the idea of creating a garden scene, someone would be the leader and get all of the actors together, and then someone would compile a draft of that scene. Then all these drafts are done and I put them together. Also, visual elements such as design are very important in the summer—equal to the acting—which is a bit different for us. The project of creating Summer Spectacles has evolved according to the interests of the different ensemble members. That's a strange and wonderful project. Still, the actor is always autonomous because the actor is responsible for their own material, completely.

Q: I haven't seen many directors—there might be some—who relate to the actor beyond the work. Beyond the specific performance work, let's say, or the rehearsal work. Somehow in sharing together the idea of theater and living culture, you were already coining this other idea in which a relationship extends beyond the specificity of a performance. In my case, I feel much more comfortable working like this, and it has allowed me to grow. I didn't come to Double Edge as a neophyte—I had years of background—so I have had other directors and also opted to work without a director at all. There is something about that relationship. You relate to the actor beyond the specificity of the performance work. The director/actor relationship is not a common one. It is rare to see a director who understands the lives of their actors and their approach.

SK: Maybe that's the starting point of living culture. I think this idea is important, although I don't know exactly how to discuss it. Let's say that the material people are working with is themselves. That's the starting point for their creation. When I said that we bring in material in the second stage, I meant that in the first stage, people are identifying themselves, and where they are, and what their questions are and what their archetypes are—or what archetypes they are working with in the present. The first stage is very, very personal. It also relates to where the person is at that time in their lives: what their struggles are. In the second stage, we would find an outside example of what those questions are. We would work with this, and grow with this. I think anybody who is in the arts is pretty crazy, and anybody who stays in the arts is even more crazy, so there has to be a benefit to it all. And the benefit is that you get to work on yourself, so you're not crazy in an institutional way.

You're crazy in a way that few people are allowed to be, where you realize yourself and don't spend your life trying to be something else.

I used to think that everyone had the potential to work this way. I was wrong. There are a lot of people who need to live in their daily routines and should not go into themselves in that way, because it's too intense; but that's a personal process that people need to go through. A lot of people quit acting. There are people I went to school with who had a fairly successful career in theatre or TV and then quit, because they couldn't stand the industry anymore. But really, they couldn't stand confronting their inner selves in the industry context. At Double Edge, the problem is a little bit different in that you always have to confront yourself and you don't get a break from that. So *The Grand Parade* is done, but the next thing is happening. To that extent, we all have to participate in making our culture present. You want to know that this imagination is possible. I want to say that every day. We all should be saying that every day.

Q: What I wonder is: when you approach your work, do you always approach it with a context in mind, or do you approach it with a vision and allow it to change? Have you ever been surprised by what you end up with?

SK: Oh yeah, I'm a pretty surprised person. I think there are certain things that are known, but there are always things that are surprising because my work involves such a collaborative process. For *Grand Parade* the music was surprising—I'm talking about the recorded music. Brian Fairley started DJing our trainings and then we had this idea that we would have audio of the century. Just those factors changed everything. Then we had the idea that we would incorporate audio-visual elements in the performance, which we had never really used before. We had never used projections extensively in our work. We used one projection in *The Firebird*. That was a huge surprise in aesthetics. One thing we really wanted was to invoke the reality of Chagall's painting, which is about juxtaposition. So while we maintained that juxtaposition, it looks very different than what I thought I wanted it to look like. I thought we would have Hayley [Brown] on trapeze and Milena [Dabova] dancing and a war scene in the background. The way this actually happened was surprising, and had to do with many factors—decisions about design, for instance. I think the live music was also a major element. I thought it was going to be different than that.

I don't plan the outcome of my work—probably even less than I should. In the summer, it is little less of a surprise. The fact that it happens and that people actually come is a surprise to me. I do have the idea of how it looks, and that it should be beautiful; the natural environment has taught me that. I knew that Amanda [Miller] and Hayley would drive the singing, but I didn't know how. The summer is probably my one opportunity where I'm painting the performance and then there are different colors than those I envisioned, but it is still my painting in some way. That's pretty different from *The Grand Parade*. We did the Garden Cycle, which was more like the first cycle of work we had, because each of those earlier works was based on preexisting material. *Don Quixote* was based on Cervantes; *Republic of Dreams* was based on Bruno Schulz, and *The Disappearance* was written by Ilan Stavans, with quotes from *The Merchant of Venice*. So that was much less surprising, although it was still surprising that we did it.

Q: Could you talk about the role of Spectacle in general, in performances like *The Grand Parade*?

A: We have been using large objects in our work since 1985, when we got the space in St. Luke's in Allston, and it was a big parish hall, the size of this barn. We started putting up rigging and flying and using spools as part of our training. We did a lot of partner work in the Women's Cycle; we did a lot of isolation work; but then we felt the need to have an object to figure out what would really drive our challenges. So somebody found these huge, wooden spools outside and brought them in, so we started working with them. We built these cement towers and tried to train on them. A bunch of crazy stuff. Fishing nets made from hemp. We would use those in all kinds of different ways. We built the Song Trilogy with all of those objects.

Then Carlos arrived, with his background in puppetry and circus. There was a meeting-point then between his work and ours, which was not apparent at first, but which soon became clear. Large objects are large objects, only we were using them for different purposes than those for which they had originally been made. We started getting interested in materials like fabrics and ended up using these for *Quixote*. That was the first time we ended up translating our large objects into circus equipment and yet we kept the same ideas. They were white in *Quixote* and people were hanging on them, so they looked like Inquisition ropes. Then, at a certain point, we started developing our training a little bit beyond what we had already been doing. Some people started going out for additional skills training, and some people started working with individual coaches. In the meantime, we found that in the summer there was a terrific need for circus. So we basically started concentrating on that every summer. When we returned to the Chagall Cycle—and circus is a primary motif in Chagall—it became very clear that the idea of circus and flight was something we all understood. We started making costumes based on Chagall's pictures of the circus. Hayley had been working on becoming one of those circus people. Jeremy [Louise Eaton] was researching all the people who were flying in airplanes and spaceships throughout the twentieth century. Milena was working on dance in the twentieth century. From those starting points, together we combined these three investigations with the reality of how they fit with the imagery of Chagall. Jeremy's character, Ameilia Earhart, merges in flight with Bella Chagall flying, as depicted in Chagall's paintings. The paintings also relate to Hayley's aerial trapeze. And then Hayley is working with discovering the inner world of that circus person, which may not be that comfortable. There is always a battle between one's attempt to fly and the limitations that ground us. That's pretty much how we got into *The Grand Parade* and circus. I would say that since the Song Trilogy started, there's been flying in every Double Edge performance. That is the representation of what we desire for our lives.

Q: What is the difference between training with large objects and training with small objects?

A: Large objects provide resistance, and they can overwhelm you. A small object can be owned and controlled. You can't just control a large object; it remains a partner rather than a prop. It's fundamental to the training of Double Edge. Working with large objects or aerial apparatuses does not mean that we are circus trainers. In fact, we bring in teachers who are experts in skills such as aerial work, vocal technique, strength and conditioning, and so forth. There are a lot of different skills you need to develop in conjunction with performance work. For us, large objects are a major bridge between our training and our performance creation.

Q: In *The Grand Parade,* it's a pretty serious performance, but there are some very comedic moments and I was wondering how comedy comes into your other performances—how have you experimented with that?

A: We had that question in *Song of Absence. Song of Absence* was primarily about the Holocaust, yet we approached it with Charlie Chaplin and other figures like the Three Stooges, because this has to do with juxtaposition. If you make something serious, it will be one-dimensional if you can't find different sides of it. The humanity of it was multidimensional. Anything that was tragic was also comic until the actor would get to the center of it, which then became neither—just present. We would work with things in a comic way and then translate them into the broader context. The century was an awful century, really. After studying it, I can't believe we allowed ourselves, as human beings, to have a Holocaust bookend and war all throughout a century. I have a much bleaker view of the century after working on it.

But the humanity of the century is still there. It's not every day that someone participated in a war, or a serial killing, or something evil. There were plenty of days—and I was part of half of the century–when I was having fun, I was having sex, I was loving, and I was in a peace march and thinking about how beautiful somebody was or how funny somebody was. It's important to note the humanity and the possibilities of flying. That's how we worked on comedy and also on flying amidst a century that was terrible. The issue is how we get people to see the possibility of flying, or the possibility of comedy, or the possibility of inventing an airplane and not a bomb. How we can do that is the serious part.

22. *Grand Parade* Training Journals (2010–12)

These journal entries date from a far later period in my career than the Song of Absence *journals. Dating from 2010, these entries reflect on the ensemble's work in co-creating* The Grand Parade of the Twentieth Century, *and they demonstrate some of the ways in which Double Edge's practice of physical training is always navigating between the historical reality of the time-period of the performance and the reality of the dreams we create.*

***

October 2010

Ease of individual work vs. partner work. No push.

Each beautiful attainment interrupted by WAR. Materialism helps us forget.

Notion of the enemy: 20th century run amok—technology so fast— FEAR

Next generation is jaded because there is no truth. The truth is not news.

April 2011

Problem between daily and work. Neuroses go into daily rather than into the work.

When working—decide who each person is in your world.

CU [Carlos Uriona]: You want to be a Master Actor and want to know but you need to see you can't know all.

MG [Matthew Glassman] make the story—the wolf makes it but still cannot control it.

Yesterday I was totally free as leader and participant.

May 2011

We did an improvisation and put up the sail. Made a journey, an odyssey, or temple, or desert. I stood on people's heads to make the sail. Watched. Danced. Then water water water. In the end wrap the sail and look at the bird of peace (HB [Hailey Brown]). Everyone comes to the tree.

Wailing Wall.

Conflict requires very special preparation. What am I missing? Drama in the action. Action and reaction. Action very precise with consciousness.

CU—stop pushing chanting.

Preparation together:

The Pole—central access point. Energy up and down. Concrete.

What is most dramatic in your life. What is in common with the life of your character.

Technical training, then creative training. With motivation. Cannot go into research privately.

Dancing—for action

These are rules for actors.

What is my research? What is this group?

We lost paradise, but we can dream of it.

Art as voice.

Not disappeared

War as lack of voice

Sensitivity and group.

2012 *Grand Parade* preparation notes:

Dramaturgy of COLD WAR in popular culture

Animal world—mythological and timeless. Impact of the entrance of the horse.

Intrusion of emotional impact

Rooster does have impact

Tension between historiography and wonder

After chaos we need CHAGALL iconography

Beginning—

Set up who we are at the beginning of the century. How do we relate to each other and animals. Building vocabulary.

Violence abstracted and mythologized. Play with the play of violence.

Concrete choices.

The end as the possible response to the beginning

The acting ensemble and I are in a period of growth with Chagall and the century. Lack of ability to label this project—"flying theatre" involving visual, projections, sounds.

Creators of theatre reinterpret and represent history according to their own fascination + proclivities, imagination, and individual conviction.

What does it mean to be an instrument of memory. In what way is asking questions using the imagination. To create theatre that is about real events a unique contribution to historical memory and accuracy?

What are the distinct characteristics of interpretive memory? Its obligations to history? Our choice is about finding an emotional voice to history rather than simply historical. To voice our human potential, identity, seeing history.

Hope is the power of will.

Memory includes emotions, attempts, creativity, identity.

23. "Defining What You Want": A Talk with Fall Immersion Artists (2018)

Repertory theatre in this country, which is mainstream, and which is as well-supported financially as anything is here, grew out of an experiment. It began with the Federal Theatre Project after the Depression, and moved toward the kind of theatre we know it as today.

Now, that theatre, for those of us who don't practice it, looks like something very different from what we're doing at Double Edge. But repertory theatre started with people who needed to create something for their communities. It has since moved away from the community and into the entertainment industry, but it was once in the vanguard. And every single thing that you probably know in contemporary theatre—Broadway, for instance—also started as something completely different.

Even the very opposite of that vanguard, such as *Cats*, which is now probably archaic to your generation, was actually the first commercial musical that adapted principles of Grotowski's work, turning physical theatre work into a multimillion dollar Broadway enterprise. I imagine that many of the productions that make a lot of money began as experiments too, just like *Cats*. But this was made possible by the fact that there had first been twenty or thirty years of people making physical theatre, just because they wanted to. There's no *Cats* without this fact. This is the rolling wheel of experimental art.

Each of you here, or let's say most of us, thinks that you want to do something more or less in the vanguard, something experimental, such as vanguard community work. That may be true, and it may not be true. You really have to find out for yourself. I'm saying this because most people refuse to place themselves in their own place, or even to look for their place. It's admirable when somebody really looks to define themselves and identify themselves beyond the mandate they've been prescribed.

I'm learning more and more about this, because I used to think that Double Edge was for everybody. And now I think that *parts* of Double Edge—the performances and some aspects of the experience—are for everybody. But not necessarily Double Edge itself. Not necessarily the acting in Double Edge. Not necessarily the training in Double Edge. Or even the community spectacle. There still is plenty that's available to people who don't want to work this hard, to people who don't want to make sub-standard amounts of money, to people who don't aspire to those things that are *our* goals in life. We have a variety of different goals in life. And they're all valid if you're honest with yourselves.

I understand these differences more fully today than I once did, now that I'm not an angry young person anymore. I'm not young. But I'm also not really angry in the same way I once was. I think this is due to the hardship it's taken to create Double Edge; I've learned through that process. I've learned how to be open, and how to be open in a way that means openness to other people. That is, not just open to *my* way, but open to other people's ways. I think that's a pretty hard thing for young people. And it's not necessarily something for you to investigate at this point. I do think, though, that being open to yourself is extremely worthy of investigation.

What do you want? What, for instance, can you take away from your experience here this summer that will help you to define and grow what it is that you want? And that will give you the energy in yourself to define what you want? That will help you face the hardship of defining what you want? I bet that most of you have spent at least three-quarters of your years being told what you want, and being told how you want it.

At this point, all of you have to go through a process of unpeeling yourselves. What is it really? Do I want to use my body? Do I want to be healthy? Do I want to work really hard? Or do I want to have more peace in my life than that? Do I want to face paradox? Do I want to build something all by myself? Or do I want to work with a group? What kind of group do I want to work with, if I want that? What kind of things do I want to make in my life? Is it social? Is it spiritual? Is it artistic? Or is it all of those things?

Another question: What am I curious about that I probably wasn't even allowed to think about? You're all coming from institutions. None of you has been out of institutions for very long. Institutions are the opposite of what I've described so far. They do not want you to define yourself; they want you to do what they've defined. Even as they're teaching you things, valuable things—I'm not saying you should quit school—they want you to mirror them rather than finding your own reflection. That's natural, and that's the way institutions survive. But I'm asking you to rethink that whole thing and ask: what is my reflection? What do I want to look at and see myself as? How do I want to grow right now?

The final aspect of this question is: how can I learn to be honest about all that? What are the impediments that stand in the way of that honesty?

This is what I think about when I reflect on how I got here, on where Double Edge is today.

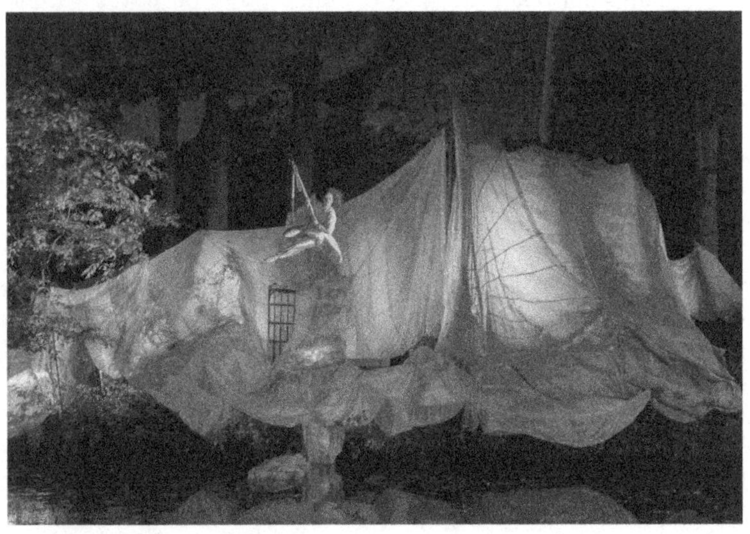

FIGURE 7 Leonora's World, *conceived and directed by Stacy Klein, with Cariel Klein (pictured), 2019. Photo by Kim Chin-Gibbons.*

24. Leonora's World (2019)

Although Double Edge has been working outdoors since moving to the Farm—training, creating Études, and performing spectacles outside—our understanding of the relationship and connection to the environment has taken many years to unfold. In the city, and particularly inside a soundproof theatre space, it is nearly impossible to learn about silence. I have learned silence from the breath between the whisper of the trees, the frogs croaking, the water flowing. I have learned how to bring humility to my images within the container of the immense fields and forests, the geese flying overhead, and the heron resting in the tall trees; my song and words are in chorus with the splashes of the pond water and the sounds of the animals, of the wind and, often, rain. I, and all of Double Edge, have learned that we are part of this natural world and not the owners of it. We have been gifted this understanding through our work, and hope to share it with our art.

✳✳✳

Double Edge's vision of an integrated artistic and community experience of culture and environment is fully embodied in our Summer Indoor-Outdoor Traveling Spectacle, which began seventeen years ago as an intimate outdoor experiment, and which the ensemble developed over the years in an explicit dialogue with our neighbors and our rural landscape. Five years ago we began touring the spectacles, to offer the blossoming of the imaginative possibilities of living culture in late spring or summer in urban and other settings. So far these have been as varied as the *Odyssey* on an ancient fortress overlooking the North Sea in Norway, or the Latin American Spectacle in the streets of the Latin Quarter in Jamaica Plain, in Boston, and in a public park in Springfield, MA.

Notwithstanding the huge rainfalls of this past summer, the summer and spring seasons fundamentally enhance the beauty, the poetry, and the sublimity of the art we create, offering the spectator an entrance into a transforming reality in which fictional and historical figures (such as W.E.B. Du Bois) as well as geese and blue herons fly over our ornamental gardens and fields and pond.

Less unique but still extraordinary experiences of the art and environment include Shaker women dancing from the top of a field amidst roaming cows and audience processions that encounter characters dancing with fish as they swim downstream.

This deep examination of the natural world and its connection to our daily life and culture is integral to the art and values of the Summer Spectacle. It has surprised us, after seventeen years, that walking in a rainy procession while listening to the sounds of crickets and whistling trees and singing voices is not only a new experience of theatre for many people, but a first-time connection to our natural world. The truth of this matters. How are we to recognize the importance of our environment if we do not experience it? (A parallel occurrence in Jamaica Plain was hearing the spectators' comments that they had never celebrated in the streets together before). How do we participate in ourselves and our relationships to each other, to other creatures and to nature?

Over the past year and a half, we have been researching the life and artwork of the British-born, Mexican immigrant artist and writer Leonora Carrington, resulting in the creation of an indoor performance inspired by her mentorship of Alejandro Jodorowsky. Carrington's deeply held beliefs about nature and all beings on this earth were presciently translated into her paintings and statues depicting a fantastic life. Her magnificent oeuvre awakened in turn an artistic vision of interaction and dialogue with nature and the natural environment not limited to the relative calm and beauty of the Summer months.

This vision acknowledges the disconnect between the contemporary thinking about our environmental crisis and an actual interaction with the elements. The possibility of confronting and appreciating the vibrant life, of moving between the light and dark forces of the fall season (and perhaps one day the winter) called to us. We set out to develop a Fall–early Winter Spectacle, opening the portals of Leonora's landscapes and surreal worlds, mazes and arctic flights in the fields, waterways, fires, and hidden forest nooks of our own rural environment. Many things occur that are unique to this creative process, born entirely in the hands of nature's impact. Icy nights, cold rains, frigid waters provoke a reality that (for the ensemble and the audience alike) takes the art to a new realm of authenticity. The same should be said for the clear skies of the full moon.

To find Leonora's World is to remember that it is in our hands to change what we must change, in our attitude toward land, the environment, and all the injustice that has inundated us today. It is local; it is art; it is community. Most of all it is the healing power of the imagination, which provides the ultimate portal to travel through in order to effect meaningful and lasting transformation.

4

Art, Living Culture, Art Justice

Introduction: From Anger to Love

I am not sure when I first started using the term "Living Culture," but I can identify the road that led to it. It began with identifying the sleeping culture that rendered atrocity acceptable, from the US involvement in South American (and other) dictatorships, to the purposeful blindness of post-civil rights-era self-satisfaction. The road led from my first visit to Auschwitz in the 1970s (which I wrote about in my "Director's Confession" for *Song of Absence*, in Section 1) to my encounter, in the streets of Cambridge and Boston in the 1980s, with the widespread capacity for ignoring injustice that wove through contemporary society. For me, this "sleep" was the result of a lack of cultural underpinning in the fabric of our lives. The streets were not a place of song, dance, gathering, or protest; rather, they were little more than a means of transportation. The culmination of this sleep culture surely had to be the Anita Hill Trial—for that is what it should have been called—which took place in 1991. This was the first of many public hearings that would normalize the degradation—and worse—of women, particularly women of color. My reaction to sleep culture was rage. This anger seeped into everything in my life. Sometimes I managed to convert my anger into art. At other times my work stayed angry. For me, it was necessary to build a strong container around this anger, and to create art that could bring me and my audience to a place *beyond* that anger.

When I toured Ukraine with Double Edge in 1994 I encountered responses to sleep culture that did manage to lead beyond anger. I witnessed the abounding possibilities brought about through the power of community, even in the face of cultural warfare. The decimation of the communities we visited and worked with had never succeeded in extinguishing their desire to gather and share in their collective existence, whenever opportunities arose—in spite of decades and decades of anti-Semitism, hostility toward Lemkos and other ethnicities, and the ruinous aftermath of Nazi and Soviet occupations. This experience transformed my work as a director. It initiated a long process of understanding how my anger could be directed toward discovering possibilities for cultural survival. It also fueled my belief that impossibility need not have the final word. To put it more simply: I learned how anger can transform itself if we refuse to accept impossibility. For me, as for the Double Edge ensemble, the imperative became to delve as deeply as possible into our potentiality as humans, instead of setting limits according to what might be considered impossible or wrong. This process had less to do with the immediate topics or themes of our work, than with our overall approach to the creative process: to resist the rage and entrapment of the world we live in by making space instead for the unknown, intangible possibilities of our inner worlds.

In Ukraine, the people we were working with had been forbidden from practicing Judaism for close to seventy years. While our discussions certainly addressed their collective trauma, as I describe in the writings below, most of our interactions involved sharing the memories, songs, liturgical music, and prayers that had survived extermination. To this day I continue to marvel at what it meant to keep these cultural practices alive for so long. During our residency we witnessed how the community gathered and shared their life stories through the resurgence of their surviving culture. This tenaciously *living* culture had survived political suppression, legal constraint, and genocidal warfare, yet it had also endured the people's own need for respite: a respite from grief, a respite from fighting.

This cultural struggle was not only present for the Jewish elders in the villages we visited. It was also experienced by the many young people who gathered with us, trained with us, and came to the Great Synagogue in Drohobycz, which had just reopened as a functioning synagogue for the first time since the 1920s. This was a place that had never before held a multicultural event involving people of all the region's ethnicities. But when we performed, the whole community gathered: Jews, Catholics, and ethnic Ukrainians (Huculi, Lemkos, and Boykos). We hadn't anticipated performing in Drohobycz, so we had no sets or equipment. We performed by candlelight and relied on the human-to-human experience of gathering in a shared space. It was a transformative moment of cultural exchange. The impossible, we realized, was possible.

When we returned to the States, our group understood our task as seeking out those inklings of culture and humanity that managed to exist between the layers of assimilation and comfort that stifled them. It became our mission to work in a "Republic of Dreams." This term, which we adopted from a 1936 essay by Bruno Schulz, the great modernist writer and artist from Drohobycz, held multiple layers of meaning for us. It meant, for one, that our work dealt with dreams and remote realities. But it also meant that we wanted simultaneously to build a real community—a republic not only of dreams, but also of liberation.

Returning to Boston after our tour of Ukraine, we felt confined by the isolation we encountered in the city. Each neighborhood (and by that time I had lived in five of them) was deeply segregated, or was in the process of gentrifying. Boston was, and remains, a strange combination of elitist and working-class cultures, with its roughly eighty colleges and universities, its transient students, and its long history of snobbery and puritanism that often renders the region blind to its own racial, gender, and economic disparities. Our neighbors would barely speak to us outside the confines of the church parish hall we were renting as our rehearsal and performance space. In retrospect, many of our problems stemmed from this Bostonian context, a city in which theatre that was physical and visceral, and which valued connectivity with the audience, was unheard of. We began to look for a home outside the city, a separate reality where we could practice and develop work without having to prove each day that our radical ambitions were valid. This new place could become our Republic of Dreams, Schulz's fictional realm of freedom in the essay he wrote only a few years before he was shot and killed by a Nazi in his hometown of Drohobycz. I fear that Drohobycz, along with the Synagogue we visited there, will be reduced to rubble in the ongoing Russian invasion that began in 2022.

In relocating Double Edge to a rural village far outside the city, we were not looking simply to recreate our magical experience in Ukraine, so much as to create a remove from the policies, bureaucracies, and isolation of city life. By freeing ourselves to communicate in and with the natural environment that now surrounded us, we could find pathways for exploring ourselves more fully and, as I mentioned above, developing a construct around our work that could accommodate anger or even sometimes let it float away. We could begin to build, and open ourselves to, a Living Culture. Ultimately we realized, albeit quite a while later, that if our separate reality remained disconnected from the surrounding community, and from others who sought this type of cultural justice, then we would become no less isolated than we had been in the city. This realization led to a multiplicity of collective projects that have emerged today as Double Edge's Center for Art, Living Culture, and Art Justice.

I want to say more about what "living culture" means to me, and to Double Edge, as a way to exist in the real, political world, as well as in the world of creativity and imagination. A lot of social movements use cultural work to create norms, which then function in the political sphere to reproduce how people act and even think. The idea of living culture is *not* to weaponize cultural change directly in the political sphere, but to create and recognize other practices that would otherwise be impossible, such as creativity, dialogue, self-identification, and collaboration. The general culture, the externalized culture of American social existence, is something very different from the culture of creation I'm describing here.

There's an internal cultural work that has to do with respect, and, let's say, love; it has to do with understanding identity. This is inner work that can transform outer, real-world practices. It is living culture because it's alive; it's happening. And it's happening with the people around you, so you're building something together. I wanted to share a cultural experience, which I felt couldn't happen without inclusivity. That's what builds trust, and that's what builds the value of imagination—as well as all the other things that are so lacking in our world, such as creativity. What we're trying to do at Double Edge is to uplift or actualize culture, which is different from being didactic or confrontational.

Culture is something that needs to be built. It's imaginative, and it's courageous, especially now. It taps into all of the aspects of humanness that are so often in the process of being extinguished. It has to do with a different side of your brain than the thinking side: it's singing, it's dancing. In some cases, it's tradition, and all that grows out of tradition. All those dynamic forms are culture.

25. Culture Can Still Be Alive (1991)

What follows is a compilation of the numerous pieces I wrote, some in programs, some in newsletters, responding to the attacks on Anita Hill during Clarence Thomas's Supreme Court hearings. As many can understand today—after the repeat spectacle of the Kavanaugh hearings and the monstrous overturning of Roe v. Wade, for instance—there is a continued refusal to listen to women's voices. This is unacceptable, yet it is nevertheless being forced down our throats. The fight must be taken out of the failed judicial system and into the culture itself—to the people.

***

Double Edge was created as an act of rebellion against the social and theatrical surroundings out of which it developed. Today we maintain the idea and practice of theatre as rebellion, although the nature of this rebellion has changed. In the context of social, psychological, political, and daily life, Double Edge understands this rebellion as a domain of questioning, of searching, and—most fiercely of all—of surviving. It also means that we are no longer, in the theatre business, strictly speaking. The past week (October 11–15, 1991) has made it clear once and for all that the politics of life, or political theatre, is best left to the senate. We know, too, that psychological theatre is deeply pervasive in the daily life of our contemporary society, and that theatre for shock's sake already plays out on tele-dramas such as *Cops*, where viewers can witness real-life murder on TV. This view holds true as well for the Theatre of the Absurd, surrealism, and the grotesque. After sitting through the senate hearings on Clarence Thomas' supreme court confirmation last week, one comes to understand that *no* working theatre company can invoke the absurd as successfully as a failed state institution like the US government.

One is left with the impression that experimental theatre has few places left to go, other than to succumb to the charges of self-indulgence or art-for-entertainment's sake that have been the call words for experimental theatre for at least the past half century. Yet even as entertainment, the theatre industry pales in comparison to the spectacle of public debates and publicized rape, murder, and child abuse we witness as political spectacle each day, or which unfolds as the absurd silencing and trivialization of acts of real violence.

So when I state that Double Edge is a rebellion, I mean that Double Edge rebels against any conception of theatre, or life, as an interpretation or embodiment of what is actualized as everyday realism, whether in approximating the news, or following a story that is little more than a description of a linear and one-dimensional transaction. Double Edge is a rebellion against theatre—or against life, or art—understood as a domain of answers, points of view, or attempts to fit into reigning sociopolitical frameworks. Theatre cannot be created by believers. Nor can it thrive as a lens of analysis through which to ascribe political correctness or incorrectness, or to enact the sociopolitical capture of our lives. What I mean by this is that theatre—our theatre—is art, and that is art consists in the rebellion of the individual against *all* preconceptions about art. This includes even the preconception that art must exist in a state of perpetual risk and discovery. Institutional environments in which prevailing rules exist as boxes and limitations make it impossible to evaluate what risk and discovery really mean.

Having stated so clearly what Double Edge is not (and what art is not), I am now faced with the necessity of stating what Double Edge is. Throughout the nine years of our existence, this has remained an enigma to me. Perhaps I feel that once we name ourselves we risk becoming one of the theatres of answers I've just described, and move on to spending our time interpreting. Even if we didn't resort to interpreting the work of an outside director, designer, or playwright, we might still end up re-interpreting ourselves.

Double Edge is a collective of artists who define themselves and identify themselves through a very long process of working alone and together. We have been called "a separate reality," and I believe this is accurate. We work for one to three years making a performance, which draws from all possible artistic spheres—including literature, art, music, and dance—and from all possible human spheres—including the physical, the emotional, the psychic, and the intellectual—to challenge our own conceptions of reality and humanity. We create in our space in our theatre, our own response to these elements. We can no longer define ourselves according to social categories; for instance, we do not wish to be measured by feminist standards alone, nor do we wish to be measured by traditional standards. Rather, we embrace cultural traditions at the same time as we explore their contradictions.

Our training, which occurs on a daily basis and includes physical, vocal, spiritual, and craft elements, is an attempt to push beyond what we have been taught to believe, and to push beyond the limitations of those beliefs. In this sense, we come back to the ideas of risk and discovery. The risk is concrete, describing the stakes of our physical efforts to supersede our skills and our emotional efforts to break our beliefs. The discovery is continuous: at each step of the way we find ourselves experiencing a living culture—one that is in fact growing and developing in us, and which is not an artifact. This work does not involve pretending. We do not try to become someone else, to imitate a character, or even to understand the inner workings of another being. Nine years ago, at the beginning of this search, we existed as if on an island, in a world that was self-sustaining. Having now found ourselves as a group, we have taken on the role of wanderers; we make our journey through various times, and through different cultures, never completely adopting the life or style of these realities but always uncovering further hints about our own. I believe that our home is our work, but that we will never be able to say truthfully that we have found a final identity. We have looked at ourselves as women and men, as sexual beings, and as culturally diverse people; most recently we have looked at ourselves in relation to Jewish culture. Yet each time we feel at home, something breaks in to warn us against the finality of an answer (Women, Jewish …). Who knows what comes next? What we do know is that as we continue these discoveries, we touch upon the truth that life is discovery and not stasis.

The genuine theatre is an art that surpasses the knowledge of the present day and reaches into new realities and experiences, to which its audiences cannot otherwise bear witness. This has always been true, and this must also be true for the explorations of Double Edge. It is for this reason that we cannot rely on preconceptions, because this is what society knows already. What we attempt to give our audience is an opportunity to witness that culture can still be alive, that truth can be sought with community (yet separately from society at large), and that it is possible to exist beyond the conditioned mediocrity of the day. We offer the audience an opportunity to witness this, though not to join it. For the object of the work is the demonstration that each person or group must seek their own reality, and not simply be content with ours.

This may sound lofty, but it is nonetheless the intent of the theatre, if not its invariable result. One Polish theatre critic said that theatre is either priestly or full of jesters. We, in fact, are both. We are full of jesters in the sense that we have developed our craft as fully as possible, as in a circus or rodeo show. And we are holy in the sense that we seek knowledge and identity that transcend the realm of theatre. Yet we must also deny both these categories, for whenever we become too embedded in our training we find it empty, and whenever we become too holy we find it laughable. Perhaps we are too immersed in the Jewish culture to accept any truths to be true.

In order to embark on this type of journey, to be a wanderer, one must have become truly bored or even offended by the business of theatre.

26. Feminist at the Core of Its Being (1987)

Written in the spring of 1987, this unpublished letter to the editors of Boston's Gay Community News *addresses an internal fight debate among various factions of the gay community in the late 1980s and early 90s. The letter is a response to the weekly newspaper's insulting review of the 1987 Boston Women's Theatre Festival (April 19–25, 1987). Titled "Women in Theatre '87— People in Theatre '88?," the review attacks statements made by the festival's director, Sophie Parker, about the artistic and political content of the festival. The review all but condemns my colleague Sophie as a traitor to feminism.*

Here's how the review opens: "In its third year, the Women in Theatre Festival once again raises questions its director, for one, would rather leave unasked. In an ominous bit of pre-publicity, Festival Director Sophie Parker declared on National Public Radio that the Festival is not feminist in intention or content. This left many wondering just what, then, is the purpose of a Women in Theatre festival—a novelty item to attract grant money?"

Sophie Parker wrote her own response to the review, published as a Letter to the Editor ("Misinformation in Women and Theatre Festival Review," May 10–16, 1987). Noting that the review's author had never contacted her directly, she clarifies that what she had said in the radio interview was that "we do not choose performers on the basis of their feminism and that I do not believe that all women have the same 'voice,' artistically, politically, or otherwise." Parker shares the reviewer's "rage at the constant discrimination against women in our society," while noting that "reviews that discuss our politics, or lack thereof, without a dialogue with us serve no one." The author of the original review responded in a subsequent letter published in the May 24–31 issue ("Leapfrogging on Our Backs?"), in which she defends her criticism and redoubles her "concern that the Women in Theatre Festival not leapfrog into the mainstream on the backs of the feminist and queer community and then abandon it." I find that these letters, both Sophie's and mine, offer a critical reflection of what is happening today in all walks of justice work. Our disagreements over viewpoints end up not in finding resolution, but in providing food for our unified oppressors to keep us from liberation. This is in no way a plea for passive agreement, but rather a demand to listen to each other in dialogue rather than attack.

***

To the Editors of *GCN*:

I can feel nothing less than outrage and more than disgust for the article printed in *GCN* and written by Mara Math about the Women in Theatre Festival. As a woman who has been working in the theatre for that past fourteen years, six years of which were in theatres with a feminist label, I feel it is time we take the responsibility to respond to dangerous and unintelligent criticism such as is at issue here—criticism which is at odds with the growth potential of artists and also of women.

In 1980 I co-produced the first women's theatre festival in this country, in Boston. The strong desire behind the festival was to give an opportunity for artists and audiences to experience creativity by women in an area which was and continues to be a male-dominated field of the arts. After producing the festival for a second year I ended my role, as did the other producers, and moved to other areas. For me the end of the festival was filled with sadness—it was a bitter disappointment to see that the very issues I was battling as a feminist existed in a profound way within the community itself.

As a producer and as an artist I am not only interested in those women who follow the book of rules and who already have awareness. Frankly I am a bit more interested in people who have not yet "seen the light." The didactic and obtuse element on the part of critics, organizers, and some audience members made it impossible to reach anyone with any real need. I remember the fights about bringing in one group or not because they employed a male technician, or another group because their teacher had been male, or yet another because their politics were not suitable. I remember equally the so-called criticism from the press. On the one hand, people complained about the heat in the tiny space being stifling and about the starting times for the performances being late. The establishment press screamed at the lesbian quality of the festival, thereby completely discouraging mainstream women from attending, while the women's press had a field day discussing anything they found "sexist" or "not politically correct."

After this experience I decided to start my own theatre, to address in a serious way the concerns I had over this battle between women themselves. You see, the establishment press did not bother me so much—this is a fight I expect, after spending my whole life facing it. It was the intolerance and oppression of the women against each other which was horrifying—where to go? The theatre began as a feminist theatre trying to address the concerns of women in every way, not only acceptable and simplistic ones. The first performance, *Rites,* was about women who change into their oppressors and enact the same sort of violence against women. The establishment press complained about the "staunch feminism" of the piece (although at least they seemed to recognize the quality of the artistic work), and the women's press and many audience members were enraged that we dared to show women who were bad on the stage.

The women's community no longer supported the work. I understood this as a sign that these people did not want to deal with their pain in the way that we presented it. I respect this choice. It is the critic I cannot respect, the critic who refuses to deal with the integrity behind the work rather than their own ego and personal political view. The pain behind this piece was quite real—a result of many years of facing oppression by women. When will we allow ourselves to see? When will we stop closing our eyes to the real oppression while we self-righteously condemn each other?

My theatre no longer calls itself feminist. I no longer call myself a feminist. Now the theatre comprises three men and four women. We do performances written by men and women. Our constructions and lighting are developed by anyone who has the interest or skills to create it. We no longer use the label or the rules, but in fact I find the theatre to be deeply and truly feminist—at the core of its being. That is to say, we now have two concerns in our work and our lives. To search deeply for questions and answers about ourselves and the world, which are not facile but offer the opportunity for expanding one's vision, and to try to work with the utmost quality and integrity so that this vision can truly be profound.

I deeply regret that I cannot call myself a feminist anymore. I have learned much in the last five years about SEXISM, ECONOMIC OPPRESSION, RACISM ... Mara, please join the world, not your textbooks. You who are fighting injustice cannot begin by accusing those who are trying sincerely and courageously to raise questions in the theatre which, albeit difficult and complex, are necessary to our growth as human beings. This is not sexism. Sexism is the fact that whereas there are now about ten women directors (artistic directors) in this city, not one of them has the funding to provide living wages for the artists involved. (At least we can triumph in the growth in the number of quality women directors.) Sexism is also the fact that whereas this is the fifth women's theatre festival in Boston, all of which have been packed by audiences, Sophie Parker and her staff are not paid anything, much less a living wage, for their work, thereby endangering the survival of the festival as well as the survival of the staff. Sexism is also the fact that my friend, who spent many years of her life raising four children, thinks about suicide because certain feminists have made her feel that her life is worthless.

Economic injustice, sexism, and discrimination are embodied in all of Mara's complaints about the festival, and those of critics before and after her. Yes, late starting times are problematic to the safety of women riding the T. Please write to the MBTA and suggest that they provide protection or later T service. They are the instruments of institutionalized discrimination. Don't complain about the festival organizers, who would gladly have earlier starting times if they could afford another week's rent. Or perhaps you would like them to cancel the performances, thereby depriving us yet again of an opportunity to see women's work. As far as the lack of parking spaces, perhaps you might address this issue to the Mayor of Boston—but you probably don't know that it is virtually impossible for artists in this city to find performance spaces, much less affordable ones. Outside the city it is more possible, but there arises the safety issue for women who are not fortunate enough to be able to complain about parking because they don't own a car. These issues, as well as the issue of access for the handicapped, should not be addressed as accusations to a festival which is attempting to better our society through art; they should be addressed to those who are responsible for them. If the critics spent half the time the festival did working for change, maybe we wouldn't have to worry about this type of discrimination. While you spend your time thinking of comfort, the festival staff, as well as every theatre of change, is fighting for survival.

From past experiences I know that it is impossible to please everyone. It does not bother me when responsible and serious criticism is leveled at my theatre or my politics or anyone else's. What disturbs and frightens me is when I read an article in CGN that sounds like it is written by the propaganda arm of the right wing. Yes, the right wing: divide and conquer. The division over mundane issues (called scapegoating) which are not even the responsibility of the scapegoat has ensured the success of fascism, from Hitler to Reagan. While we are all fighting and accusing each other of everything, we are too busy to discuss and work on the real issues at hand—the content, the issues involved in the work at the festival. This has, again, ensured the survival of sexism, racism, and discrimination. No unity, no change.

I would like to say that theatrically, and probably politically, I share little agreement with the festival. I am an experimental theatre artist; the festival is traditional. But I applaud the festival for this very fact—they present a challenge, with integrity, to my way of life and my thinking. This is the battle I am interested in—one which challenges me to grow and to reconsider. I am not interested in seeing anything which merely restates my position. Theatre is an art which must trigger the audience, in whatever way, to a new experience, a questioning and a reconsideration.

I applaud the fact that Parker continues to do the festival despite the lack of understanding and support which is to be found in the article concerned.

I applaud the fact that each year in March I have the opportunity to see the work of women that I have few opportunities to see otherwise.

I applaud the fact that Parker and staff have the courage to stop using labels so that more women will have access to the festival. The courage to present diversity of opinion and style in a world which encourages sameness and banality—in other words, the courage to face hostility because of their choice to challenge.

Most of all I applaud the fact that each time I go to the festival I see a huge range of all types of women and men, sharing each other's work. This is unheard of.

This year Parker's company and mine will co-produce a festival of experimental women's theatre from companies around the world. We will work together because of our differences, not our similarities. We have recognized that women (and men) must collaborate to understand more, not only to maintain the status quo of our particular little society.

Mara—to you I say—yes, to challenge with depth, meaning, and intelligence; no, to challenge which merely serves one's own ego with little else to offer.

27. Art, an Endangered Species (1993)

In March 1993 Double Edge invited theatres from around the state to a performance of Song of Songs, *followed by a discussion about cultural policy in Massachusetts. The proposed subject was whether establishing quotas could effectively challenge a lack of equity and diversity, and how such a policy would affect the arts, as well as artists. Several misconceptions surfaced during this meeting, partially due to the lack of a common definition of the words* art, artist, quota, and cultural policy. *The following text is my response to that meeting.*

My writing, like the original gathering, was an argument against tokenism. It takes issue with arts funding agencies that treated diversification and social justice as "current events" to be addressed through the ticking off of boxes rather than through creating communities that actually work and create together in dialogue. Rather than approaching arts funding as the practice of dividing up of a "pie" of limited resources, this article advocates for expanding the basis of arts funding so that it can be predicated on a broader representation of marginalized artists and communities.

Finally, it addresses the white-liberal guilt politics in a Culture War context that continues today, and, even before the violent dismantling of DEI initiatives, continues to promote a vastly inadequate pie and an astounding lack of genuine equity. This article was written in protest against the expectation that art and arts funding would be the place to solve all the inequities of our society, which still continue on a massive level in corporate and political structures. In other words: rather than reparations, the policy-makers and funding agencies sought to give artists of color a tiny sliver of a tiny pie. My essay protests against this limitation, particularly because it diminishes the essential value of art and culture—which to my mind is a fundamental part of awakening an equitable reality.

Below I have written and used the word "quality" many times. For me this meant, and still means, breaking barriers artistically and building connectivity in ways that are heretofore unexplored, or which have long been held back from exploration. For instance, ritual performance, which has now been brought forward as an art form deeply related to community involvement, was, in the 1980s when this piece was written, practically banned by every critical or funding institution. Yet it stands a prime example of what I refer to as the quality of cultural expression. Different cultures have different ways of expressing art. My feeling, looking back, is that I could not quite articulate my objection to this inequitable "equity," but even today I believe that although changes are being made, the mainstream is still holding nonconforming artists hostage, as far as art and funding go.

***

Art is created because it is necessary and essential, in and of itself, for human development and human existence. Since the beginning of human life people have made art in order to transcend their limitations and to discover what is unknown and concealed in themselves and their reality. Art gives testimony to the creative forces of humanity. For this reason alone it is a necessity, without which most of the testimony that survives our lives would represent destruction. Art is irreplaceable: it is beyond both the expectation and the capability of the viewer.

The subject of art can be anything. Topical, timely issues such as diversity, AIDS, and politics, or religion, culture, and sexuality, may all be part of the artistic process, but only if the work transcends what is already known about these issues and gives birth to new questions of human existence for the audience and the artists. If theatre simply restates what is known—politically, historically, or aesthetically—it uses itself as a form of mass media: reproducing information, it gives up the necessary component of creativity. This may be an indication of why theatre is not a necessity in the United States today, because it tries from the beginning to replace the newspaper, rather than to emanate culture.

Art for art's sake (or culture for culture's sake) should be viewed as a fundamental layer of existence. It is not a sin, nor is it synonymous to calling for aesthetics for aesthetics' sake. Throughout the world, and throughout time, people have fought for the right to create and to experience creation, sometimes at great personal cost, as essential to their societies' existence. Yet today we in America must continually battle the opposite: a prevailing attitude of lethargy toward art and its processes, and an insistence on viewing art as a form of entertainment that reflects, rather than leads, the fantasy or reality of the day. The United States uses its art as an agreeable reflector of trends and censors it when it goes beyond the standard-issue rhetoric of freedom that we have all come to accept.

Today much artistic work does not arise out of the culture that surrounds it, but instead preaches given norms about these cultures, propelled on by prevalent standards for language, vogue fashion, or societal malaise toward and censorship of any challenge. In seeking to educate rather than to create art, or to provide a social service rather than to create art, the artist can finally feel worthy of attention. It turns out we have only fed the enemy: we have accepted and encouraged the notion that art and culture are not important unless they serve another function, whether social, informational, or educational, and therefore that art—that which is *beyond* the expectations of the viewer—has become obsolete.

The only way to fight this is to find our way back to culture, away from prescriptive conditioning, to escape from bureaucracy, and to create from the deepest places in ourselves. This means that we must stop reformulating the problem as it has been handed to us by society, and look instead to the living complexity of our own culture and of ourselves when we are free as artists. It is substantially different to write about AIDS, the Holocaust, sexuality, or racism as something we witness or read about, than to ask the question of how we ourselves participate in these phenomena, how they become embedded in our complex cultural life. The first way provides more information for the converted. The second challenges us to transcend our limited ability to see our own roles in life.

The view we hold at Double Edge is that only work of the highest quality in form and content (as determined by the community and culture it arises from) can change the place of the arts and culture in the United States. Only when art does this can it change from an instrument of complacency to a shaper of inspiration and aspirations for all human potential. Truth is fundamental to quality, even if it is not always agreeable.

Several statements have been made, surely by bureaucrats and not by the artists themselves, which seem absurd and yet which must unfortunately be addressed: these are (1) that artists do not deserve to be paid and (2) that people should not apply for public funding if they do not agree with given standards of arts service agencies. Payment should not be based on agreement with standards of funding or agreement to standards of acceptability. Artists cannot create in order to promulgate or agree with public policy, but rather in order to move the society beyond "cultural policy." Once you agree as an artist to embody the role of an administrator, you have given bureaucratic demands the role of leader and shaper of your art, your artistic materials, and your process. I cannot underscore how ridiculous, compromising, and even dangerous this attitude is. THINK: to have artists following the demands of bureaucracy, or for that matter, of anyone else, is to completely eliminate the nature and role of art as transcendental, unknown, and essential, and to replace this with the role of an entertainment weekly or a school newspaper

Since the beginning of time religious organizations, courts, societies, communities, aristocracies, and villages have funded and supported their artists, sometimes in tandem with their role as entertainers and sometimes exclusively in their role as artists. If the work inspired people, restrictions and given quotas were *secondary* functions and not the primary judge of the work! Left in bureaucratic hands, however, work can only be mediocre, as this is the function of bureaucracy: to make information palatable for all. The result is the reproduction of museum culture rather than the pursuit of living culture.

In this state [Massachusetts], it seems that artists have been convinced of the righteousness of cultural policy to such a point that disagreement is neither allowed nor encouraged. What is everyone afraid of? I say that culture is not something to be created, but something that exists, positively and negatively, wherever there are people. It must be reflected honestly as it exists, and not as you would wish it to be. And further, art *only* exists if it is allowed to be free and not forced into the mold of the well-intentioned.

Double Edge believes and lives with the knowledge that each of us can create life anew, rather than reflect dead forms. This is essential and important not only for us, but also for the world around us. The Theatre Culture meeting held at our theatre was not a gathering of artists discussing the trappings and problems of artistic creation in our society, but rather a meeting of administrators and bureaucrats trying to define public policy. WAKE UP: if theatres are completely controlled by administrators, and if theatre survival is defined by bureaucrats, rather than by artistic vision, then artists are no longer the leaders or inventors of the theatres—and it is possible that ultimately there will be no art at all. In this case, artists become another quota for the administrators to fill. Hirelings and trash: disposable, replaceable, and no longer human.

We must fear for this situation, in which people are afraid of the title, "artist," and lose the ability to recognize the value of *art*.

28. Letter to the Advisory Board of Double Edge (1986)

*My passion for the work of Double Edge has led me sometimes
to fight and sometimes to extend an olive branch. This has
recently become a literal tree branch, as my* Hidden Territories
of the Bacchae *(2022) was filled with the wonder of saplings
and strong tree trunks. When I wrote this piece, the theatre
company was four years old and we were fighting for survival.
We had performed many of the plays from the Women's Cycle,
gathering a community of supporters who desired the intensity
and creativity of the performances. The Board signed on eagerly
to our experiment, but as I learned, they were not as passionate
as we were, and sometimes did not even attend our performances.
That lack of support really hurt. When one devotes oneself 18/7
and gives one's all, there is an agonizing feeling of disappointment
when people are not true to their expressions of commitment. This
is particularly true regarding the importance of Double Edge's
cultural mission.*

*Honestly speaking, all this remains problematic for me, even
today; but I do understand now, as opposed to then, that building
these relations and this shared commitment takes long-term work
similar in duration to that of the artistic work itself. It's a risk—
for all. Importantly, I try to learn not to take it so personally,
and am more or less successful at this proposition. Sometimes
it gets lonely working the way we do. Sometimes I think that if
somebody would just* understand, *then we could do all this great
work together. I share this text mostly for readers at the beginning
of their own questioning: to know that you are not alone, and that
you will find those who will work together with you.*

✳✳✳

April 10, 1986
To the Advisory Board of DOUBLE EDGE:
   DOUBLE EDGE is currently enjoying one of the most fulfilling
periods of growth and concrete success in our endeavors to become
a center for theatrical experimentation. Our goals—to develop our
own work, to teach, and to produce extraordinary experimental

theatre artists—are all being attacked vigorously and are beginning to bear fruit.

We are training and developing the actor's art in new and exciting ways: we performed Kroetz's *Request Concert*, which was extremely well received by audiences and critics, and we are in rehearsal for a "reconstruction" of Beckett's shorter plays.

We are teaching on a continual basis and have started to become known for our unique type of training. We will sponsor a workshop and performances by the Theatre Association GARDZIENICE from Poland in May and July, and performances by the Swedish Company JORD CIRCUS in June. These are two of the most well thought of alternative theatres in Europe.

In addition to all of this, we are currently publishing a newsletter, the last edition of which got an extraordinary response from readers, and we are now beginning to grow financially. We have received several grants, from the *Boston Globe* and finally, from the Massachusetts Council for the Arts. Double Edge has done all of this with no salary, working full time (which means eighteen hours a day) for four years. We now plan to start paying members of the company a minimal sum, which will hopefully increase with time.

All of this is very exciting to us. Unfortunately the reason I am writing to you is because I feel that we are not exciting to you. We have performed two productions in the last two months. Out of eight board members, two of you came to a rehearsal for the *Chehov Project*, three of you came to a performance, and three of you did not attend at all. One board member was at the opening night party, which is intended as outreach to the audience. The same board person invited five people to the production. Noone else invited anyone. *Request Concert*, performed last week, was not attended by any one of the board, nor did any of the board encourage other audience members to come.

I want to say that we have had many discussions about what the board should do and how we can communicate with a board. I have tried, through letters and personal meetings, to keep you each informed about us and also informed about our needs. No one on the board has tried actively to address any of our concerns or be a part of our work. But even this has been acceptable because each of you showed support financially, or through a contribution of materials or skills. This kind of support has been much appreciated and we of DOUBLE EDGE had decided to be satisfied with a supportive, if inactive, board.

But we are a theatre company and the purpose of all our work, and all our struggle, is to create theatre for an audience. If DOUBLE EDGE cannot assume that our board will be interested in seeing our work and bringing friends and colleagues, how can we possibly say honestly to ourselves that any audience will be interested?

It is very painful for me to have to write this letter to you—on a personal level, for each member of DOUBLE EDGE, and also in terms of theatre in general. We are thriving in so many ways and yet it is always a struggle to communicate to an audience. There are many battles to conquer, including our location, the prominence of A.R.T. (American Repertory Theater) and other money-making theatres, and the allure of film and television, not to mention our society's laziness and lack of concern for no-glitz quality art and experimentation. We do not complain about the long odds we face. But the fact that our board is uninterested in our work, both the successes and the failures, makes it difficult to continue to believe. The ironic part of this question is that now DOUBLE EDGE has more to believe in than ever.

Do you believe in DOUBLE EDGE? Are you really interested in us? In experimentation? In the theatre?

Please ask these questions of yourself. If you feel committed to us, come to see our work and believe in it enough to bring other people. Call us if you can't come so we won't think you just don't care. Call us to find out what is going on, or at least respond to letters we send you. Each of you are on the board because we respect you and your work—we want to hear what you have to say and most of all we want to see you at our work. We need this.

If you ask these questions and find you don't care, then you must reconsider your role on the board. Again, I cannot convince someone off the street to come to our theatre if I cannot convince you.

I try to see whether I write too roughly, and I can only say that this work that DOUBLE EDGE is trying to do is too hard, artistically and financially, to have to add to that self-doubt because of an uninterested board. Yes, it is true we could not continue without your financial support, but with no audience there is no reason to continue because there is no theatre.

With much regret in my heart,
     Stacy Klein
     Artistic Director

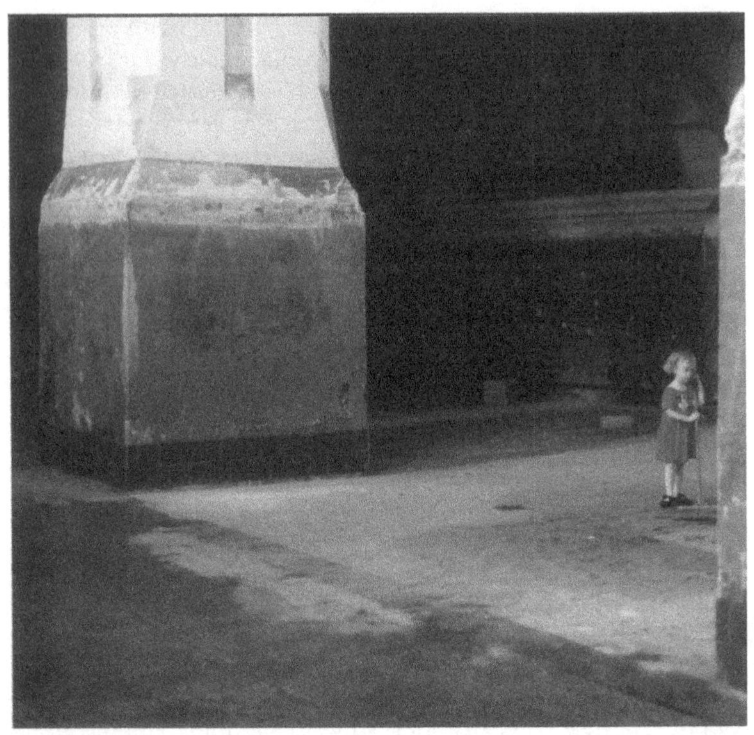

FIGURE 8 *Drohobycz Synagogue after the collapse of the Soviet Union, during the "Republic of Dreams: Hidden Territories" project, 1994. Pictured: Tadea Klein. Photo courtesy of Double Edge Theatre Archive.*

29. Toward Living Culture: Writings on Ukraine (1994–5)

"Republic of Dreams" is a short essay by Bruno Schulz that describes Schulz's family visit to a sanatorium and hot springs (common in Eastern Europe in summertime); the visit takes place in a context of repression, including both the murderous political climate and the restrictions of his family's traditional Judaism. During this trip Schulz goes on an inner journey and creates his own imaginative adventure, in spite of the context.

When Double Edge traveled to the Ukraine to visit Schulz's hometown of Drohobych/Drohobycz and delve into the near-extinct (but once flourishing) Jewish culture there, we named the project the Hidden Territories of the Republic of Dreams. *It seems fitting that when we started looking for our own imaginative place—through the company's move to Ashfield, where we could endeavor a life of possibilities rather than impossibilities—we would refer to it as our own Republic of Dreams. This was also a period in my life when I had small children and realized that my anger needed to take a turn, possibly as fuel for making the impossible possible, in both my life and my art. Without overlooking the realities of repression and cultural extermination, I began to understand a way of creating that begins with hope.*

✻✻✻

i. The Republic of Dreams (1994)

Narrative for *The Republic of Dreams* documentary, 1994.
The Gardzienice Theatre Association of Poland/ Kadmus Theater/ Double Edge Theatre Central European collaboration originated as an expedition to the Carpathian Mountains of Ukraine. Until 1991 these regions remained inaccessible to both Eastern Europeans and Americans. The intention of the 1993 expedition was to examine the Huculi and other Carpathian mountain cultures, and the remains of the Jewish culture. Gardzienice led this first four-week expedition to the Huculi village of Krasnolia. The group was invited to several

local events including a Huculi wedding. In addition to these events, important exchanges happened in individual homes around the village where participants were housed.

From the expedition it became apparent that there is no "living Jewish culture" in the areas we visited, and that there are very few Jews remaining in the villages at all. Although it was to be expected that the Jews, unlike other ethnic groups, would consist of a sparse population and many graves, the extinction of the Mountain Jewry was an unexpected discovery.

In February 1994, through contact with the Symposium on Jewish Life, sponsored by the Carpathian Mountain Society, we met Dora Kacnelson, an elderly Jewish scholar from Drohobycz. She was conducting research on the Jews of Ukraine and knew of several villages where the rebuilding of Jewish life was taking place.

The second part of the *Republic of Dreams* took place in Ukraine in September and October, 1994. The expedition took on a unique form in that it was focused not on traveling, but instead on a continuous contact with the daily life of the people involved.

Double Edge Theatre, together with the Charlestown Working Theater, spent three weeks in the town of Drohobycz. Drohobycz is a town of 100,000 in Western Ukraine, approximately 50 miles Southwest from Lvov and 40 miles East of the Polish border. Drohobycz was also the birthplace of the great Polish/Jewish writer Bruno Schulz, who was killed by the Nazis in 1942. Schulz was a central source for Double Edge's performance, *Song of Absence*, and he wrote the essay from which the project's title was taken; the essay is about a place where all things could be possible. The town was once the center of one of the largest Jewish populations in Galicia, Western Ukraine, with five Synagogues, a Talmudic Center, and a thriving Jewish life that spanned the breadth of the culture.

> Sealed in a self-sufficient microcosm, that town and its countryside
> have installed themselves at the very brink of eternity.
> —Bruno Schulz, "Republic of Dreams"

The community that housed the local theatre was located at the foot of the Carpathian Mountains and it's a truly multicultural community: there are many different native cultures living together, respecting each other's cultures, and sometimes, infrequently, sharing them. But still living with respect. We were trying to find out how Jewish culture influenced, and was influenced by, the surrounding cultures.

In Drohobycz and the neighboring towns of Pidbuzh, Boryslaw, and Chernovsky we found thirty old, very old, Jewish people and many young, very assimilated Jewish people. Most of the people in between were either dead or had emigrated to Israel or America.

The whole atmosphere was absolutely stuffed full of stories. You only needed to lay a trap under this sky full of ghosts to catch one.

—Bruno Schulz, "Republic of Dreams"

Here are some of the people:
Alfred Schreyer is a conductor and music teacher in the secondary music school. He was a student of Bruno Schulz's.

During the Nazi occupation, Scheyer was taken from the Drohobycz ghetto and sent to Dachau, where he spent the last period of the war. Later, in Berlin, he appealed to the Red Cross for permission to emigrate, explaining that he had an uncle in Argentina. They asked him for his address, and since he didn't remember it, they told him that he had to stay in a transitory camp until they checked it, which would take at least half a year. "I looked at these barracks, and they were exactly the same as those that I had just left in Dachau. So I thought that I'd better go home."

I remember in particular a certain condor, an enormous bird with a featherless neck, its face wrinkled and knobby, it was an emaciated ascetic, a Buddhist lama, full of imperturbable dignity in its behavior, guided by the rigid ceremonial of its great species.

—Bruno Schulz, "Birds"

Maurice Weiss: a distant relative, a second cousin or so, of Schulz. He escaped the Holocaust because he was drafted into the Soviet army, and he still wears his medals of decoration.

Most of his life he worked as the head economist in the crane factory. A loyal party member, he still addresses the congregation as "comrades." As the leader of prayers he performs the service with a profound sense of mission, stressing the importance of preserving continuity. He is the only person able to read Hebrew, and for that reason he is the central figure in the life of the Jewish community.

Little Rosa: She works as a bookkeeper out of her house. She escaped with her parents from Belarus to the Ural Mountains—

leaving behind her grandfather, a rabbi, and her grandmother, who refused to leave their home.

After the war her family relocated to Drohobycz, where her father continued his religious practice, gathering in private homes, until his death at ninety-three in 1992. He thought that passing on his beliefs and practices to his children was useless, since the Synagogues were either closed or destroyed. Rosa wanted to bury her father's prayer book with him, but some of her friends dissuaded her. They have no need for the book at the synagogue now because they have new books. "And when I find my end, what will become of the book then?" She gave the book to actor Nachum Cohen.

We sat in their homes, which themselves were testimonies of discontinuity. There were no old family photographs on the walls, no old books, no things made before the war. It was as if the entire material culture had been annihilated, evaporating without a trace.

Schteinberg Fania Gregovna: She tells of her classmate Mr. Kojenikov, who hid her for twenty-nine months in his home in the suburbs of Kerograd. He cut out a space behind a bookcase for her to stand in when anyone came to the house. "I lost all faith in my friends," she says. Once when I was walking through town, trying not to be noticed, I saw an old school friend. She asked me how I was and where I was living. I was afraid, and I told her an incorrect address. When she looked into my eyes I knew she knew I had lied. She put her hand on my shoulder and asked if I would stay with her.

Jack London: Mr. London was eight years old when the war began. He lived in the village of Zegophzka, which had a Jewish population of 250. Miraculously, no Jews in this village were killed. The Ukrainian villagers protected their neighbors by giving the Nazi soldiers food. Seven kilometers away in the town of Finsánuka, all of the Jews were killed.

The individual dimensions of the Holocaust appeared omnipresent. Not a single person managed to survive intact; there was always some personal tragedy in the background. "This is very hard for us to remember; it comes to us at night as a dream."

We also tried to gather and collect any songs they remembered from the last time they were allowed to sing them—which was forty-five to fifty years ago. Most of the time we ended up singing the Yiddish and Hebrew songs we knew because they had never heard them before.

Our expedition took place during the High Holidays.

We sang in the synagogue for several services, including Yom Kippur, the day of atonement and the most holy of Jewish holidays.

It was the first time the community had used the synagogue since they had taken it back from the Soviets in 1992. The Drohobycz temple is an impressive brick building dominating this part of town, a reminder of its Jewish past and former well-being. During the war it became a stable where the Germans kept horses; then the Soviet authorities turned it into a furniture store. We sang liturgical songs to the forty or so members of the congregation, mostly elders. These songs had not been heard in the synagogue since before the war.

Members of the synagogue made a special holiday dinner following the Yom Kippur fast. During this occasion memories of the customs and music of pre-Soviet Drohobycz were brought to light. The members of the Jewish community invited Double Edge to present two performances of *Song of Songs* in the Synagogue.

It was a difficult situation at first, as the City Director of Culture, the head of the Palace of Culture, was more than skeptical about helping us if we performed in the Synagogue, for they could not believe that the work would be anything but religious propaganda. After they saw our work demonstrations, and attended the Charlestown Working Theater's performance in the Palace of Culture, however, they were convinced otherwise.

We immediately began cleaning and preparing the space for the performance, with the generous help of the young people we met, as well as many gracious neighbors.

To me it was very touching to enter the synagogue and to start to work there, in a sense to sanctify the place, to scrape the floor and to clear it out; it wasn't a daily act of cleaning, there was something extraordinary there that I felt—maybe to elicit the memory again, or to invite the spirits.

—Actor Nachum Cohen

Accompanied by the ghosts of the past, and in front of a very present and enthusiastic audience, the performance was changed and deepened in a way that will never be lost. This was, for all of the theatre, a defining moment of artistic work.

With feelings of great satisfaction and enjoyment, with my breath withheld, I watched the musical performance *Song of Songs* presented by your theater in the Drogobych synagogue. Although this performance has a very modern character, it was understood and exceptionally well received by all spectators, regardless of their interest, nationality, or points of view. Amazing was the director's invention, owing to which it was possible to present in the empty space of the synagogue such a magnificent show.

    —From a letter to Double Edge from Alfred Schreyer

Through these encounters, the potential for theatre and in-depth cultural contact to break through cultural isolation, antisemitism, and nationalism became evident. So too did we become aware of the relationship between the forced assimilation of the Soviet state and the frail assimilation that exists in our own country, which hides or devalues the strong inner realities of a culture.

The way of our theatre is to attain the ultimate potential of the artist as a human being, and to recognize the distinctions between people as the ultimate weapon for this struggle. These are the principles at the heart of the work on *Keter: The Crowning Song*, the final segment of the Song Trilogy, and they are accompanied in every way by the precepts of responsibility, choice, and human potential that are at the heart of all of our work.

Each of us has a memory of our values hidden inside. Through our work a slow awakening happens. Perhaps it is a small touch, or perhaps it comes back to someone after years. It is a ghost of our memory, the shadow of life. We have the ability to extend our hand, to make our choice, to decide to create a new life of recognition and sharing, and of tolerance. This is the *Crowning Song*.

Today those remote dreams come back, and not without reason. The possibility suggests itself that no dreams, however absurd or senseless, are wasted in the universe. Embedded in the dream is a hunger for its own reification, a demand that imposes an obligation on reality and that grows imperceptibly into a bona fide claim, an IOU clamoring for payment. [...] We are all of us dreamers by nature, after all, brothers under the sign of the trowel, destined to be Master Builders.

    —Bruno Schulz, "Republic of Dreams"

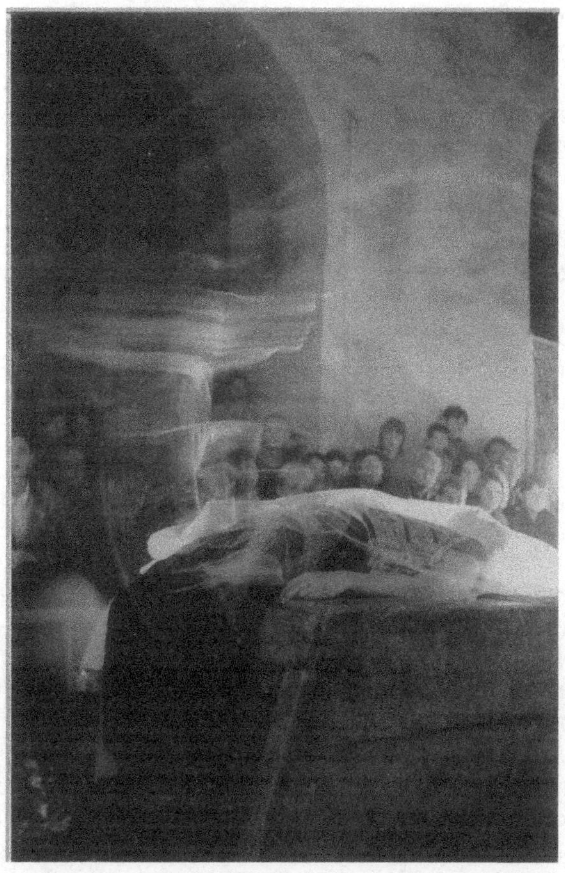

FIGURE 9 *A performance of* Keter, the Crowning Song, *in a fortress in Ciasnadora, Romania, outside the Sibiu International Festival, 1997. Performance conceived and directed by Stacy Klein. Pictured: Jennifer Johnson, supine; and John Peitso, left, in a swirl. Photo courtesy of Double Edge Theatre Archive.*

We have begun the process of building our own Republic of Dreams, at the Double Edge farm in the small town of Ashfield, Massachusetts. Through the hosting of gatherings and the encounters with international collaborators who have visited, we have come to understand our own Republic of Dreams, a Center of Living Culture.

ii. Notes from the Director on Authentic Culture and Double Edge (1995)

"Real life in the Republic of Dreams," as we began to describe the circumstances of the people of Drohobycz as well as our own, has become much more than a representation of the type of work Double Edge has created in communities in Poland, Scandinavia, Germany, Wales, and the United States in the areas of cultural exchange and performance. It is also a provocative and adamant reminder of the reasons for Double Edge's existence, and ultimately for my own life and work as the theatre's director.

In Drohobycz, we sang Jewish songs garnered from previous research and expeditions and performed *Song of Songs* in the ruins of what had been the most glorious synagogue in Galicia. Turned into a horse stable by the Nazis and a furniture factory by the Communists, the synagogue was recently taken back by the handful of remaining Jews in the town. The tears of the elders upon hearing songs lost to them for over fifty years, and the ethnic songs sung for us all night after the performances by the young people from a variety of Western Ukrainian cultures, sprang forth out of a cultural, spiritual, and personal isolation so deep it could only have been penetrated by the most intimate and powerful reaches of art and cultural mutuality.

It has been several years since I have experienced such a defining moment, free from all outside frameworks, labels, and social discussion, which crystallized the absolute necessity of art and theatre for human existence. This is what I want to bring to my peers, my students, and most of all to the community of people who see the work of my theatre.

The ability to transform an audience—to reach beyond cultural stereotypes, ideologies, and alienation, to awaken the unexpected and hidden realms of our innermost worlds—is a direct outgrowth of the unique methodology and work practice of the Double Edge ensemble, which we call "living culture."

Double Edge is a group of eight actors, musicians, technicians, designers, scholars, humanists, and a director from four countries that creates theatrical art and cultural exchange based upon the distinct identities of the members of the group, half of whom are Jews, originating from both the Sephardic (Middle Eastern) and Ashkenazic (European) traditions. Yet given that we speak eight languages and encompass other Western and Eastern backgrounds as well, our work speaks from the Jewish experience in the context of surrounding societies.

The Song Trilogy, Double Edge's present performance cycle concerning the two-thousand-year Jewish Diaspora, is a living example of the theatre's juxtaposition of the realities of cultural isolation and extinction with the possibilities of its preservation and mutuality. *Song of Absence* evokes the world of pre-war Hasidic and assimilated Jewry in the context of Central European culture, and *Song of Songs* springs from the inner life, imagination, and spirituality of the Spanish Medieval Jews, Moslems, and Christians. All of the work drawn from the history, anthropology, music, artwork, and tradition of Diasporic communities, as well as our own present-day exchanges with them; our creative work begins at the moment when these factors meet the individual and artistic vision of the Double Edge ensemble members in confrontation with our audience. Thus, the intrinsic nature of the theatre is that of dialogue or creating "living culture."

The resonance of Double Edge is born from the open, exposed, and often defenseless dialogue that we aim to create at each performance within the clearly defined structure of a theatrical presentation. It is a fact that we use our differences as the foundation of the work. We do not whitewash distinctions or attempt to create a common cultural vision, but instead clear a common ground for a unique, deep, and authentic meeting of people. This is achieved through a unified way of working developed by the eight members of our group over the past ten years, training physically, vocally, and intellectually with each other, with our long-term collaborators, and with our community. An example of the artist-identified culture for which Double Edge is recognized is the sensorial work, developed largely by one of the company's core actors and its training leader, who is blind. Sensorial work is a visceral mode of physical training that incorporates touch, taste, smell, hearing, and sight, which are generally not all involved in the training process at the same time.

The life of the work is continually renewed through this type of dialogue. So too is it renewed through the constant juxtaposition of disparate realities or circumstances, as in the battle in Double Edge's performance work between tradition and contemporary life waged theatrically by hundreds of glimmering candles and torches burning against harsh stage lighting, live choral singing bursting forth out of recorded music, old folk dances struggling with the beat of "The Boulevard of Broken Dreams," and Christian imagery enveloping Jewish ritual.

The complexity of the performance experience and the subsequent necessity of a highly precise physical setup for the work have led us to develop a new performance practice called Études, a combination of the fixed structure of performance with open narration, which allows us to actively react to the audience and include their response in the event. The simplicity of Études has given Double Edge an opportunity to introduce itself to new audiences in rural areas, at homes for the aged, and in schools, churches, and other places where theatre would not normally occur; the dialogic nature of Études also enables us to deal more intimately with our established audiences, including audience members with disabilities, immigrant groups, artists, and people of different ethnic backgrounds. At the same time the mutuality implicit in Études allows us to gather and develop material for our new performance, *Keter*, the Crown.

The third and final performance of the Song Trilogy, *Keter*, brings together all of the current work of Double Edge in a multi-layered collaboration and international vision. Partners for this work will include the Ukrainian choir, with their range of multi-cultural music from the Carpathian region; the Charlestown Working Theater, from the working-class community of the same name in Boston, who have been students of our theatre for two years; and a Klezmer band from Massachusetts.

These groups will come together to create *Keter*, a performance challenging the growing isolation of today's world, on Double Edge's new one-hundred-acre farm in the rural hilltown of Ashfield, Massachusetts, where we are presently developing a Center for Living Culture to function in conjunction with our Boston performance space. This Center will ultimately host international and US guest artists from all forms of artistic expression, who will have the unique opportunity to create work on a long-term basis, develop and store archives of hidden and nearly extinct culture saved and revitalized through artistic exchange, as well as document international theatrical work of excellence. The Center will also enable students of Double Edge to live and work with us on a semi-permanent basis, as well as enable us to conduct enduring cultural exchanges and bring theatrical performance and activity to a local community where it has never existed before, inaugurating a meaningful and long-term process of co-existence. The dialogue is enhanced by the challenge of maintaining our own theatrical and ethnic culture while also developing mutuality and trust with the surrounding community, as we are "strangers in a foreign land."

Whether performing, touring, making Études, producing developing artists or international events, building our rural center, or creating exchanges, we measure our success strictly by the artistic quality, depth, and honesty of the experience, as seen from the perspective of the ensemble and reflected in the eyes of our history and our spectators. This is not as easy to measure through numbers—there is no known metric for artistry. The silent stillness at the end of a performance; the deep astonishment and even deeper inner regions touched and written on people's faces; the long-term relations we have with our audiences, who return over and over to the same performance; the students and professional artists who come back to us from across the country and from around the world as a reminder of the humanity and possibility of theatre expression; the people from the town of Ashfield helping us build our theatre; people from the town of Drohobycz giving us their food, and the long-forgotten song shared timidly during the Étude: all this bears witness to Double Edge Theatre's ability to transform isolation and reveal the human need for art which, once discovered, is absolute.

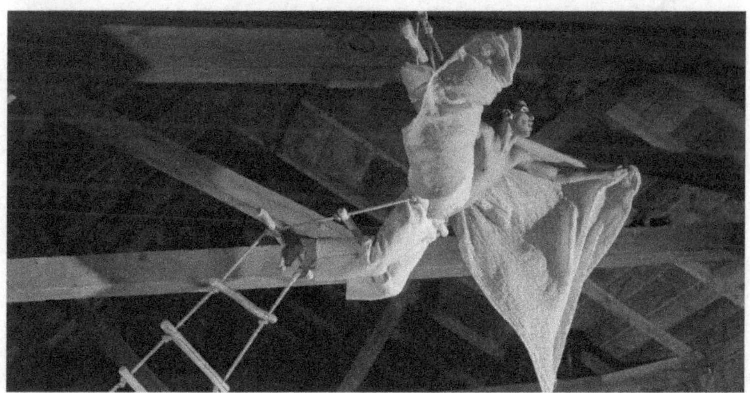

FIGURE 10 SUGA, *conceived and performed by Travis Coe, directed by Stacy Klein (2018–19). Photo by Kim Chin-Gibbons.*

30. To Connect with *This* Community (2021)

Stacy Klein and Maria Shevtsova in Conversation (excerpt)

This conversation took place on the winter solstice, December 21, 2020, a date that Maria Shevtsova, Editor of New Theatre Quarterly, *had chosen symbolically. It was transcribed by Kunsang Kelden and edited by Shevtsova. The current text has been excerpted from the full interview, which was published in* New Theatre Quarterly 37, *Issue 4 (November 2021), pp. 299–322.*

***

Maria Shevtsova: What are some of the features of the parades you put on with Double Edge? Presumably, you have stilt-walkers, for example. People flying, musicians playing, people singing, and you'd presumably have the townspeople following you back to Double Edge on foot through the parade.

Stacy Klein: Well … not always. Take the *Ashfield Town Spectacle and Culture Fair* (2017). It was all over the town. There was a scene in the cemetery, there was a scene in the Town Hall, there was a scene on the commons, there was a scene somewhere else, and so forth. There were people, actors, walking on the streets, looking, and relating to the history of the town.

MS: Is this phenomenon of parading in the town part of the beginning of Double Edge's history with the town? The Farm is Double Edge's space and so having audiences come there is a different matter from sharing town space. Double Edge is a more intimate space—it's not public in the way that the town is public. Audiences coming to the Double Edge Farm are offered spectacles by the water with all those wonderful, magical, and sometimes completely ecstatic scenes that you create. You are offering your home, in which you dream.

SK: You have made a connection between the parade and home, and to that I would add "community." The parade may have been the culmination of explorations concerning mine and

Carlos's different histories. I had been working on a ten-year project from 1988 to 1998 whose research was mainly concerned with Jewish communities in Central Europe. The project was *Republic of Dreams*, and the research took place across five Central European countries: Ukraine, Poland, Bulgaria, Hungary, and Romania. It included oral history, singing liturgical songs in the synagogue as a way of connecting, many community gatherings, eating and drinking with groups of people, and training future artists. Our approach was influenced by Rena Mirecka, but it was developed with some connecting links to Gardzienice's idea of expeditions.

   When we came to Ashfield, we tried some of those things. Musical gatherings—they weren't for Ashfield; they were more suitable for a different community. We quickly realized that we could not just transplant something from a different culture into our community here. We had to find out how to connect with *this* community.

MS: Connecting with the community couldn't have been easy. You came from Boston, you bought a farm, you were outsiders. You were coming into a community that had a history from 1743 when two African American land track settlers put their roots down here.

SK: There's a history before that, going back like 10,000 years!

MS: You're referring to the Indigenous peoples of the area and particularly to the Nipmuc Nation, and we'll be talking about this aspect in a minute. There were also other communities in this region long before colonial settlers came and imposed. But here you were in the mid-1990s, arriving in the country—city slickers, as they might have thought of you.

SK: Oh yeah. We were called "the City."

MS: Then, for three years, you commuted between Boston and the Farm, and this wouldn't have looked good. Local people would have seen that as a sign of not making up your mind. Who are you? The question then is: How did you start building relations with the existing community to the point where we started this conversation, when we talked about how wonderful the community was and how supportive it is of you in 2020? What did you do to build relations? One of my thoughts was parades, or a form of them. I take it that the Summer Spectacles were—and continue to be—a way of involving the community physically and more viscerally in your artistic work?

SK: In 1997, we opened the Barn with the final work of the Song Trilogy. [This cycle ran from 1987 to 1998.] We got an audience. Carlos was here by then, and he would call people up on the phone and ask them to come. The piece really had nothing to do with anybody here. It was being made to premiere in Boston. Carlos could get people to come, but we weren't doing anything related to the community. But we had started to make some inroads by hiring local people to help us with building. That was the first thing.

MS: Very important, too.

SK: We started a project called the Consortium for Theatre Practices, which was a collaboration with Gardzienice [1999–2001], where we would take our students—maybe ten students—and Gardzienice would have ten students. We held the first collaboration for three weeks in Gardzienice's center in Poland. The second one was held in both places; the students went back and forth [between the United States and Poland] but we did not. We started working with them outside. This led, in the third year, to our doing an outdoor performance. There were three scenes: one by the pond, one in the field and, I think, one in the Barn. It was the *Saragossa Manuscripts* (2002), which was great because we could create disparate scenes that didn't need to have a narrative except for how its main character voyages through different realities. And I love that book [*The Manuscript Found in Saragossa* by Jan Potocki, written at the turn of the nineteenth century] because it's what I believe about reality. *Saragossa Manuscripts* basically came out of Carlos and me combining our work—his street theatre, popular music, percussion.

MS: You mean people's theatre.

SK: Yeah, and this went together with our ensemble work, as well as our much more intimate, one-on-one gatherings with community members. We did this work first with our students from the Consortium. Then, when we started doing performances outdoors each year, we would have gatherings afterwards so that, even if people didn't totally get what we were doing, they would still be able to commune with us. That whole Summer Spectacle project came out of the partnership between Carlos and me, while Matthew Glassman, an ensemble member who came to Double Edge in 2000 as a student, worked with us in developing it more fully. Alongside this, we were growing into the town: many of us were living in town, the kids were going to school in town, and we were hiring only local people. Eventually people would come from elsewhere and stay in the local bed and breakfast. The bed and breakfast "industry," let's say, started growing restaurants; there's a general store now, and there's lots of local development in Ashfield. Right now, we're the largest business in Ashfield.

MS: I'm not surprised, given that rural communities are generally dying, aren't they? I mean, small subsistence farming is dying while the big mega-farms, the industrial farms, are swallowing them up. So I'm not surprised in the slightest that you have become the biggest enterprise in the town. Is this partly what you mean when you talk about the power of art—theatre, in your case—to transform the community? Is it this economically and socially developmental aspect that you have in mind when you talk about transformation? I take it that you also see this as a cultural transformation: people discovering something about the world of mixed arts, of the visual arts, music, word, and more, and your geographic space, your outdoors, for instance—that is the form of theatre that you do. I am tempted to think of your form of theatre as in part ecological—certainly insofar as you fully integrate your natural environment in the very aesthetics of your outdoor performances. The environment is not just a backdrop.

SK: I call everything that you have just said part of "living culture." Living culture, as in: the culture of the whole community. It starts with art and the imagination and it goes from there—people see that art and theatre are not just about some people getting up and talking about something that is not theirs, which has nothing to do with them, and which puts them to sleep. The first time our main contractor, whose family has been here since whenever, came to a performance was when we had to drag him to one. Adam

[Bright] dragged him in. He had been working with us since we got to Ashfield—a beautiful guy, Ray Gray. The performance was *The Odyssey* and, when the sailors turned into pigs, and they literally did—the sailors dropped off the back of a roof, and out came the pigs—he couldn't believe it! He could not believe it! He just started laughing, and he's a very circumspect guy; you would never know what he was thinking. He was laughing so hard that he had to step away.

MS: That's hilarious. Real pigs flying out: he didn't expect that, did he? I bet nobody did!

SK: Oh my God, no! And Ray Gray is a farmer. Every year after that, he says, "I miss the pigs." People think that we just work for a couple of hours a day and then we're finished. They have no idea what a culture of theatre is, but now, they're part of it. Ray worked so hard on the *Ashfield Town Spectacle*. He dug up every old machine to place all over town, such as Ashfield's original fire hose, which people had to walk over to any fire. It was unbelievable. He got a crane—his own crane—and we used it in the performance to lift somebody up from the audience and suspend them over the street: it became theirs. They own it, and they're part of creating it. This is what a living culture is to me, as opposed to getting people into buildings and charging a huge amount of money, which has nothing to do with the person except for the fact that they are being entertained.

MS: Would you accept the appellation "community theatre" to describe this kind of work?

SK: I don't mind it, but I prefer "living culture." It definitely is community theatre, but I don't use the term because it has been so horrifyingly abused: it has ended up describing an excuse to gather socially, but it doesn't actually specify a cultural element. The cultural element has to be engaged. That, to me, is the difference. And that's the growing problem in our century: we aren't using our creativity as humans *with* each other. We're very separated.

MS: Community theatre has been instrumentalized. It has also been exploited by NGOs. I can't bear those institutions, which are usually large or influentially "big" institutions, because when they come in and basically tell groups of people, existing communities, what to do, they destroy the sense of the living together-ness in which culture is formed and where people create together, in time and place and space.

I can see why you would prefer to use "living culture." I'm going to move to the last part of this conversation, which concerns the Indigenous peoples of Western and Central Massachusetts. In August 2020, I viewed the two video podcasts from Double Edge that featured the Ohketeau Cultural Centre. I watched with great attention and wanted to ask you what stimulated your partnership with Indigenous groups.

SK: When we started working on the *Ashfield Town Spectacle,* we started researching the history of the Indigenous people of our area. We worked with the Ashfield Historical Society and gathered a great deal of information. One of the things we found out was that the first settlers of Ashfield were African American freed slaves who were given a tract of land: you have already referred to this. The second thing we learned was that the first two women ever elected to public office in the United States—this was in 1855—came from Ashfield. Amazing, right? The staff of the Ashfield Historical Society refused to acknowledge that there were any Indigenous people in Ashfield. They said that they were all just migrants.

MS: Migrants from where?

SK: Migrants, you know, people who were just moving through the region. I don't know. "Migrants" was the word they used, but I didn't think it made sense, so we started researching. We met Rhonda Anderson, who is a Native Alaskan Inupiaq-Athabaskan. She was raised here and has lived here all her life. Because we wanted to learn, she told us to go and attend the various lectures that were happening here and there. We asked her to suggest someone who could tell a Nipmuc story during the *Ashfield Town Spectacle*; it ended up being Jasmine Rochelle Goodspeed who did that, and then circled the Ashfield Lake in homage—because water is life.

We were then introduced to Larry Spotted Crow Mann, who is a Nipmuc elder. He came to one of our gatherings on "Art and Survival," and sang healing songs. We asked

Rhonda and Larry what they needed so we could help do something to redress the disappearance, the invisibility of Indigenous existence Ashfield. You can say that freed slaves founded the town, but this does not acknowledge the area's 10,000 years of history.

They said they needed space that was not institutional, explaining that they had no place but the universities "for our people to gather and do their traditional things—traditional plants, medicines," and other cultural practices. Double Edge decided to donate a barn we were renovating so that it could become an autonomous Indigenous space, which they would run. This Ohketeau Cultural Centre took three years of work to build, following the *Ashfield Town Spectacle* in 2017. It has since opened and is active. Currently, it is the only Indigenously owned and run cultural center in the whole of Western and Central Massachusetts.

We are the Ohketeau's fiscal sponsor, which means that we're assisting them administratively as well as helping them get grants. They need to speak for themselves. We also want to teach the people in Ashfield and beyond that the Nipmuc and other Indigenous nations are still *here*: they were not completely exterminated. As the new US Secretary of the Interior said yesterday, "You tried to exterminate my people, but we're still here." Ohketeau and Double Edge joined forces to create an educational series about the Indigenous peoples of this region titled "Living Presence of our History." We are also collaborating artistically.

MS: Do you know how many Nipmuc people live in Ashfield and the immediately surrounding area?

SK: In Ashfield—no. There are larger groups in Western and Central Massachusetts. There's a big community in Springfield and a pretty substantial one in Worcester, and because of this population the gatherings at the Ohketeau Cultural Centre are always full.

MS: Are there also African American groups in the Ashfield area? I seem to remember from my years in the United States that there's an African American community in Springfield—quite large, I seem to remember. Is that right?

SK: There are African American and Latin@ communities. Springfield is where we performed *Cada Luna Azul* in a park, where audiences followed us around. It was incredible.

There were so many people that they couldn't fully hear us—about 800 people!

MS: Do you have direct working relations with African American and Latin@ artists? Do some of these artists work with Double Edge? Do you ask them to be teachers? Do they come as students? To workshops?

SK: Well, Travis [Coe] is Afro-Latinx. He came from New Jersey and he's now our Associate Artistic Director. Carlos and I started mentoring him when he was an intern and he quickly became part of the ensemble. He's been here for five years—a brilliant, super-talented young man. I directed his solo piece *SUGA*, with James Baldwin's novel *Giovanni's Room* as our guide. Travis was exploring his background, his relations with his father, and his investment in queer performance. We worked together for over a year, just the two of us, training and improvising, and bringing up parts of his life through movement.

MS: One can perform solos in Covid times. What is hard to do in such times is collective ensemble work; yet what you are indicating is that Double Edge hasn't folded. It's alive, well, and busily working. Tell me about your residencies.

SK: Baraka Sele became one of our three Art Justice consultants around four years ago, and worked with the ensemble and me to update our new mission values and create a Case Statement. Our current artists-in-residence include Shey Rivera, who is creating a performance titled *Antigonx*, which we have planned for our fortieth anniversary festival in 2022. There is Deidra Montgomery, a musician who took up a residency and who is now one of the composers for our future performance *The Bacchae*—and who is also a performer in it.

We also have a larger partnership with Ebony Noelle Golden, who is the head of Betty's Daughter Arts Collaborative, based in Harlem. She began doing artist residencies with us five years ago. Together we launched the Art and Survival Fellowship, a three-year learning program; we will premiere her Afro-feminist piece *In the Name Of* along the stream at Double Edge. We have hugely developed over the past five years, as far as collaboration is concerned, and it's been very exciting. We received a large grant to finish a number of buildings, so we now have spaces for other people and can be more than a little cocoon.

MS: You're going to have more studios for people to work in and thus to have much more of a studio-style approach to developing projects, which is very important for everybody's artistic development, as it also is for introducing your audiences to new perspectives. It's vital to bring out the tremendous interconnections between the artwork that you are making and the social and cultural frame that feeds and transforms it, while the art likewise transforms the social frame.

SK: Absolutely. It's a pleasure to talk with you—someone who understands the essential relationship between art and Art Justice. [Klein is here referring to Double Edge's particular understanding of the latter phrase, as articulated in the company's April 2021 Case Statement: "Our dedication is to face isolation and erasure; to face despair and pain that can translate into personal incapacity and political paralysis. To uplift. We call this 'Art Justice'."]

EXCERPT FROM A JOURNAL: ASHFIELD TOWN SPECTACLE, 2016

Place: how do you dramatize the place—birds, environment? Time of who is on the land. Stories of Indigenous people, women, the Underground Railroad, the whole identity of Ashfield. The story of Ashfield: music, dance, art, religious freedom. Direct democracy. Participation. Activism.

As we navigate our new government, think about how direct democracy can apply to culture—we are making a spectacle in which each person can have a voice and make a living culture.

Nobody ever agrees. Openness instead of competition. Different ways of collaboration based on imagination. Consensus is not for art, find the way through the art. Challenges of work, not just positive. How do we get along and do something for society—for agora?

31. Art Justice at Double Edge Theatre (2018)

As I note in the conversation with Maria Shevtsova above, our visit to the Ashfield Historical Society yielded two shocking statements. The first was that the town of Ashfield had been founded by liberated enslaved people. The second was that no Native people had ever lived in this area, whether historically or in the present. The first statement was true, and it led to major questions about why the town is almost exclusively white today. The second statement was blatantly false, and that falsehood needed to be rectified. In our subsequent research, we found out that the Black and Indigenous populations throughout New England were exiled to the cities during the 1850s. We needed to immediately engage in the work of cultural reparations, partnerships, and contributions to land justice.

✳✳✳

Since its roots thirty-six years ago Double Edge has created art based on the identities and backgrounds of the artists involved in the performance creation. As the ensemble has grown and transformed from an urban performance laboratory into a rural-based center of living culture—which includes performance creation, site-specific traveling performances, touring, and collaborative, multidisciplinary arts and culture—so too have our ideas about identity and background expanded.

Our notion of community stems from the deep-rooted relationships that have been forged in our rural town, from artistic collaborations with visual artists, designers, seamstresses, and musicians, to cross-sector collaborations with farmers, food systems providers, businesses, contractors, youth, and town government. From volunteers to exchanges, from employment to audience participation, all are part of the living fabric that comprises our cultural life. To summarize: a shared resource wherein life, art, and culture interlace erases the borders of each compartmentalization.

Our rural town is primarily white, and in developing these in-town relationships the missing link—of inclusion based on the composition of our ensemble and our collaborators—has been apparent. We thus needed to tour with a focus on urban centers and to apply the same sense of diving deep into community across all sectors and all disciplines.

During the past year, Double Edge formally created an art justice advisory board, composed of our international ensemble and long-term collaborators working in the intersection of art and justice. The projects we are engaged in range from training exchanges and scholarships to freedom singing, from producing to work on access, equity, and inclusion in our rural area as well as in communities around the country. At the same time, we have donated a dedicated space to the Indigenous organization, the Ohketeau Cultural Center, along with a land share agreement for Native American programming. We have also launched an Emerging Artist Studio dedicated to performance development for visiting artists, with a particular focus on rural, working class, LGBTQ and/or African American artists. We also have begun an exchange with local people to work on improving access for people with disabilities, in order to facilitate participation in this growing culture.

Art Justice at Double Edge is a commitment to transforming the way in which we build a living culture. It is a statement of necessity that without addressing disparity and inequity according to race and gender, age and ability, and rural/urban residency, we are not able to create a genuine living, breathing, and flourishing culture. Art Justice is built into the entire fabric of Double Edge's way of life, from training, performance, and programming to our connections with our community and the environment, and it is helping us see a way of establishing a truly creative future.

Art Justice leaders at Double Edge include the leaders of our four partners groups: (1) co-founder of the Ohketeau Cultural Center, Larry Spotted Crow Mann, a Hassinamisco Nipmuc Citizen; (2) Ebony Golden, Artistic Director of Jupiter Performance Studio and CEO of Betty's Daughter Arts Collaborative, for educational and ritual theatrical performance exchange; (3) Tonasia Jones, director of programming at the Theater Offensive, our LGBTQ POC residency partner; and (4) Andre Strongbearheart Gaines, Nipmuc Citizen and No Loose Braids founder. It also includes our dramaturgs Amrita Ramanan (consulting in DE/

Ohketeau's Indigenous Playwright Lab) and Morgan Jenness, as well as artist-in-residence Harold Steward (NEFA Executive Director) and independent consultant Baraka Sele, along with the Double Edge ensemble and company, who are committed to this outcome.

EXCERPT FROM A JOURNAL: EBONY NOELLE GOLDEN WRITING WORKSHOP, WITH THE DOUBLE EDGE ENSEMBLE, 2016

Respond to your body in this moment:
stiff, gentle, sensitive, aging, strong. Breath, anger.

Respond to the word "hope":
Despair. Expectations. Not active. Wanting to believe. Resist.
Risk

Did MLK hope or work toward belief?
Respond to the word resistance:
YES. Resistance is blessed power, a place to train, the meaning
of training, a place of dialogue. A partnership. Resistance is
justice, voice.

Breath:
A practice

Future:
Double Edge island of many ports; love; resistance. Fight.
Awake and Sing. Awareness

Land:
Under constant attack, not ours, we don't own it; we need to
understand it. The Earth is the owner and we share. Ownership
is a human construct.

Risk:
Take a risk with yourself, stop trying to make things work out.
Risk, new, give voice. Know that you know. Face the dark side.

5

A Hidden Secret: Double Edge in and as Theatre History

Introduction

Looking back on the history of Double Edge through my writing has been an unsettling, albeit profound, experience. I write about horror and history in a way that clearly speaks directly to today's world. As Gabriel García Márquez would say: a death foretold. Each time I write I truly believe I am writing about life—or that I am about to—but then circumstances overwhelm me and I end up writing about how we must fight to achieve that life. Another way to look at the writing in this book is as an act of resistance that calls upon the courage to imagine, the courage to create, and the courage to claim the 80 percent of life that has nothing to do with the media or politics or the events that overwhelm the headlines. For it takes a monumental act of courage to see and hear and feel the songs of the people, the awe of the natural world, the insights of art, and the kind and furious rebellion many of us are undertaking on behalf of justice. Each day the struggle to choose these practices becomes harder, and each day it becomes all more essential.

32. On Beauty (2023)

I had written about beauty some time ago, maybe during the early 1990s, after an encounter that was full of wonder, but which also had to come to an end. The encounter related the experience of working in the fading Jewish community of Drohobycz, but it also related to a personal experience. That writing, like its subject, is now lost.

My colleague Matthew Glassman, lead actor/co-creator from the Garden and Chagall Cycles, was always interested in learning about my research into those lost places. So I attempted to revisit my earlier thoughts about beauty and loss. Beauty is ephemeral, and relates in many ways to its own memory, as well as to the sadness that comes from its loss. I cannot hold on to the beauty of these experiences, but in their transmission a memory can be still be passed on from generation to generation.

***

i. On the Farm at Double Edge

When all is said and done, there is silence. This silence reveals all.

It is so important for me, and for our audience, to walk in the field, to take steps toward the silence, which reveals that we humans are not the only thing in the field. We are the heron that comes down and eats the fish: it's the same for us. Before flying we need to descend. The ascent may enable us to gasp, but the descent gives us breath.

Our music, our dance, our images, our puppets can help us move toward the silence, which can offer us our place in the reality that includes all life.

Can we begin to see our place in the context of the world, rather than the world in the context of ourselves?

ii.

We spent many years in the wastelands of extinction. Not just environmental extinction, but cultural extinction. In Poland, in

Romania, in Hungary, and most prominently in Ukraine, we tracked the Jewish people and their vibrant history, as well as other minorities including Roma and Lemko. We found cemeteries and traces of songs and laments of what once was. Moving to Ashfield at the end of this nearly fifteen-year journey, we found another community that was nearly gone. When we arrived the farm that is now thriving was on its last legs, the buildings falling down, the farmer too old to repair them, and younger farmers unable to compete with industrial midwestern farms. From Ashfield's nearly eighty farms only two remained. The farmer wanted us to take over to make something alive, and not to let a 250-year-old farm go barren.

We learned by trial and error. We learned to honor the land. We walked on the land, we trained on the land. We grew (in our case, primarily theatre making, but now also farming), and shared with the community. That was part of growing.

One could not exist without the other. We turned dilapidated buildings one by one into new facilities; from the unused one hundred acres we made gardens, vegetable and ornamental, grazing fields, an animal barn; and most importantly for the community, we made art. The project is a living culture. Local people come and make stone walls and towers, mosaics, ornamental landscapes, retaining walls for water flow, massive paintings, costumes, fabrics, and facades, using a combination of their work and trade and a desire to rebuild the very purpose of the land. There are countless other exchanges with artists, tradespeople, and community members who engage collectively every summer.

I have come to think of this as an example of how beauty and creativity can rebuild things. From serious degeneration to a thriving community, this is the opposite of cultural extinction. It is a different approach than what followed the destruction of Jewry in Central Europe, where the attempt to rebuild Jewish life has been based on confronting the Holocaust and on imitating an old culture, rather than trying to discover what Jewry could be now.

Reinventing culture means giving birth to renewed life, and it is not and cannot be exploitative. It is an actuality of exchange based on the needs and desires of all involved.

iii.

I am trying to move away from an art of destruction and violence. These are the forces that surround us, that we see on the news, that we witness on the streets, that have engulfed our very being. It seems much harder to find the forces of creativity, of natural life and death, of nature and survival. These are the forces I am most interested in. I want to call beauty to the surface of my work. I want audiences to be confronted with the power of a song, or a color, or an image. Yes, I want to face death, and express courage, and engage in protest, but it is becoming increasingly important to examine our world and find where imagination, invention, and love have gone. Making art that searches beyond the waste and destruction seems to me the most radical and empowering choice. And it is very difficult. Amidst daily confrontations with hate, brutality, and waste, to attempt a theatre of human potential is to confront anew the existence of love.

iv.

We, those who seek beauty and life, are the 80 percent. We have been inundated with fear and taught to believe that politics, war, and mass media are the dominant parts of existence. Yet I see around me dozens and dozens of experiments and centers of art, culture, justice, and sustainable models for living—in this country and throughout the world. These are local, growing, and healing places. They are unsung. They are the source of hope and courage, and the understanding that beauty is a possible, if difficult, choice.

33. Under the Perfume of Analysis (On Eugenio Barba) (1988)

This piece is the Introduction to my Ph.D. dissertation on Eugenio Barba and his production Oxyrhynchus Evangeliet (The Gospel According to Oxyrhynchus), *first performed by Barba's Odin Teatret in 1984. I saw the production twenty-five times. It was a beautiful mix of the actors' work with that of the director, all of whom were freely creating and taking ownership of their creation. To me it was essential that this type of performance could be studied and described as a way of working. I had to fight with the institutional powers that be to write about a living director, particularly on a non-conventional model. Although I believe it is acceptable these days, the University system continues to deny so many of the values of learning, leadership, and equity that make this piece, regrettably, sound very contemporary.*

***

To write analytically is ultimately to be limited by a set of guidelines or laws. The exception is when the writing achieves the level of art, which in most cases takes a lifetime to master. Yet to leave the words within these boundaries requires a pattern of thinking which is in direct confrontation with the artist.

Is it possible to capture the depth and spirit of a rebellious artist while at the same time following the law? How can one write about Eugenio Barba employing the same methodology as would be applied to the cases of Shaw, or Kissinger, or Einstein? The familiar languages of art, or psychology, or politics cannot be applied to a living rebel. To write only from the analytical side would not be betrayal but surrender. To ignore the side of passion, to create distance from one's own methodology, that of personal experience, is to deny the deepest type of understanding. A total annihilation of freedom.

Through a decade of higher education it has become clear to me that this type of surrender is almost total. All parties even agree to discuss its acceptance. Yet I remember Barba's words to me before I left the Odin, words full of various connotations. "Please protect your word." I have chosen to take those words in the most honest way that I can: to rebel—to fight the passivity. In this case it is not by being true to the artist, but rather by being true to the age and the conflicts of my University experience. This means that I must put restraints on my own attempt to speak to Barba, knowing at the same time that it is in the response to his work that one finds the truth, and not in its analysis.

Under the perfume of analysis the raw smell remains, waiting to be exposed. My debt to the University, for teaching me the precious lesson of how to reject, will be paid by leaving behind a trace of my scent that others might catch. Perhaps they too will choose to seek. Barba is virtually unknown in American universities. He is just one more example of how we ignore living art in deference to the museum.

Sometimes I believe that one should never seek knowledge but only the unknown. This, in reality, has been my experience of true learning.

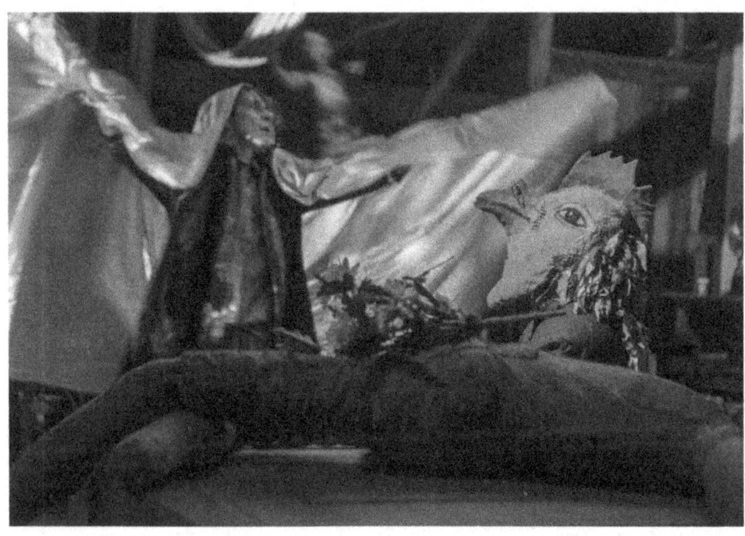

FIGURE 11 The Grand Parade, *conceived and directed by Stacy Klein, with Carlos Uriona (left), Hayley Brown (above), and Matthew Glassman (as the rooster), 2015. Photo by David Weiland.*

34. On Marc Chagall and The Grand Parade of the Twentieth Century (2010)

As for art I often talked about color, which I love. I think that you too think of the same things. And I love to dream that it won't be a voice crying in the wilderness.

—MARC CHAGALL*

Color-splashed worlds were the playground of recurring motifs in the world of Marc Chagall. The world of circus, the theatre, larger-than-life musicians—the world of simple daily life, the Shtetl (centuries-old Jewish villages), Paris streets; the world of ancient myth, universal folklore, religious symbols, and fantastical transmogrification. These are the places where the rich figures of the tragic and the triumphant, the humorous and the absurd, would meet. The overwhelming and the hopeful coexist with the solemn and the beautiful, where color explodes and death and life converge.

Today it is common to avoid nature as far as possible; this looks to me like people who avoid looking in each other's eyes.

—Marc Chagall*

At a time when cultural responses to our fast-moving, inundated, and dangerously out of control contemporary reality have been largely factual, scientific, ironic, and cold, there could be no richer, more radical place to confront the paradigm of the early twenty-first century than the rich human vision of Marc Chagall, a painter whose ninety-seven years of life spanned the twentieth century, who lived through and amidst five wars and great personal tragedy, and yet intensely embraced the world around him.

Perhaps the change in the social order, as well as in art, would have been more certain if it had emerged from our soul, not just from our head.

—Marc Chagall*

In the current cultural and economic climate, people have begun to question and redefine their worlds, realities, and choices. Double Edge's work pushes audiences to examine their role and participation in creating a living culture, occupying the environment in a sustainable way and elevating the question of how we can transform ourselves and our world into a functional, creative reality. Traveling through the labyrinth of Chagall's art, a mythic, metaphoric mirror to the contemporary world, the work will explore the role of the individual in creating culture, and the role of the community in developing a sustainable reality.

I cannot refrain from saying that art of a scientific nature or art for enjoyment's sake, like nourishment, is not a living value.

—Marc Chagall*

*Quotations from "Color, which is Love (A Word for America)" by Marc Chagall, 1964.

34A. EXCERPT FROM JOURNAL: EARLY *GRAND PARADE* 2010

Here is something I shared with Milena:

Grand Parade *is an opportunity to view yourself very intimately and personally within a larger context of history.*

A couple of instances: Cassandra may have seen herself as someone who was catatonic, hysterical, and uncommunicative as a woman; but history sees her as a prophet who could not speak because a god cursed her.

When we look at folktales we see a magician who can't die (Houdini is still being talked about as alive!!!! But what if this is more like Dracula, a real count in a real woodland who actually tortured and dismembered boys?)

Myth is something that is definitely personal at the beginning — Agamemnon's agony at finding his wife with another man became a huge myth, as did Medea's murder of her children. Or as Chagall paints the personal in the context of war, and in the context of the village.

What is your context? Where do you relate to the 20th century—in the 50's there was so much energy, so much hope—but there was also the idea of the Cleaver family—the perfect family which led many people's children into a lifetime of therapy. Meanwhile there were people being imprisoned across the world in the name of different political movements.

Anyway, where do we each see ourselves, who we are, and how do we find ourselves in the context of another time (as we cannot find ourselves in the context of time)—and what do we want to say through the lens of the 20th century?

A myth or a folk character or tale or legend ...

I am thinking about following Chagall's life and times in some way as a guideline of our story. It came from Milena talking about communism, and I realize Chagall lived through all the major events of the 20th century until right before communism fell, and he fled from event to event in an interesting way from the tzar, from Lenin, Stalin, from the war, from the second war, from the post U.S. postwar McCarthy era, and from and to his own culture.

So I thought people could choose a period of time that interests them, or an event, or a dance form, or a person in his life, or an event they are interested in.

This could be the story of a man of a century. Anyway, I hope this is of interest, it seems to follow what I have received from those of you who have written as well.

35. Why Devise? Why Now? Creating the Impossible (2005)

When I was first asked to contribute an article to a special journal issue on devising, I don't even think I was familiar with the term "devising." I had been creating performances with the Song Trilogy ensemble since 1986, and adapting scripts before then. Do I devise? The word remains somewhat artificial to me. My way of writing performances with the actors/co-creators in the room has more to do with "sweat, blood, and tears" than with a contrived set of procedures or systems.

Words can be elusive. I therefore agreed to explore my creative process using the journal's terminology.

What follows was originally published as "Why Devise? Why Now? Creating the Impossible." Theatre Topics, vol. 15 no. 1, 2005, p. 69–72.

✳✳✳

In the aftermath of September 11, 2001, despair overtook me and I began to find my work empty and ineffectual, incapable of changing the world or even touching just one person. I decided, along with my partner Carlos Uriona, to work on *The Adventures of Don Quixote*: a novel written in far-away times but with unfortunately similar dilemmas and ominously parallel questions about idealism and fanaticism, cultural wars and social decay, and individual honor and the nature of patriotic rebellion. In conjunction with this research I began to explore a new way of creating, combining physical imagery and emotional intensity with spectacle, flight, comedy, and a circus-like dynamic. I found that I had reached a unilateral place with my previous work, starting to settle for answers instead of asking questions, and I thought I was too young to let my work die in this manner. I wanted to move away from the anger and heaviness that was starting to take over the duality of the Song Trilogy, and begin to find the play and therefore the lightness which must exist in any art whose purpose is not didactic. I must admit that the last thing I could bear to be at the time was unilateral.

The UnPOSSESSED, based on this Quixotic investigation, exists in the juxtaposition between the external nightmare that we have created and the impossible dream that we must risk creating. Although I have spent my life trumpeting the necessities of art, never before have I felt so convinced that without it, our descent into chaos is inevitable. For it seems clear that hope lies beyond our frail attempt to "understand," and art is one of the few realms that can deal with the world beyond this "understanding."

I founded my theatre group, Double Edge, over twenty years ago with this idea. There must be a place in our society for those who want to ask questions, and a means of expression for those who seek what is beyond words. Through three cycles of work—including the Women's Cycle (1982–6), a series of adapted plays on the duality of women as victims and victimizers; The Song Trilogy (1987–98), an exploration of the Central European Jewish culture in relation to its surrounding societies; and my present work, The Garden of Intimacy and Desire—I have attempted to minimize or even destroy the word as an answer, a mask, or a pretense of the truth as a whole.

In the beginning of my work as a director, I attempted to use plays, albeit in adaptation, in combination with the intensive physical training I had learned from my teacher Rena Mirecka, the founding actress of Grotowski's Teatret Laboratorium. As I began to pursue this training on a full-time basis, and with the dedication of a permanent group, I came to the understanding that the words of the play were a barrier, or wall, to the imagination, soul, and autonomy of the actor, and therefore to the creation of a living theatre. Later, from a place of creation beyond words, I also understood my work as the creation of a living culture, one which defines its own reality—or, as Barba put it, "a floating island." When I was still in the reality of words, or a previously created construct, the already provided answer of the words did not allow for the expansiveness of discovery of human potential, with all the sights, sounds, smells, and tastes that go along with this approach. To devise is deeper, more personal, and intimate, and ultimately demands a visceral investigation of content rather than another rehashing of forms. This process of creating a living culture, drawing upon the individual's autonomy and potential, upon genuine relations to the world and to each other, is what I consider to be the process of art. And art should not necessarily be confused with theatre, as they are not always synonymous.

I have spent my directing career dedicated to the investigation of this human potential. The ability and need to see through the many, many superficial and daily layers of existence beneath which human beings have managed to hide, and to extract the vast imaginative and creative potential which lies within, is my unique ability (and sometimes, curse) as a director. This has meant pushing myself and my group of actors to go to the ends of ourselves to uncover all of the enormous possibilities of our hearts, minds, and souls—to break the boundaries that exist in ourselves and with our audience. In order to do so, the group uses a three-tiered approach that begins with a highly vigorous physical training as a means to surpass each person's limits. Running, jumping, partner work, and acrobatics have all been used as a path to tap the actor's energy—the source of creativity beyond the daily or, as it is named within the group, "beyond what we already know exists." In the second phase of work, the actor uses objects, usually retrieved from the trash or found in the surrounding environment, that have included large electric spools, fishing nets, fire, puppets, and rolling cow feeders. In the dialogue with the object, the actor confronts the "other" and through this confrontation loses the normal ability to control or manipulate, thus creating a situation of alertness, risk, and discovery. Simply stated, this induces the dynamics of "presence."

Drawing upon this heightened state of being, the actor enters the third part of the process, the world of the imagination. Using the energy and presence garnered in the first two stages, the group improvises upon a theme or a question that will continue to challenge any pre-existing definitions and concepts. The group creates a reality heretofore unknown, one with its own language— for instance, in this country everyone walks on spools, or in this land, people speak primarily through song. This reality generally looks more like a world of dreams, devoid of the logic of order, and full of the logic of emotion, image, and irrational connections, akin to magic realism, or jazz, but understood through a complexity of raw emotion expressed in spinning, twirling, poetry, laughter .... Each time of work, we must be able to say that "we never knew this could exist." From these created and unknown worlds come the first pieces of performance. These pieces are essential to Double Edge's view of art—something that is created anew that brings the audience to a different experience of and view of the self—a mirror which challenges rather than reflects what is already seen. The essence of this work is the essence of living culture—to discover and create and perform and move and breathe in a place that the audience cannot themselves go. That is the reason to devise—otherwise the theatre is just a slightly technically better imitation of life—so why not just live life instead?

Although it would seem that in this state of being or presence, one's cultural make-up (and therefore the differences between cultures) would be obliterated, the process functions exactly in the opposite manner. What surfaces throughout these three stages of training/energy, objects/presence, improv/world, is an exacting reclamation of "identity"—the psycho-physical, emotional, creative, imaginative, and cultural aspects of each individual actor, normally trapped by words, are released to the surface.

This process has carried Double Edge through an intense and viable dialogue between individuals and cultures throughout the world of our work, which has taken place internally in our work space and externally in the United States, Central Europe, and South America. Projects, or journeys, have been undertaken alongside our performance cycles. The five-country Jewish American-Central European *Republic of Dreams* took place in five Central European countries, and used oral history, song, dance, liturgy, and performance as a means to tap the energy and presence necessary to create a new world composed of the group and the community. In the US/Argentine Spiral Mirror project, training was exchanged between theatre groups, which forced the Argentine spectacle theatres to re-examine their depth while at the same time pushed Double Edge to re-investigate its ability to play. Finally the US/ South American/ European/ Central European *Ex-CHANGE*, a multicultural indoor-outdoor performance, combined training, circus objects, intimate theatre, and raw, swashbuckling spectacle, such as a pirate attack in a river (from the *Saragossa Manuscripts*) or an organ-death cart-funeral procession (*Master and Margarita*) or a dance through a door leading up a mountain (*Quixote*).

Each of these projects or journeys has undertaken similar means to create cultural exchange as that which takes place in the inner regions of our performance work. The parallel is such—the cultural project, Double Edge's meeting with another culture or community, uses the same means as the performance process, the creation of a separate reality which is used as a mirror to open the audience's awareness. Using music, song, dance, food and drink, interviews, spectacle, and ritual, the theatre and its audiences attempt to move beyond the normal and often stereotypical exchange into the risk of the unknown or the discovery of a new reality.

In Double Edge, we do not ask questions "about" a culture, or offer answers or defenses on behalf of our own culture, but rather we participate in an essentially nonverbal dialogue that is an exchange of culture and individuals. In parallel to the process of training, this movement—beyond concept, beyond form, and into the irrational, or the mysteries of what is possible between people—creates an artistic dialogue, which is the rediscovery of the story of the human being.

This story, which we are presently calling *The UnPOSSESSED*, is, although complex, dark, and incomprehensible, certainly one of hope. I have witnessed this hope in the eyes of my collaborators and my audience, from strangers in Central Europe who dared to move beyond their sometimes nationalistic beliefs, to the extent that for the first time in seventy years non-Jews came to the Jewish Center to witness a theatre performance, to young people in rural Ashfield, Massachusetts, who abandoned their daily despair and engaged in the creative act of performance.

In this manner I have managed to find that the despair of the incomprehensible reality in which we live, and which Cervantes embodied, is in a constant and determined dialogue with the foolhardy playfulness of the unending dreams and hopes of his (and my) alter ego, Don Quixote.

36. Women and the Unknown (2018)

Leonora, la maga y la maestra was the beginning of a new performance Cycle on Surrealism; it was also a fully circular invocation of Double Edge's Women's Cycle. Since the first two pieces in this new Cycle, I have also directed and co-created two others: the first is SUGA, a solo performance co-created and performed by Travis Coe, an autobiographical performance centering on gay Afro-Latinx experience. The second is the Hidden Territories of the Bacchae, *a matriarchal rendering of Euripides' 500* BCE *play, co-created by Jennifer Johnson and Milena Dabova. All these performances are related attempts to break out of the entrapments of a patriarchal definition of reality, and to reidentify and redefine ourselves as the fully expressive artists we intend to be. I wrote the following piece thinking of my daughters Tadea Klein (costume designer and farmer at Double Edge) and Cariel Klein (co-producer and aerialist at Double Edge), whom I have the joy of working with in what I hope is the building of a new and more just reality.*

What follows is excerpted from a speech originally published in Medium, *as part of "Anger / Appetite / Ambition / ART"—a Symposium on Women Innovators in the Arts, curated by Baraka Sele, which took place at Montclair State University on March 28, 2018.*

***

I would like to start from today and move backwards, from where I am to how I got to this moment in time. For the past seven months, I have been immersed in the world of Leonora Carrington, a painter, sculptor, writer, and profound contributor to the art and magic of the twentieth century. She died five years ago in her nineties. I created the performance *Leonora, la Maga y la Maestra,* inspired by her work, with my ensemble and particularly with Jennifer Johnson, who played Leonora. It premiered last weekend at the Kasser Theater. I wrote in my program note how it came to be that the performance was based on Leonora. After the US election and the misogyny that led up to it, I decided I would never again create a piece of theatre without a female lead. On the other hand, I did not want to abandon the Latin American Cycle I was creating based on Alejandro Jodorowsky's writing and the experiences of my partner and co-artistic director Carlos Uriona under the Argentine military dictatorship. I sought out women artists of Latin America, and Leonora Carrington appeared. A British-born aristocrat, Carrington escaped from a Spanish asylum where she was incarcerated at the beginning of the Second World War and sought refuge in Mexico, where she remained for seventy years. What we didn't know at the time was that Carrington and Jodorowsky knew each other, and had worked together. Carrington was the mentor and Jodorowsky her apprentice.

Serendipity (or perhaps we should call it magic) had a huge role in the process of creating this performance. We did not predict or even seek out the possibility the story of Carrington's life and work would intersect so deeply with so many, many women, nor that we could openly create a work of magic, mysticism, pain, beauty, and very importantly, the Unknown. We did not realize that it would be so singular to create a work with a female, crazy (or maybe not?) artist in the leading role, nor that almost all work on these subjects tend to be about men (think of *A Brilliant Mind,* or any movie you know about artists, like *Pollock*, etc.—but unlike many of these film-worthy, brilliant male artists Leonora never raped, abused, or used violence as a methodology). It never struck us that having a woman lead a man, and mentor a man apprenticed to her, as Leonora did with Alejandro, would be so unique.

Had I realized all these things, the magic and mystery probably would not have worked out as well. Or I might have been afraid to reveal them.

We dove deeply into Leonora's writings about her time in the asylum, and uncovered an artist who refused to capitulate to the torture she experienced in receiving regular injections of Cardiazol and in being told to control herself. Rather than stop creating, a short time after she chronicled these experiences she transformed them into a magic realist story called *The Hearing Trumpet*. This depicted a group of old, wise women locked (or thrown by their families) into an asylum, who, rather than giving up, go forth in search of a mystical journey to the Arctic (the North). Ten years later, she wrote an unabashedly mystical book called *The*

Stone Door, delving into the Unknown with a courage that fully captured my own lifelong search.

Having lived in Leonora's world for these many months, I have learned that with each step I take in my art and my life, I must garner my own courage to survive, to speak (usually through art), to continue creating, to form creative (and loving) partnerships, and to dare to confront the Unknown and to share this experience with those who see my work and exchange with me.

Upon reflection, I am in awe that I never knew that courage was a daily process. I spent my artistic life, and indeed my adulthood, fighting to gain back the rights I was raised with by my dear parents, who did not understand I might face limits as a woman. Thus began a life-long dichotomy between a world of imaginative journey, wonder, mystical yearnings, freedom, and art, juxtaposed with the strong reality of doubt, struggle, limitation, and just plain fighting.

In my career of forty or so years, I have been called "iron lady" by authoritarian producers shouting at me to listen to them as they tell me what to do in my performances; I have been described by *American Theater* magazine as a pale, petite, intense woman, and I have been told off and written about repeatedly as someone who doesn't smile. OR as a witch or a bitch. OR as too intense to approach. These are only the minor insults. I wake up every day wondering if today is the day when I will descend again into craziness, be violated, or give up my soul for survival. Which women have I encountered who believe with confidence they can ask men for work, or ask for the same fees as their male counterparts? There is an institutional creation of inferiority with regard to women, but when I cannot sleep at night, or wake in dread that someone won't understand me, I cannot see the institution, but only my own fear. Then I force myself to go to work in the Unknown; I seek the courage of my passion, I live in the natural world, I walk in the snow, I plant the seeds of art on my theatre farm. The hurricanes are coming; we have made sure of that. The sick game of battle with control is being lost. I must continue the radical act of imagination. We all must become citizens of the imagination. We must feel, hear, smell, taste, sing, dance, and paint our future. With courage.

EXCERPT FROM A JOURNAL: LEONORA, PHASE II 2017–18

Ensemble training—a different constellation each time. How to build? How to work without controlling each other, but by demanding?

What is the interior of the image? Building the alchemy of imagination. You cannot approach this intellectually.

Magic is the flight beyond hardship or fantasy—imagination is worth fighting for.

Magic of the unexpected: Is it an incarnation of something I don't understand? Is it something of revelation? Is it unknown to me?

The political act of magic—anti-colonialism, Indigenous, feminist—animals (we are not alone) environment

Location of forces present. Active practicing witch. All ritual magic is theatre.

Repression comes from fear. Internalizing the craziness of the world. Why does she remain vulnerable?

37. "The Next Layer of Essential Imagination": A Letter to the Double Edge Community (2023)

Friends,

I am writing on behalf of Carlos and me to share some wonderful news, for Double Edge, and for the future.

As of the reading of this letter, Carlos and I will step aside from our roles as Artistic Directors of the theatre, and our work will be focused on making art and continuing the vision of DE's future. I will formally be known as Vision Strategist, Founder, and Artistic Director Emerita, and Carlos will be Cultural Strategist.

For me it is an enormously exciting time, when I can refocus on directing and devising performances after many years of combining this work with the daily labor of running the theatre. I will also have the opportunity to concentrate on working with our partner organizations and on cultivating our survival, continuing to develop our full vision for our site in Ashfield as well and the economics of that vision. Carlos will focus on the national and international vision of his grassroots work, which has brought so many, many people to Double Edge since he came to the theatre in 1996, as well as continuing to develop local connections and resources. And of course he is already deeply at work on three artistic projects and engaged in the mentorships he has grown over the course of his life's work.

What we will not be doing is "running the theatre," which has become a huge responsibility with our twelve ensemble members and twenty other staff, fifteen buildings, year-round performances and festivals, partner organizations, and residencies. Since its founding in 1982, Double Edge has been a multigenerational ensemble and, through the process of moving to Ashfield twenty-nine years ago, it fully embarked on its course as a collective, and finally as a collective of collectives, with our four partners running their own distinct organizations. I am happy to say that in the past several years I have witnessed Co-Artistic Directors Jennifer Johnson, Milena Dabova, and Travis Coe taking over the daily artistic leadership of Double Edge as they each establish and grow their own amazing creative processes. Alongside our Producing Executive Director Adam Bright, my dear partner heading Double Edge's business for the past five years, our Co-Producer Cariel Klein, and our Director of Artist and Community Engagement Hannah Jarrell, the team leading the theatre is not only solid, but also has the means and energy to carry the theatre into its next forty years.

These six people are lifted up, as Carlos and I have been lifted up, by the other four members of the Ensemble, who share in shaping and visioning what Double Edge is and will become. They are Jeremy Louise Eaton, John Peitso, Amanda Miller, and Tomantha Sylvester.

In celebrating my 40th and 41st anniversary performance, *Hidden Territories*, I had the pleasure of working with one of the founders of Double Edge Theatre, Daina Robins, which brought me full circle to the meaning of Ensemble. All of us have worked, whether for forty-one years, or thirty years, or eighteen years, or seven years, on trying to identify ourselves as artists and as human beings in the context of the other people who are struggling, sometimes joyfully, sometimes not, to do the same. It is an artistic home we have built, a family, not just for ourselves but for all of you who participate with us. These things have lost value in our culture—long-term artistic paths, ensemble creation; even the word "legacy" has become fraught—but, especially in these deeply disturbing times, they constitute a singular process of healing and of creation.

I am proud of what we have accomplished and prouder still of those who will take the lead on accomplishing more. I look forward most of all to spending my time inside Double Edge's incredible barn, making ensemble performances, finally separated from my constant organizational companion, my smartphone, devising and dreaming up the next layer of essential imagination.

Carlos, as always, wants to share some words borrowed from the Uruguayan poet Mario Benedetti, which invites us to continue walking the path together.

Te Quiero

Si te quiero es porque sos
Mi amor, mi cómplice y todo
Y en la calle codo a codo
Somos mucho mas que dos.

Tus ojos son mi conjuro
Contra la mala jornada
Te quiero por tu mirada
Que mira y siembra futuro

Tu boca que es tuya y mía
Tu boca no se equivoca
Te quiero porque tu boca
Sabe gritar rebeldia

I Love You

If I love you it is because you are
My love, my accomplice and my
everything
And in the streets locking elbows
We are much more than just us two.

Your eyes are my magic spell
Against the terrible days
I love you because your gaze
When looking is sowing futures.

Your mouth that is yours and mine
Your mouth is never mistaken
I love you because your mouth
Knows how to scream rebellion.

With so much love,
Stacy and Carlos

38. Hidden Territories: from Ukraine to the Americas (2023)

In 2022, I returned to the Bacchae for the second time in my artistic career, with the Hidden Territories of the Bacchae. *This time around, I knew the things I needed to work on to delve into the reaches of matriarchy and the ancient expressions of women long forgotten. As the fortieth anniversary of Double Edge turned into the forty-first, I began to explore where I wanted to go in the future, and how I could work with the ensemble and our partners to get there. At the same time, the full-scale Russian invasion of Ukraine in early 2022 brought back memories of the town I lived in during my first* Hidden Territories *journey—Drohobycz. If life is a spiral, then these two parts of my life continue to move powerfully around it. My reflection below lies at the center of this territory.*

From the Program Note for Hidden Territories of the Bacchae, *2023:*

Dionysis was the Greek God of ecstasy, wine, and theatre, also called Bacchus, who traveled through distant matriarchal lands with women claiming their rites of duality, liberation, and joy. In

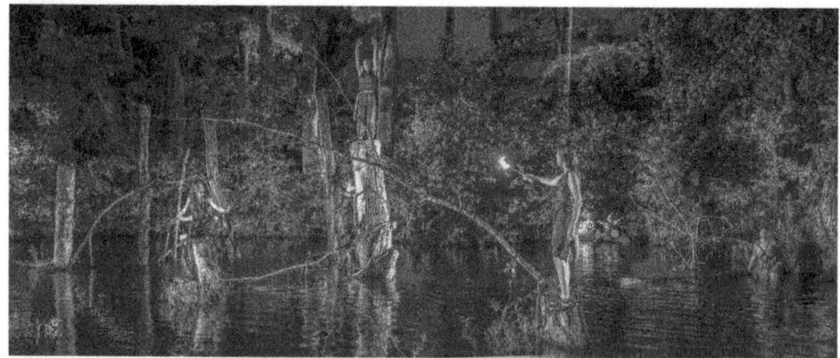

FIGURE 12 Hidden Territories of the Bacchae, *conceived and directed by Stacy Klein, 2023. Pictured, from left to right: Milena Dabova, Cariel Klein, Jennifer Johnson, Mica Farias Gomez, Desirée Graham. Photo by Doug Mason.*

our version of Dionysis' return to Thebes in Hidden Territories, *the Bacchae (women gathered from around the world) are led by the female Dionysis, played by co-artistic director Milena Dabova, in rematriating their own languages, rituals, ceremonies, and story, including Anishinaabe-mowen, Bulgarian, Polish, Kechua, Aramaic, Yoruba, and Spanish, in addition to English. In Euripedes'* Bacchae, *the focus is on the story of Pentheus, the patriarch who condemns women for asserting their rites (and rights); in Double Edge's 1982 premiere production of* Rites, *written by Maureen Duffy based on* The Bacchae, *the drama focuses instead on Agave, Pentheus' mother. In our current version, over forty years later, we have brought a community of women out of their hidden territories to celebrate the power of their voices, songs, and, ultimately, their passionate expression for freedom and a just world.*

As I embark on creating the indoor version of the Hidden Territories of the Bacchae, *I wanted to explore again the idea of language, both spoken and nonverbal, and its relationship to a process of rematriation.*

✱✱✱

What is language? It is not limited to words; it can be a physical gesture, an image, a song, a dance, the sound of trees whispering. Language is art and expression and imagination. When our authentic language is liberated from the Hidden Territories—those territories of existence which for so many reasons have been suppressed—imagination and love can EXIST.

When I first heard the Nipmuc language, as spoken by Larry Spotted Crow Mann and Andre Strongbearheart Gaines, I felt an immediate sense of the land upon which I stand. Aquene, meaning greetings and peace … Motompan wunne … good morning … This was strange to my ears and yet, at the same time, deeply familiar. I was told that the words came from the land; they are the land, at the same time as the trees and the birds sound with the land. And yet, distressingly, this language, like so many other Indigenous languages, is close to extinction, wiped out after years of being rendered forbidden and illegal.

I later encountered the language of the Anishinaabe, Anishinaabe-mowen, through Tomantha Sylvester. Their people left the Nipmuc and their other Algonquin cousins thousands of years ago, due to a prophecy of destruction on the East Coast. I learned that there is no word in the Algonquin languages for Art, that art is contained in everything. Art is its own language, without a need for verbal codification.

This evoked in me feelings and memories of the Hebrew language, an ancient language that rose alongside Aramaic. Until the early twentieth century, Hebrew was a hidden language, as a result of its own suppression and near death on account of the Roman Empire's laws forbidding its use. Those in exile created Yiddish, a combination of Hebrew and European languages (particularly German), and Ladino, the language of the Sephardic Jews, which were all but fully swept away and buried after Inquisition and Holocaust.

Throughout Double Edge's Song Trilogy, a cycle inspired by research in Eastern and Central Europe in the late 1980s and 1990s, I insisted on having these languages—Hebrew, Ladino, and Yiddish—spoken and sung in our performances, although the majority of the audience would understand meaning through sound and image rather than the words themselves. Then in the 1990s in Ukraine, our encounter with local attempts to unbury the nearly wiped-out Jewish culture led to the naming of the Hidden Territories project. Could we attempt to raise the language and culture out of their secret domain? This desire grew to include many other cultures that were near extinction, such as the Carpathian mountain Lemkos. Our research extended to Bulgaria, where we actually found and spoke to the last surviving Ladino speakers (along with reading and hearing Ladino liturgical songs and texts).

Double Edge has always created non-verbal language from our art and dreams as well as using the spoken languages of our Ensemble—Bulgarian, Argentinian Spanish, Polish, English, and Hebrew. These languages are not hidden, yet we learned from our journeys into the nature of extinction that all language is essential to our identity. Language is not only the words we speak but also how we dream, and how we understand ourselves and others.

The effects of the loss of language—whether through assimilation or extermination—demand a crucial process of grief and mourning. When a language is exterminated, there is no choice in this process. The loss can rip out a piece of the soul and the heart, and maybe the Art.

The Algonquin Peoples speak one of the languages of this American land, Turtle Island, and we must insist that these languages be used in their fullness. As we honor the languages of this land, we also want to remember those peoples who dwell here who were forcibly removed from their place and who have been left with little access to the language of their ancestors.

Nipmuc and Anishinaabe, and the lands they grew out of, continue to move me. I want to include these languages, the languages of my Ensemble and my partners, in my performances. In the *Bacchae*, the languages spoken and sung include Anishinaabe mowen, as well as Aramaic, Krymzcek, Ladino, Kechua, Yoruba, Spanish, English, and Bulgarian. To include these languages is to begin to re-connect to the land, to reaffirm that resistance to the forced and continued disappearance of a people's voice is possible. Extinction is not acceptable. People must have the freedom to speak and sing and act in their own language, the language of their heart and soul.

How, then, can we transform extermination into imagination, and unearth forgotten and disappeared languages into our ART and DREAMS, as a manifestation of LIFE?

A NOTE: *THE BACCHAE* AND *HOWLING AT THE MOON*, 2021

Hello Milena and Jennifer. Please also push yourselves with regard to freedom, to physicality and to voice. I am not so interested in smooth and pretty bodies or voices, but in the guts of the matter and the guts of the voice. That is why we have moved forward with texts, so that we can push beyond the choral.

Conclusion: Transitions, a Radical Love Story

My life in theatre is always in transition. Even as we try to escape the unknown and cling to the answers available to us, the process of theatre-making forces us to embrace the ephemeral in art and culture. When I write that my work is a search, not a form or a method, I mean exactly that:

It is a continued state of evolution, transition, movement, embodiment, breath, and struggle.

I hope this book has offered a means for sharing many of the transitional movements in my work, which have continued to evolve and expand in spiral form, from well before 1982 through the present and into the future.

This book is an ascending spiral: its ethics are my own, which means making sure that nothing stops these enormous transitions from becoming full and honest and wondrous (by which I mean: magical).

My life in the theatre has been an ongoing struggle to remain true to my humanity, and to prioritize listening and learning above all else. To remain true to the embodiment of the creative process and the full life of the ensemble. To allow for growth, even at the cost of comfort.

Transition, for me and for my theatre, has meant multi-generational work. It has meant moving out of the city to a healthy, albeit challenging, rural area, finding quiet and yet staying fiercely connected to our community.

Growing community: This has meant developing an interdependent structure alternative to the extractive capitalist model. It means sustaining a place where we can reconnect to the *why* of what we do and how we do it, and where we can reconnect to our roles in the community, our accountability to the community.

I have always insisted to actors and students alike that we will work on transitions more than any other part of a scene. Transitions are the way we move from one place to the other. In our artistic work, we cannot ask the audience for the courage of their imagination without moving intentionally through the transitions of a performance. In life, too, we may spend time trying to deny the transitions of age and life and death, but they exist nevertheless.

I have learned—and I have sought to share in words—that performance, culture, and life are all intertwined in a beautiful state of mutual transition. The spiral evolution of Double Edge proceeds along an ever-reaching, if always fragile, path. We, and I, have grown from a dedicated group of few to a community of many. We care about our art, but we care equally about our collaboration, our growth, our food, our housing, and our environment. This all defines the language of justice.

So rather than writing a how-to book, I wanted to share the distinctive stops on this spiral of transitions, from before the beginning into the future. This story is primarily an artistic story, although my writings should be understood in the context of struggles in the world around us. I have learned that facing these struggles is my way to be able to flourish in the joy of the journey.

INDEX